Intelligent Information Systems – Vol. 4

Adaptive Cloud
Enterprise Architecture

INTELLIGENT INFORMATION SYSTEMS

Series Editors: Da Ruan *(Belgian Nuclear Research Centre (SCK.CEN) & Ghent University, Belgium)*
Jie Lu *(University of Technology, Sdyney, Australia)*

Intelligent Information Systems – Vol. 4

Adaptive Cloud Enterprise Architecture

Asif Qumer Gill

University of Technology, Australia

 **World Scientific**

NEW JERSEY · LONDON · SINGAPORE · BEIJING · SHANGHAI · HONG KONG · TAIPEI · CHENNAI

Published by

World Scientific Publishing Co. Pte. Ltd.

5 Toh Tuck Link, Singapore 596224

USA office: 27 Warren Street, Suite 401-402, Hackensack, NJ 07601

UK office: 57 Shelton Street, Covent Garden, London WC2H 9HE

British Library Cataloguing-in-Publication Data
A catalogue record for this book is available from the British Library.

The author is the inventor and owner of The Gill Frameowrk® copyright.

Intelligent Information Systems — Vol. 4
ADAPTIVE CLOUD ENTERPRISE ARCHITECTURE

Copyright © 2015 by World Scientific Publishing Co. Pte. Ltd.

ISBN 978-981-4632-12-6

Printed in Singapore

To my lovely family.

Endorsements for the Book

"Mass movement to digital business and cloud computing is changing the way businesses and government adapt to digital disruptive forces. Emerging trends now show 40% of the IT budget being spent by the business. New digital leadership is required to meet head-on the challenges of convergence of services in highly integrated as-a-service landscapes. We are starting to notice the transformative nature of cloud and digital business impacting both the supply side and demand side of the IT services marketplace. In this heightened period of change 'adaptive' is the new black. 'Adaptive sourcing' is already emerging as a key to market services. Being agile and flexible is a business 'adaptive imperative'. Defining business and IT strategies and roadmaps for cloud and digital business requires new 'adaptive thinking' and frameworks. The Gill Framework addresses this emerging niche with the 'Adaptive Enterprise Services System' (AESS), a systems-of-systems framework. What sets the AESS framework apart from others is the practical application of the Adapting, Defining, Operating, Managing, Supporting (ADOMS) life-cycle management approach. Adapting to change, as a result of pressures of digital business and cloud, requires a new response with new capabilities around agile. This book is a body of knowledge which is a must have handbook for adaptive business and IT thinkers and leaders."

Dr. Pedro Harris
Executive Director, ICT Strategic Delivery
Department of Treasury, Office of Finance and Services, NSW

"Going digital is far more than the App or the web portal or the social media channel, it's the ability to realise effective business presence, the ability to stay obsessively close to the customer and the ability to swiftly adapt and innovate both in the physical and digital worlds. It's about both your mission systems that delivers your organization's purpose and your support systems that enable its existence. It is also about being able to innovate and adapt these systems to remain competitive or to gain that edge over the competition. Enterprise architecture is about realising organisational strategy through deliberate design, assembly and change of all elements of the enterprise. Just like an architect designing a building for a particular purpose, an architecture will ensure that the emergent property or competitive advantage desired by designing your business in a certain way will emerge from your investments in change. This book provides a playbook for the architectures and critical considerations to designing and embedding desired properties required into your business through cloud and other digital enabling technologies. Asif's book is a must read for digital leaders embarking on digital transformation and to an adaptable cloud enabled enterprise."

Christopher Organ
CTO, HAMB Systems

"Asif has produced an insightful and thought-provoking look at how we might better structure and run our organisations to create predictable outcomes and greater responsiveness in what is a challenging period of technology-driven change. It gives us the 'conceptual glue' that can be used to join the myriad of frameworks and approaches together without the need for radical change within each of those disciplines."

Darryl Carr
EA Specialism Advisory Group, ACS

"Demystification of the 'cloud' and clarification of its critical role in business. This book is a must read for anyone involved in business architecture, technology decision-making, or wanting to understand the paradigm technological shift underway and how the accelerating rate of change in business is being enabled. Asif's book provides a comprehensive perspective of enabling architecture and technology driving digital disruption, which all organisations will be required to adopt. Asif's framework provides a meaningful foundation for the development of appropriate strategy, governance and planning to gain traction in this complex and rapidly evolving environment. The cost of not implementing such a framework is not optional."

Dr. Alex Kokkonen
Global executive, author, researcher, and motivational speaker

"The future of many organizations is dependent on their ability to have a vision and more importantly the ability to transform the organization towards that vision. As such, a number of Enterprise Architectural frameworks have been introduced, however these frameworks have challenges. Asif states in this book, "Traditional top-down approaches to enterprise architecture development and management are continuously challenged by the dynamic business environment. Enterprises are lagging behind in harvesting agile or adaptive enterprise architecture capability. The applications of traditional top down approaches to enterprise architecture are criticized for not delivering or showing the value early as the traditional top down approach takes few months to year to develop and effectively operate enterprise architecture capability". This book introduces a much needed approach that helps to deal with this challenge. Asif does an excellent job at introducing the Gill Framework, which is a meta-framework that works with existing Enterprise Architectural frameworks.

The book is easy to read and understand. With Cloud Computing being a major focus of many organizations today, the book gives an easy to follow description on how to adapt, define, operate, manage and support an adaptive cloud enterprise architecture capability. In this book, Asif describes the issues and challenges that many organizations face, where there is lack of alignment. He states that whilst most organizations have well established agile or adaptive Project Management capabilities, they are not agile or adaptive in other areas of the enterprise. Asif argues that being agile or adaptive in one area and not agile in another area such as enterprise architecture will cause misalignment and inconsistency in the enterprise. He highlights that even the architecture work products or enterprise architecture design need to be adaptive as well. So, this is an essential book for those considering the adoption of the cloud and with the use of the Gill

Framework, will help the enterprise align their capabilities as they transition the enterprise."

Dr. Bernard Wong
CEO, Denbigh International
CEO, PMI Queensland
Director, Enterprise Strategy Consulting

"This book is a must-read for those business decision-makers wishing to successfully build enterprise adaptability and agility into every aspect of their organisation. Fuelled by technology-led disruption, the pace of change is accelerating. This further increases the pressure on business leaders and owners to meet the challenge of change head-on in order to remain relevant in our increasingly competitive, globalised markets. Through this book, Asif offers a proven framework and approach that will be invaluable in giving business leaders the capabilities with which to successfully manage their organisation's transition to one of intrinsic adaptability and agility. Ensuring that the adoption of new, emerging and disruptive technologies (such as Cloud computing) by organisations delivers sustainable, tangible business value with known risk and without compromising effective ongoing governance is crucial. This book provides that assurance as you transition your business to becoming truly responsive and adaptable – both critical success factors in our increasingly volatile and competitive environment."

Rob Livingstone
Fellow, University of Technology, Sydney
Consultant, industry advisor, mentor, author, speaker and former CIO

"Dr. Asif Gill's "Adaptive Cloud Enterprise Architecture" is a book which provides a comprehensive coverage of the Cloud ecosystem. Chapter 1 – Introduction coverage of concepts, definitions and benefits is encyclopedic. Asif's "Meta-Framework" which provides a back drop for adopting and managing the lifecycle of an EA capability for cloud architecture no matter what the underlying EA framework is, is discussed in length in the subsequent chapters. In the final chapter, Asif provides a succinct conclusion with scenarios demonstrating the value of his Meta-Framework. This book is recommended reading for anyone who wants to undertake a serious activity in Enterprise Architecture of the Cloud ecosystem."

Krish S. Ayyar
EA Consultant and Trainer
Martin-McDougall Technologies Pty. Ltd, Sydney

"We are going through the second machine age and may I say – the most defining. The core engine fuelling this revolution is digital technologies. Cloud is the heart of digital. Whether you are an enterprise architect focused on business, application, information or technology architectures or a IT practitioner or simply work within business, it has already impacted our lives and yes – our careers in more ways than we know it.

This is not the first book on this subject nor has the last, however, Asif managed to demystify the topic from average business users to business leaders and veteran cloud practitioners to enterprise architects to allow us to make sense of this all. The risks and rewards are much too high for anybody to let this wave pass by. This book is a must-have reference for anybody who has just begun exploring the topic or has a skin in the digital game. Professionals outside the consulting practices will enjoy a step-by-step guide, framework and method to establishing an internal cloud capability or engaging the service providers like a pro."

Salman Gillani
Digital transformation practitioner
Enterprise architecture consultant and evangelist

"This book arrives at a critical time. Many organisations are struggling to effectively manage the combination of people, process, culture and technology to allow them to deliver value. In Incrementalism has taken hold, with managers and staff barely able to keep up with their day jobs, looking to 'go with the flow' as much as they can. Frustrated, leaders attempt transformation programs that look good in the boardroom but are found wanting when it comes to implementation; locking the organisation into a negative spiral of mistrust: management and staff complain of a lack of planning and consultation, leaders complain of inflexible and uncooperative managers and staff. As the transition of computing systems to the cloud continues, leaders, managers and staff across the organisation will increasingly need to be able to understand and communicate strategies to deliver customer value that fully embraces the power of technology. It's time to adopt a new way to break down barriers to collaboration. This book outlines a framework to build a language for collaboration, one that creates the syntax for thinking and better decision making in organisations. From the creation of the collaborative adaptive mindset, this book outlines the policies, processes and tools to build a technology-enabled future. The book is serious, deals with complex issues and requires very deliberate reading, and a strong bias to action to adapt and execute on the ideas that form The Gill Framework. The reward is that of a handbook for the future of your organisation."

Brian Bailey
Technology Innovation Manager
The University of Sydney

"Cloud computing and technologies is no longer a futuristic concept that we can dream about. These technologies and business models are present, well established and available. However after many years it is still a concept that is broadly recognised by Australian businesses but not well understood. While this technology can deliver improved business performance, staff productivity and reduce Operating expense, there is still lack of clarity for Australian Corporates and SMEs around how they can achieve these outcomes using Cloud technologies. The 'Gill Framework' developed by Dr. Asif Gill allows Technology and Business teams within a business to understand, adapt and utilitse this technology with an aim to deliver integrated change management capability and better business performance. This 'must have' book will appeal equally to the business readers interested in this subject, technology experts and technology driven change consultants."

Amir Saleem
Sr. Project Manager, Business Improvement & Advocacy
Telstra Corporation

"Enterprises are scrambling to keep up with the demands of the modern customer-led environment. Digital transformation, customer engagement, customer experience management (CEM) and omnichannel are common buzzwords we hear allied to the big melting pot of big data, cloud computing, mobility, 3D printing and wearables. Just when we have got used to that cauldron of potentially disruptive technologies, along comes the IoT or the internet of everything offering more connectedness than ever before and data measured not in petabytes, exabytes, or even zettabytes, but yottabytes the equivalent of 250 trillion DVDs and over the next ten years potentially brontobytes as the IoT becomes so deeply embedded in all our lives.

How do you plan for a tsunami of change like this? And how to you get the business community, employees and IT to build the future together?

Well rather than panic or keep trotting out industrial age command-and-control recipes, the smarter organisations have got their strategic thinking caps on and are finding new ways to plan and collaborate and mobilise their people, processes and technologies to go after the emerging opportunities and to be the disruptors not the disrupted. My focus at Ovum over the last few years has been to answer a simple question. How can we as an enterprise remain and increase our relevance to our customers? Successful organisations will be highly adaptive, customer-adaptive and act more like organisms able to sense, respond, adapt at the right frequency to create new value for their customers and remain relevant. Technology has a massive part to play in this once the fundamentals of visionary leadership that commits to the customer above all, an engaged and highly collaborative and emancipated workforce that has the power to make a difference to customers through great experiences and innovation in value. But to get to this level of organisational coherence and agility, every enterprise will need to master the art of designing, developing an adaptive, not a static, enterprise architecture. This is a process of continuous renewal and in this book Dr. Asif Gill gives us through his The Gill Framework® the planning framework to create this level of enterprise coherence and the environment for continuous adaptation at the right speed to remain and increase our relevance to the customers, citizens and patients we hope to serve. In my work on what it takes to become a customer-adaptive enterprise, one of the 8 core attributes that underpins customer-adaptive capabilities is an adaptive enterprise architecture, Dr. Asif Gill puts the meat on the bones of what that means."

Jeremy Cox

Principal Analyst Customer Engagement Practice

Ovum

"The fundamental challenge of IT architecture is to define core business requirements, and construct the IT solution to meet those requirements. Seemingly a simple concept, but most enterprises find it hard to comprehend it and went way off course in the past decades. IT exhausts by trying all the maneuver starting from "Waterfall" to application architecture type approaches. The time it takes to move from the requirements to the final deployed is months if not years. By that time the business requirements likely to be changed, require going back to drawing board and caught up in endless loop. Therefore, IT is not addressing the objectives and expectations of the business. According to Gartner the four nexus of forces i.e. Cloud, Mobile, Social, and Information will obsolete the existing architectures and application strategies within next five years. This will expand business engagement with IT but in a different way. So the question is what core benefit IT should provide to achieve this fundamental shift. IT should be able to allow the agility and as a result enterprise should be able to adapt to rapidly changing business requirements and opportunities. Thus, businesses can move quickly into newer and more profitable territories. IT leaders, architects, and developers have an enormous challenge in front of them to remodel the IT.

This book is an important contribution for IT community who successfully wants to steer their enterprise through adaptability and agility journey. Asif established the agile or flexible or adaptive enterprise architecture by introducing The Gill Framework®. This book uses the capabilities of The Gill Framework® for assessing, designing, improving, and transforming agile or adaptive enterprises. It defines an agile enterprise as an Adaptive Enterprise Service System (AESS) and use ADOMS approach for lifecycle management. Asif supplemented the book with four fictional case studies and applied The Gill Framework® from adaption to supporting an agile enterprise. I am sure the concepts defined in this book will help IT executives, architects, and managers to begin the journey that finally meet the needs of business adaptability and agility. This book is not only useful for IT community but also an excellent text book for academicians to use in their class room."

Shoaib Alam
Enterprise Integration Architect
News Corp Australia

"In this book Dr. Gill provides a mechanism for companies to address the issues that are faced working in a period where technology change is the constant and the ability to be flexible and adapt to changes is critical for business success. He provides a comprehensive method, the Adaptive Enterprise Service System (AESS), which can be used to not only address these issues, but provide a foundation with business value delivery at its core. This book describes how this is achievable with an approach that addresses all factors from system component agility and interoperability the role social architectures play in the business and customer environments. The need to constantly monitor and learn essential for any person working in IT. Obsolescence is something that can take months not years and this is the same for businesses where changes in the marketplace's adoption of technology is often faster than that of many businesses. Dr. Gill has clearly identified this need and presents a framework where automation, machine learning, self-adapting systems can be adopted into company landscapes. The AESS can provide a solid framework for any business needing to grow their IT capabilities and deliver business value quickly in a volatile technology era."

Tristan Gutsche
IT Architect, Director TelSoc

"This book moves beyond the normal hype that usually surrounds the use of agile techniques in an enterprise. Instead, Asif offers a new framework for building adaptability and agility into the enterprise at multiple levels. This framework provides a basis for enterprises to address the twin challenges of agility and adaptability as they face the growing competitiveness of their market. The enterprise today faces an environment of continual disruption. Much of this disruption is caused by new technologies, but new ideas and concepts can be just as unsettling to an enterprise and its strategic and tactical plans. The move to a service based strategy can give an enterprise a more sustainable approach, but this move can be fraught with danger if approached haphazardly. The Adaptive Cloud Enterprise Architecture offers the enterprise a method of moving forward to adapt these new technologies without compromising the proper governance and risk management that are required. This book will help to move the enterprise to a more agile and adaptive stance with the confidence to face the disruptions that are certain in today's competitive market."

Dr. Peter White
Adjunct Lecturer and Enterprise Technical Architect

"Being adaptive and agile is extremely important in today's digital landscape where organisations are focused on achieving modern day targets for cost savings and efficiency. The Gill Framework is an excellent meta framework to guide integrators and developers in the provisioning of cloud technologies."

Steve Schmid
Manager OTF, Australia and New Zealand

Foreword

Cloud computing is an alternative way to offer, source, develop, test, deploy and use computing resources on-demand as services. Industry is showing significant interest in adopting on-demand cloud services to meet dynamic customer needs. The adoption of cloud services is not an ad-hoc or isolated local change initiative. The adoption of cloud services is a transformational change. A holistic strategic enterprise architecture driven approach is appropriate to guide the systematic adoption of cloud services. One may contend that enterprise architecture is not necessary for certain cloud services such as the public cloud. In fact the opposite is true. More than ever, enterprise architecture capability is required by organizations to understand and analyse how internal and external cloud and non-cloud services and related processes and data flows would be integrated to operationalize the complex and dynamic enterprise environment.

Enterprise architecture is a strategic discipline for developing and realising strategic business initiatives and roadmaps. There are a number of frameworks TOGAF, Zachman, DoDAF, FEAF etc., which can be adopted to develop the requisite practices, roles and techniques into an enterprise architecture capability. But enterprise architecture practices defined by these frameworks are, especially from the perspective of small medium enterprises, often considered to be overly bureaucratic, time consuming, expensive and document driven. Enterprise architecture is needed to enable organizational agility rather hinder it. An agile enterprise architecture capability is called for – one that is capable of dynamically configuring cloud and non-cloud based services to align with business strategies. It is required to produce just-enough or viable coherent architectures to deal with the complex changing business and technological environment.

There are a number of books on cloud computing, cloud computing architecture and enterprise architecture. This book offers something different. It discusses a novel and comprehensive meta-framework, The Gill Framework®, for designing agile enterprises as adaptive enterprise service systems. In particular, it provides guidelines on establishing the agile or adaptive cloud enterprise architecture capability using the meta-framework such as The Gill Framework®. The Gill Framework® offers an adaptive enterprise service system metamodel and a lifecycle management approach, which can be tailored and used to adapting, defining, operating, managing and supporting a context-specific agile capability such as the adaptive cloud enterprise architecture capability.

This book highlights the necessary integration and alignment between the adaptive enterprise architecture capability with other management capabilities such as the adaptive enterprise strategic management, project management and service management capabilities. Such an integrated adaptive cloud enterprise architecture capability enables adaptive adoption of incremental architectural complied strategic cloud solutions in line with business growths. In sum, the topics covered in this book will provide readers with essential information, steps and examples to establishing the adaptive enterprise architecture capability for strategic cloud adoption. Hope you will enjoy learning from the book.

Professor Eng K. Chew
University of Technology Sydney
Former CIO SingTel Optus
Author of the Knowledge Driven Service Innovation and
Management

Preface

The on-demand cloud services offer several benefits over traditional IT services. There is a growing interest among enterprises to adopt cloud services such as software as a service (SaaS), platform as a service (PaaS), infrastructure as a service (IaaS) and facility as a service (FaaS). Cloud adoption is not merely a technology initiative. Cloud adoption requires a strategic adaptive or agile enterprise architecture capability to realise the strategic cloud adoption initiatives. This book is titled "Adaptive Cloud Enterprise Architecture" to emphasize its novel approach. The adaptive cloud enterprise architecture will provide a platform for creating the cloud service-centric agile or adaptive enterprise. The adaptive cloud enterprise architecture differs from traditional enterprise architecture approach, which is perceived to be overly bureaucratic, technology focused, heavy and mechanistic. The adaptive cloud enterprise architecture is a human focused light-weight and adaptive business architecture driven approach to cloud adoption.

The challenge is how to establish an adaptive cloud enterprise architecture capability? This book discusses the application of the adaptive enterprise service system (AESS) metamodel and lifecycle management approach (ADOMS) from The Gill Framework® to adapting, defining, operating, managing and supporting the adaptive cloud enterprise architecture capability. The Gill Framework® is a meta-framework. It has its foundation in agility, design thinking, services and living system principles. It does not replace the existing enterprise architecture frameworks (e.g. TOGAF, Zachman). A basic stance of this book is that no single enterprise architecture framework or method can be universally applied. They all have to be tailored, integrated and adapted to suit the enterprise context. The existing enterprise architecture frameworks have their own best practices. These practices can be combined by using The Gill Framework® for establishing an adaptive cloud adaptive cloud enterprise architecture capability and integrating it to other capabilities such as adaptive enterprise strategic, project, service and requirements management.

In last 10 years, I worked on a number of agile (adaptive) and cloud projects. I also published a number of articles in this important area. This book provides a broader and consolidated intensive experience and research based view on designing and implementing cloud architecture using an adaptive approach. This book is intended for enterprise strategists, enterprise architects, domain architects, solution architects, researchers, and anyone who has an interest in enterprise architecture and cloud computing.

Dr. Asif Q. Gill

About The Author

Dr. Asif Q. Gill is a result-oriented experienced author, coach, consultant, educator, practitioner, researcher, speaker, trainer, and thought leader.

Asif has extensive experience in both agile and non-agile environments, displaying a deep appreciation of their different perspectives in a number of IT-enabled business process improvement and transformation industry projects of varying sizes. The focus of his work is to help teams and organizations to define, improve and transform their human business, social, information and IT capabilities by leveraging lean agile practices and emerging technologies.

Asif is the author of The Gill Framework®, and a number of books, book chapters, white papers, and conference and journal articles. He is often invited and involved as a professional speaker, conference chair, organizer, and reviewer for a number of quality academic and industry conferences. He has a PhD Computing Science, MSc Computing Science and Master of Business. When completing his PhD at University of Technology in Sydney, he was awarded the Australian Postgraduate Award for Industry (APAI). Certified in ITIL, Lean Six Sigma, TOGAF, and Project Management.

Disclaimer:

All the material contained in this book is provided for educational and informational purposes only. No responsibility can be taken for any results or outcomes resulting from the use of this material. While every attempt has been made to provide information that is both accurate and effective, the author does not assume any responsibility for the use or misuse of this information.

Acknowledgements

This book is a result of many years of practical and research work. This book would not have been possible without the support of my almighty God, family, friends, colleagues and reviewers.

I would like to thank my parents Mr. and Mrs. Gill, sisters and brother for all the support and unconditional love they provided me over the years for allowing me to pursue my passion. I would like to thank my wife Saja for being patient and standing beside me in the arduous journey of writing this book. I thank to my kids Riyad and Junaid for the weekends I spent writing this book instead of playing with them in the backyard. I really appreciate and thank to my extended family Mr. and Mrs. Moussa, Mr. and Mrs. Kannan, and Mr. and Mrs. Sabbagh for the continuous encouragement.

I want to thank my colleagues, proof readers, editor and reviewers who reviewed the manuscript, and provided criticism, ideas and suggestions – especially Dr. Bernard Wong, Darryl Carr, Dr. Ghassan Beydoun and Prof. Vijayan Sugumaran. Finally, I would like to extend my special thanks to Professor Jie Lu for all the academic guidance and support in writing this book.

Acknowledgements

Contents

List of Tables

List of Figures

Chapter 1

Introduction

1.1 Introduction

A traditional computing environment requires organisations to purchase and install expensive on-site upfront computing resources, such as a platform (e.g. an operating system, a development platform) and infrastructure (e.g. network, storage, processing and memory devices) for the development, testing, deployment and maintenance of software applications (e.g. financial, supply chain). Organisations are under enormous pressure and are increasingly becoming interested in adopting technological innovations in order to deliver agile, economical and quality solutions to meet the ever-changing requirements of their customers. Organisations are seeking on-demand and less expensive application development and management alternatives to avoid upfront investments and unpredictable returns (Hai and Sakoda 2009).

The emergence of on-demand cloud computing allows organisations to quickly source, develop, test and deploy X as a Service (XaaS) to meet the dynamic business needs of their customers (Salesforce 2008; Armbrust et al. 2009). The character 'X' can refer to a range of computing resources such as software, platform, infrastructure etc. Organisations have shown a significant interest in the adoption of economical and shared cloud computing environment. Although cloud computing seems to offer several advantages (e.g. scalability, pay-as-you-go), it also poses a number of new challenges. Before jumping on the cloud bandwagon, organisations need to understand the fundamental differences between the traditional and cloud computing environment. Instead of a silo or ad-hoc cloud technology adoption, they may need a strategic adaptive or agile cloud enterprise architecture capability to guide the strategic business-driven organisation-wide effective and less risky cloud technology adoption.

This book discusses the application of the adaptive enterprise service system (AESS) metamodel and lifecycle management approach (ADOMS) from The Gill Framework® to adapting, defining, operating, managing and supporting the adaptive cloud enterprise architecture capability. The adaptive cloud enterprise architecture provides a platform for creating a cloud service-centric agile or adaptive enterprise. Before discussing cloud architecture, this chapter discusses the following basic cloud computing concepts, evolution and constructs.

- Cloud computing
- Cloud evolution
- Cloud characteristics
- Cloud service models
- Cloud deployment models
- Cloud stakeholders
- Cloud adoption benefits
- Cloud adoption challenges

1.2   Cloud Computing

Cloud computing is continuously evolving. There is no single globally agreed definition of cloud computing. There are a number of definitions which attempt to describe cloud computing characteristics. The 2010 European Commission (EC) report defines cloud computing as "an elastic execution environment of resources involving multiple stakeholders and providing a metered service at multiple granularities for a specified level of quality (of service)".

This definition of cloud computing highlights that the cloud is not only concerned with the use of computing resources over the network, it is an elastic or scalable environment that has the ability to cope with the dynamic high and low capacity demands of metered computing resources over the Internet, based on an agreed service quality or service level agreement. Similar to the EC report, Gartner (Plummer et al. 2008) describes cloud computing as "a style of computing where massively scalable IT-enabled capabilities are delivered 'as a service' to external customers using Internet technologies".

The Open Cloud Manifesto (2009) explains the characteristics of cloud computing from a technological perspective and defines cloud computing as "a culmination of many technologies, such as grid computing, utility computing, SOA, Web 2.0, and other technologies", but it also states that "a precise definition is often debated". Similar to the Open Cloud Manifesto, Forrester (2015) describes cloud computing as a standardised IT environment in which "a standardized IT capability (services, software, or infrastructure) is delivered in a pay-per-use, self-service way." This definition highlights the important pay-per-use and self-service mechanisms of provisioning IT services without human intervention (different from traditional IT service provisioning). As indicated in this section, there is no precise standard definition of cloud computing. In 2011, the National Institute of Standards and Technology (NIST), a body which describes technology standards, provided a more comprehensive and acceptable definition of cloud computing, as follows:

"a model for enabling ubiquitous, convenient, on-demand network access to a shared pool of configurable computing resources (e.g., networks, servers, storage, applications, and services) that can be rapidly provisioned and released with minimal management effort or service provider interaction. This cloud model is composed of five essential characteristics, three service models, and four deployment models".

This book is focused on adaptive cloud enterprise architecture. To complement this widely accepted NIST definition of cloud computing, this book provides the following architecture-driven (based on ISO/IEC/IEEE 42010) definition of the cloud:

"The fundamental concepts or properties of an adaptive cloud service system in its environment embodied in its elements, relationships, and in the principles of its design and evolution".

This book defines the cloud as an adaptive service system that offers services. Fundamental to an adaptive cloud service system is its design and evolution principles, external (e.g. local, national and international) and internal relationships, and on-demand self-service configurable software and hardware (physical or virtual) computing resources or elements that can be rapidly provisioned and released as secure adaptive services with minimal management effort or service provider interaction.

1.3 Cloud Evolution

Cloud computing provides an environment for offering services over the Internet. The concept of the "Internet" or the "Cloud" is not new; new, if anything, is the ability to access and use the on-demand pay-as-you-go shared multi-tenant cloud services over the public network. The history of cloud computing can be traced back to the 1950s' mainframe and utility computing. The term *mainframe* refers to large computing and storage resources housed in large cabinets or frames. The UNIVAC I[a], the first mainframe computer which was about the size of a car garage, was used by the U.S. Census Bureau. The concept of utility computing, similar to other utility services such as telephone and electricity utility services, refers to the use of computing, network and storage resources as metered services on a pay-as-you-go basis instead of a flat rate. John McCarthy mentioned at the MIT Centennial in 1961 (Garfinkel 1999):

"If computers of the kind I have advocated become the computers of the future, then computing may someday be organized as a public utility just as the telephone system is a public utility".

The term *Internet* refers to the large global public network of computers. The origin of the Internet can be traced back to the 1960s US government research project ARPANET, which developed an advanced resilient computer network and communication environment. This work evolved in the shape of a global computer network over a period of time and was fully available for public commercial use in the mid-1990s (that

---

[a] http://www.thocp.net/hardware/mainframe.htm

is, the final restrictions on commercial traffic were removed), which is now known as the "Internet". Concepts such as mainframe, utility computing and the Internet are the fundamental building blocks of cloud computing. The origin of the modern constructs of cloud computing can be attributed to the Salesforce.com platform in the late 1990s and the Amazon Web Services platform in early 2000. Since the late 1990s, a number of new ways of offering cloud computing services (e.g. SaaS, PaaS, IaaS) and deployment models (e.g. public, private, community and hybrid) have emerged to deal with the complex computing requirements of the 21st century. This section discusses cloud evolution from software development, hosting and provisioning perspectives.

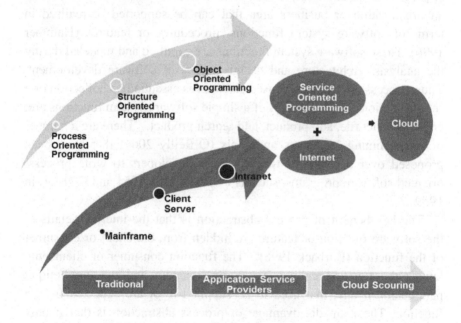

Fig. 1.1. Cloud evolution.

1.3.1 *Development*

The software application development process involves analysing, architecting, designing, coding, testing, and deploying software programs by using an abstraction model or design paradigm (Berzins et al. 1986;

Theodorakis et al. 1999). Software development is supported by the appropriate development platform, including programming languages and tools. An abstraction model is a logical view and representation of real world entities or problems and their solution in terms of software programs, such as process-oriented, structure or data oriented, and object-oriented (Burback 1998). There are four key software application development abstraction models (see Fig. 1.1), namely process, data, object and service.

1.3.1.1 *Process*

A process abstraction is a logical view or representation of activities of an organisation or business area that can be supported or realised in terms of software system functions, procedures or features (Hammer 1996). These software system functions are captured and modeled during the analysis, architecture and design phases of software development. Thus, process-abstraction-focused software is essentially a collection or a set of functions. The examples of a simple software system functions are: create product file, add product, and search product. There are a number of programming languages and tools (O'Reilly 2004) that have been proposed over a period of time to allow developers to write process-oriented software programs, such as FORTRAN in 1954 and COBOL in 1959.

The key benefit of process abstraction is that the internal details of the software function or feature are hidden from the client or consumer of the function (Burback 1998). The function consumer or client only knows the function calling syntax or signature and the input/output parameters, if any, that need to be supplied to or are expected from a function. The main disadvantage of process abstraction is that it only focuses on the activity aspect of the organisation and does not focus on data re-usability or a custom definition of complex business data structures. In process abstraction, there is also no clear separation between the data and the function that processes the data.

1.3.1.2 *Data*

A data abstraction (Jackson 1975) is a logical view or representation of the data of an organisation that can be supported or realized in terms of data structures or properties. These data structures are captured and modeled during the analysis, architecture and design phases of software development. Examples of simple data structures are: product, customer, contract and sales order.   A data structure is a set of data elements or properties. A number of programming languages and tools have been proposed over a period of time to allow developers to write data-oriented software programs, such as C in 1971. The key benefit of data structure or data abstraction is that the internal details of data elements in the data structure may not be visible to the data consumer or client. Data abstraction also supports data structure re-usability by providing a clear separation between the data and the function that processes the data.

1.3.1.3 *Object*

An object abstraction (Larman 2004) is a logical view or representation of a business entity that combines process and data abstraction concepts in terms of software classes. These entities are captured and modeled during the analysis, architecture and design phases of software development.   A class is a container that encapsulates both the data elements and methods (e.g. functions are called methods in a class), which is used to instantiate class objects. A set of objects is represented by a class, which is called an abstract data type. An object-oriented software system is a set of classes, objects and their interactions. A number of object-oriented programming languages and tools (O'Reilly 2004) have been proposed over a period of time to enable developers to write object-oriented software programs, such as C++ in 1983 and Java in 1995. The key benefit of object-oriented abstraction is that it allows the management of both data and related methods in one re-usable container (e.g. class). It also supports several other features such as inheritance, polymorphism, messaging, aggregation and association to represent the interactions and complex relationships between classes and objects (Burback 1998; Larman 2004).

1.3.1.4 *Service*

A software service is a contractually defined behavior that is a logical view or an abstraction of a business process for carrying out business-level operations (Krogdahl et al. 2005). A software service is identified and modelled during the analysis, architecture and design phases. It is developed and offered by a service provider to support business services. A software service can be used by other services or service consumers in compliance with a service contract. A software service is the application of resources, which can be implemented in terms of web services (e.g. Java web services). A service is publishable and discoverable with an externalized service description (Arsanjani 2004). For example, a published service description is available for searching, binding and invocation by a service consumer. The service provider provides the service description implementation in alignment with the quality of the service requirements. A service system is a configuration of resources that offers services, interactions and inter-connecting patterns (Nickull 2005). The key benefit of service abstraction is that it supports a dynamically re-configurable architectural style, which is governed by declarative policies. A service-oriented software system is designed to support a standard interface and a flexible collaboration contract, and can communicate in any mode at any time (Tsai et al. 2006).

1.3.2 *Hosting*

Software applications and development platforms are deployed in some kind of hosting environment (Berzins et al. 1986; Theodorakis et al. 1999). A hosting environment allows software developers to develop, test (e.g. development and testing environment) and deploy (e.g. test, staging, and production environment) software applications to be accessible to users or clients. There are four key hosting constructs which led to the emergence of cloud computing: mainframe, client server, intranet and Internet.

1.3.2.1 *Mainframe*

Mainframes provide a computing environment to centrally host applications and large sets of data, which is accessible to users via a thin client. The history of the centralised computing environment of the mainframe can be traced back to the 1950s (as discussed earlier). There are a number of mainframe providers, such as IBM and Unisys. Mainframes have been mostly used by large banking, insurance, travel, manufacturing and government organisations. In a traditional mainframe environment, "all the processing capacity, all the memory and disk storage, resided on the mainframe; only a "dumb terminal" sat on the user's desk" (Chalem 2000). The key benefit of the mainframe is that it provides a secure and centrally controlled computing environment for large organisations requiring high speed processing and very large storage. Mainframes do not seem appropriate for small organisations with low processing and storage needs.

1.3.2.2 *Client server*

A client server (Orfali et al. 1994) provides a computing environment to host applications and data in one or multiple servers, which is accessible to users via a thin or thick client. A server can be a server or client at the same time, which is known as a peer-to-peer client server computing environment. The history of the client server computing environment can be traced back to the 1980s, when there was a noticeable shift from expensive centralized mainframes to low cost personal computers distributed over a secure network (client and servers) (Chalem 2000). The mainframe community shifted their focus from mainframe central systems to distributed client server systems. The key benefit of the client server model is its flexibility and ease of maintenance. It allows the applications and data to be distributed among several independent computers (servers) that are connected to each other via a secure network interface. The main difference between the mainframe and the client server is that with the client server, all the processing capacity, memory and disk storage do not need to reside on a single computer (e.g. the mainframe); rather it can be distributed on multiple server computers and is accessible via thin or thick client computers as opposed to only a "dumb terminal". Unlike mainframes, the client server model seems appropriate for small to large size organisations with low to high processing and storage needs. The main disadvantage of the client server model is the loss of central control over data and applications.

1.3.2.3 *Intranet*

An intranet (Callaghan 2002) can be considered an extension of a client server model and provides a network environment to securely share applications and data within an organisation. An intranet is internal to an organisation, and is accessible to users from the local network of the organisation or from a remote location via a virtual private network (VPN). A VPN is an "extension of an organisation's private network to connect remote users over a shared or public network" (Odiyo and Dwarkanath 2011). A private network or intranet can be extended to form an inter-organisational network, which is known as an extranet. The history of the intranet, also called a private Internet, can be traced back to the 1990s. The key benefit of an intranet is that it provides a private platform to the employees of an organisation to discuss and communicate information and issues that could lead to innovation, productivity and a better quality of products and services offered by that organisation.

1.3.2.4 *Internet*

The concept of the Internet emerged in 1981 with world-wide interconnected TCP/IP networks, which was an extension of the ARPANET. However, the Internet was first truly commercialized in 1995. The key benefit of the Internet is that it bypasses the complexity of personal computer operating systems while providing a simplified browser-base cross-platform approach to access applications and data from anywhere in the world wherever the Internet is available (Chalem 2000). However, a number of issues emerged with the use of the Internet, such as the security of applications and data that are available or accessible over the Internet.

1.3.3 *Provisioning*

Provisioning is a mechanism to acquire, support and deploy computing resources in a production environment for operational use (Dehaan 2008). There are three key aspects of provisioning that led to the emergence of cloud sourcing: traditional, application service providers and cloud sourcing.

1.3.3.1 *Traditional*

Software applications and platforms are acquired and hosted on the organisation's local premises (in-house) in a traditional provisioning environment. The key advantage of traditional provisioning is that the consumer organization has complete control over their computing environment. The main disadvantage of this approach is that it requires a large number of IT staff, heavy upfront licensing, and configuration and hosting costs (Carraro and Chong 2006).

1.3.3.2 *Application service providers*

Software applications are centrally hosted and provided by application service providers (ASP) to consumers over a network or the Internet. ASP "entails the hosting and provision of the applications to customers, the actual servers on which these application reside, and the network connection that enables the delivery of the application over a network" (Kern and Kreijger 2001). The key advantage of the ASP approach is reduced upfront license and support costs (Kern et al. 2001). The main disadvantage of the ASP approach is the loss of control and dependency (Kern and Kreijger 2001).

1.3.3.3 *Cloud sourcing*

A service is a logical view or an abstraction of an on-demand software computing resource that is deployed and accessed as a hosted service in the cloud via an Internet client. Cloud computing builds on the service-oriented paradigm and Internet computing, and establishes a distinct paradigm of its own together with additional characteristics, such as service metering, self-service, multitenancy etc. A cloud provider provides measureable cloud services such as XaaS (e.g. SaaS, PaaS, IaaS) in alignment with the service level agreement to service consumers. Cloud services are accessible on demand, without direct interaction with the service provider over a network, such as the Internet. Traditional sourcing is based on a single tenant model, where one consumer organisation has a dedicated computing environment. Cloud sourcing supports the pooling of computing resources that can be dynamically assigned and reassigned to multiple consumer organisations according to demand in a shared multitenant environment (see Fig. 1.2).

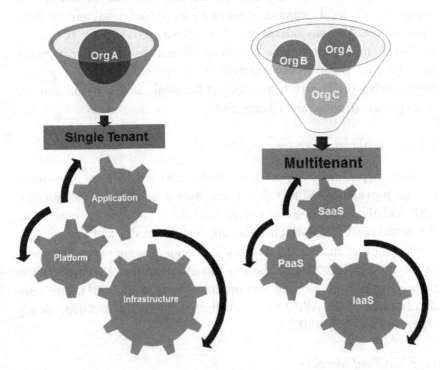

Fig. 1.2. Shared cloud multitenant environment.

1.4 Cloud Characteristics

NIST describes five essential characteristics of cloud computing: on-demand self-service, broad network access, resource pooling, rapid elasticity, and measured service. In addition to these five characteristics, this book also includes three additional cloud characteristics: service orientation, security and virtualisation. This section discusses these eight essential characteristics (see Fig. 1.3), which are fundamental to cloud service system architecture.

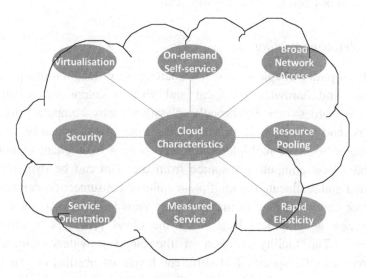

Fig. 1.3. Cloud characteristics.

1.4.1 *On-demand Self-service*

Cloud computing resources can be registered, made available, provisioned and deprovisioned on demand and without unnecessary human intervention and interaction with physical resources. A self-service cloud service can be deployed or hosted over an Internet cloud server without the need to locally install or run it. It can be deployed outside or behind the firewall of an organisation. This characteristic of cloud computing offers consumers a high level of control over the resources and their consumption.

1.4.2 *Broad Network Access*

This cloud computing characteristic refers to the ability to offer and acquire computing resources over the network. Broad network access to computing resources requires a standard mechanism(s) to facilitate the use of resources by a range of heterogeneous clients and interfaces. A cloud resource can be accessed over the Internet via a thin or thick client. A cloud resource can specify the specific network and bandwidth requirements for access. A cloud resource may support multi-channel interaction or interfacing i.e. mobile, iPad.

1.4.3 *Resource Pooling*

Cloud computing enables access to a shared pool of location-independent software and hardware (physical and virtual) computing resources. These resources can be broadly classified into compute, storage, network, and memory categories. Cloud service instances can be created and pooled to serve multiple consumers using a multitenant model. A reusable cloud computing resource from the pool can be dynamically allocated and reallocated to multiple-tenants or consumers on demand. A tenant or consumer may or may not have knowledge of or control over the precise geographical location of the cloud providers' computing resources. The facility location of the cloud providers' computing resources can be specified at different levels of abstraction, such as country, state, city, suburb, building, floor, room, cabinet, and rack.

1.4.4 *Rapid Elasticity*

The size of the cloud computing resource pool may grow or shrink in response to demand. The ability of the cloud to scale in and scale out, and scale up and scale down offers immense flexibility to consumers. This gives an illusion to consumers that the resources are unlimited and will be available for provisioning at any time and in any quantity. A cloud service can be deployed across multiple physical or virtual machines or clusters for load balancing in order to maximize throughput, minimize response time, and avoid overload.

1.4.5 *Measured Service*

Cloud computing has its foundation in utility computing, where computing resources are offered based on the pay-per-use or pay-as-you-go pricing model instead of a traditional flat rate. This requires the ability to measure the use of the cloud computing resource at some level of abstraction. For instance, processing or computing resources can be measured in terms of cycle time; a storage or memory resource can be measured in terms of bytes; and a network resource can be measured in terms of bandwidth. A resource needs to be monitored to measure, control, and report its use to concerned parties. Resource usage can be monitored by attaching a metering capability at some level of abstraction appropriate to the type of resource. Resource usage can be controlled by attaching a controlling capability at some level of abstraction appropriate to the type of resource. Similarly, resource usage can be reported by attaching a reporting capability at some level of abstraction appropriate to the type of resource.

1.4.6 *Service Orientation*

Fundamental to cloud computing is service orientation. A cloud service is the application of resources. A service is the fundamental unit of exchange in cloud computing. Cloud computing resources are packaged and offered as services: software as a service (e.g. software application), platform as a service (e.g. operating system software, web server software, development tools) and infrastructure as a service (e.g. hardware and virtual devices). This book also includes an additional essential resource, facility as a service (e.g. physical and virtual). A facility is more than a location, it is a whole geo-spatial environment where infrastructure resources are housed.

1.4.7 *Security*

Security is one of the paramount characteristics of cloud computing. The successful adoption of multitenant cloud computing is largely driven by security. The security of a cloud service can be ensured through a number of mechanisms, such as encryption and firewalls etc.

1.4.8 *Virtualisation*

Virtualisation is a way to offer physical resources, such as logical or virtual resources. A cloud is considered as one type of virtualisation implementation. Virtualisation could be applied to create multiple logical versions of a single resource. For instance, a physical server can be virtualised to create multiple logical servers. Virtualisation is done to achieve optimal use of the physical resources.

1.5 Cloud Service Models

The NIST cloud computing definition highlights three cloud service models: software as a service (SaaS), platform as a service (PaaS) and infrastructure as a service (IaaS). In addition to these three cloud service models, this books provides a fourth service model, which is called facility as a service (FaaS). These four major cloud service models are shown in Fig. 1.4).

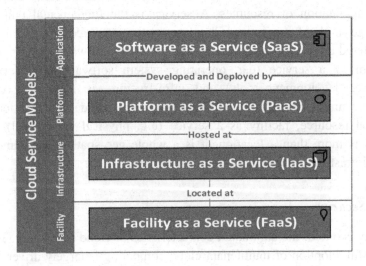

Fig. 1.4. Cloud service models.

1.5.1 *SaaS*

SaaS is a software application which is developed and deployed or run by the underlying PaaS. There are a number of SaaS providers, such as Salesforce.com, Concur, Fios, LucidEra, Taleo, Spring CM, and NetSuite. The SaaS instances are accessible over the network through a client or API interface. SaaS clients do not have control over the underlying PaaS, IaaS and FaaS layers. The SaaS instance can be customized for a particular client, however, the customisation is subject to the governance limitations imposed by the SaaS provider. SaaS can be offered on a pay-per-use basis (e.g. active number of accounts or the number of users using the SaaS application).

1.5.2 *PaaS*

PaaS is a platform which is hosted at IaaS. PaaS includes both system software and an integrated development environment (IDE). It includes programming languages, testing tools, web servers, application servers, database servers, file servers, APIs, integration utilities, and infrastructure software. There are a number of PaaS providers, such as Amazon SimpleDB, Salesforce.com, MS Azure Platform, Informatica on–demand, and Collabnet. PaaS clients do not have control over the underlying IaaS and FaaS layers. However, PaaS clients do have control over the applications developed and deployed using PaaS with some limited access to the configuration settings of the underlying IaaS hosting environment.

1.5.3 *IaaS*

IaaS provides a pool of compute, network, storage, memory and other related infrastructure resources, which are located in a particular facility. IaaS houses PaaS and SaaS. There are a number of IaaS providers, such as Amazon S3, Amazon EC2, RightScale, and Elastra. IaaS usually has two layers: physical and virtual. The resources can be virtualised through a type of virtualisation technology (e.g. Xen, VMware, and Virtual Server). A physical server can be virtualised to create more than one logical or virtual server. There are a number of ways to virtualise a resource. The IaaS client has access to virtual infrastructure resources, which are supported by the underlying physical resources. IaaS clients can deploy and run their own system software, software development tools and applications on the IaaS virtual resource. IaaS clients do not have control over the underlying physical infrastructure and facility, however, they have control over their own virtual infrastructure instances and the deployed system software and applications.

1.5.4 *FaaS*

FaaS provides a facility or site to house cloud IaaS resources. A facility is not only a location, it could be a datacenter building or an office, floor, room, cabinet or rack. The datacenter facility may be located at a local or off-shore site. A facility could be a primary or recovery site and has energy, cooling, fire and security components. FaaS clients have access to virtual facility resources, which are supported by the underlying physical facility resources. FaaS clients do not have control over the underlying physical facility resources, however, they have control over their own infrastructure IaaS, PaaS, and SaaS. This book includes FaaS as an important cloud service model, which is a part of the overall adaptive cloud enterprise architecture capability discussed in this book.

1.6 Cloud Deployment Models

The NIST cloud computing definition highlighted four major cloud deployment models: private cloud, community cloud, public cloud and hybrid cloud. There are a number of other deployment models as well. However, this book only discusses the salient features of these four major cloud deployment models.

1.6.1 *Private Cloud*

A private cloud is provisioned specifically for a single organisation (see Fig. 1.5). A private cloud consumer organisation or provider or a combination of both can establish, operate, manage and support the private cloud. The private cloud resources may or may not be located on the private cloud consumer organisation facility. There are a number of ways to establish a private cloud. A private cloud can be established by consolidating and virtualising the existing computing resources of an organisation. A private cloud can also be established by dedicating specific computing resources of a public cloud to a single organisation. A private cloud service model seems appropriate for large organisations, such as large banks and public organisations. A provide cloud is also referred to as an enterprise private cloud.

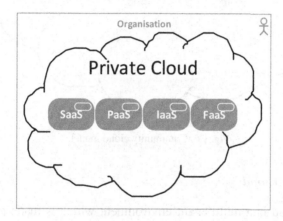

Fig. 1.5. Private cloud model.

1.6.2 *Community Cloud*

A community cloud is provisioned for a specific community that has mutual goals and requirements (see Fig. 1.6). The community cloud members come from different organisations. One of the members of the community (e.g. a lead community member) or provider or a combination of both, can establish, operate, manage and support the community cloud. A community cloud can be established as a private or public community cloud. A community cloud is appropriate for organisations which want to share the cost and benefits of the cloud through economies of scale. A typical implementation of a private community cloud can be done for government agencies. Government agencies may provision a private community cloud to share computing resources, cost and benefits. A government private community cloud can be managed by the lead government agency.

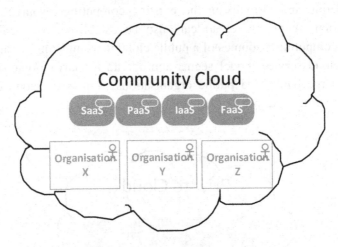

Fig. 1.6. Community cloud model.

1.6.3 *Public Cloud*

A public cloud is a multitenant environment which is made available to consumers over a public network, such as the Internet (see Fig. 1.7). A public cloud is architected and implemented to support a range of consumers. A public cloud has a pool of virtual and physical computing resources that can be accessed by consumers on demand. A consumer does not have control over the management of public cloud resources. However, a consumer can control their own use of public cloud resources. A public cloud is established, operated, managed and supported by cloud service providers. The public cloud service model is appropriate for organisations which cannot afford or do not have a business case for establishing their own private cloud.

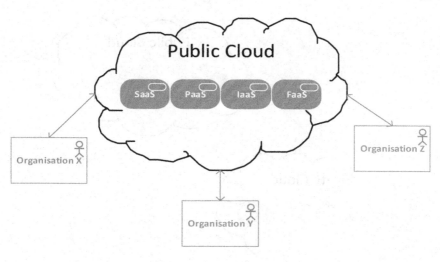

Fig. 1.7. Public cloud model.

1.6.4 *Hybrid Cloud*

A hybrid cloud refers to an environment that combines two or more cloud service models (see Fig. 1.8). It is possible that an organisation may provision some services from a public cloud and some services from a private or/and community cloud. For instance, a private cloud can be used for managing sensitive information and a public cloud can be used for managing less sensitive information. While it is practical to have a hybrid cloud environment, this may spark the need for additional integration requirements between public cloud, private cloud, community cloud (inter cloud) and non-cloud resources.

In summary, cloud computing offers these different service models, hence organisations should carefully evaluate their requirements and these models before committing any resources to cloud adoption. It is also emphasised that the selection and adoption of a specific cloud service model is a transformational change. It should be treated as a strategic change as opposed to a routine operational change. While considering cloud adoption, organisations should also develop contingencies for cloud de-adoption.

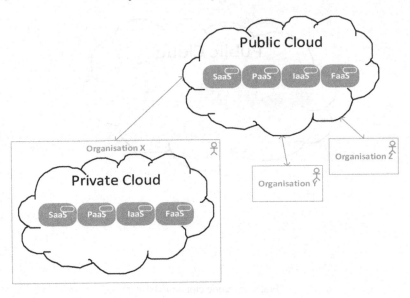

Fig. 1.8. Hybrid cloud model.

1.7 Cloud Stakeholders

Cloud computing not only involves technology adoption, it also involves a number of stakeholders or actors who interact with each other, play different roles and engage in relevant activities in the cloud environment. An actor could be a human or non-human individual or organisation. These actors can play different roles, such as cloud customer, user, developer, manufacturer, provider, tester, integrator, manager, owner, administrator, carrier, broker, auditor, regulator, observer, partner and competitor. Table 1.1 provides a description of key cloud actor roles and their activities.

Table 1.1. Cloud stakeholders.

Ref. #	Role	Activities
1	Customer	Cloud customer pays for the cloud service.
2	User	Cloud user or consumer uses the cloud service.
3	Developer	Cloud developer develops the cloud service.

Table 1.1. (*Continued*)

Ref.	Role	Activities
4	Provider	Cloud provider provides the cloud service.
5	Manufacturer	Cloud manufacturer manufactures the cloud service.
6	Tester	Cloud tester tests the cloud service.
7	Integrator	Cloud integrator integrates the cloud service.
8	Manager	Cloud manager manages the cloud service.
9	Owner	Cloud owner owns the cloud service.
10	Administrator	Cloud administrator administrates the cloud service.
11	Carrier	Cloud carrier provides the connectivity and network to connect the cloud service.
12	Broker	Cloud broker manages the interactions between cloud actors.
13	Auditor	Cloud auditor conducts an independent audit of the cloud service.
14	Regulator	Cloud regulator provides the standards and regulatory compliance requirements for the cloud service.
15	Observer	Cloud observer observes or monitors the cloud service.
16	Partner	Cloud partner supports the cloud provider.
17	Competitor	Cloud competitor is in competition with another cloud actor.

1.8 Cloud Adoption Benefits

There is a growing interest among public and private organisations in adopting cloud computing. Before jumping on the cloud bandwagon, it is important to understand both the benefits and challenges of the cloud.

This section provides some insights into the benefits of cloud computing. Cloud computing claims to offer several benefits over traditional computing. Some of these benefits are:

- reduced cost
- reduced carbon emission
- enhanced enterprise agility
- improved resource utilisation
- improved availability
- improved reliability
- improved economies of scale

1.8.1 *Reduced Cost*

There are two broad cost categories: capital expenditure (CAPEX) and operational expenditure (OPEX). Cloud computing seems to reduce the upfront capital cost of new IT resources and the cost of ongoing ownership. Cost is not only incurred due to IT equipment or software, it also includes human resources (e.g. competency and capacity). Organisations do not have to own the resources, rather, they can use the cloud provider's resources on demand and on a pay-per-use basis. However, the resource rent or lease or fee may increase the operational cost. Organisations need to carefully assess their circumstances when investing in the cloud.

1.8.2 *Reduced Carbon Emission*

Consumers do not have to keep their computing resources up and running all the time. They can source cloud computing resources from the cloud provider on a need basis, and switch them off when they are not required any more. This reduces the idle time of the resources and may consequently help reduce the consumer organisation's carbon emission. However, this does not guarantee that the cloud provider can also achieve the same benefit of reduced carbon emission. A cloud provider may need to keep their resources up and running to meet unpredictable consumer demands.

1.8.3 *Enhanced Enterprise Agility*

Cloud computing claims to enhance enterprise or business agility. It provides flexibility to an enterprise to quickly scale up and down (vertical scaling) and scale in and out (horizontal scaling) in response to dynamic business needs. Vertical scaling is the ability to reduce or increase capacity by replacing existing resources on demand. Horizontal scaling is the ability to dynamically allocate and de-allocate resources in response to changing business demands. Hence, changes in resource demand can be quickly accommodated through vertical and horizontal scaling, however, such flexibility does not suggest that an enterprise should not undertake resource capacity planning, rather, instead of up-front fixed detailed capacity planning, an enterprise needs to undertake adaptive capacity planning in response to changing business demands. Cloud services also provide some programming flexibility or an adaptable service meta-model for consumer-specific cloud service configuration. It is important that a cloud service should offer specialised technical knowledge and the skill support required for service configuration and management.

1.8.4 *Improved Resource Utilisation*

A fundamental to cloud computing is the virtualisation of physical resources. Virtualisation enables the creation of a number of logical resources from the same physical resource with a view to improving physical resource utilisation. For instance, a physical server computer can be virtualised to create a number of virtual servers. Each virtual server can be used independently by humans or software programs. However, the good health of virtual resources depends on the good health of the underlying physical resources. There are a number of virtualisation strategies, however, a detailed discussion of such strategies is beyond the scope of this chapter.

1.8.5 *Improved Availability*

Cloud computing allows cloud consumers to pay only for the required availability times. It increases the ability of a cloud consumer to minimize unwanted downtime or interruptions due to planned or unplanned changes. The underlying resources of the cloud can be dynamically changed without interrupting the cloud consumers. This means that a cloud service hosted over a cloud server can be maintained without the need to locally install service upgrades in the service consumer's machine. It is easy to make changes to a service through automatic upgrades, such as patches, plug-ins or add-ons and a cloud provider normally provides flexibility to cloud consumers to choose between the different available versions, patches, plug-ins, or add-ons of a cloud service. All changes, disruptions or unavailability of a cloud service can be supported by automatic service change notifications to service consumers.

1.8.6 *Improved Reliability*

Cloud computing is a complex environment encompassing several different types of resources. These resources allow consumers to quickly identify, adapt and recover from a failure or disaster situation. For instance, a cloud consumer may put their backup and recovery site resources on the cloud, which can only be sourced and paid for throughout the duration of the disaster situation. Further, in order to make the service more reliable, cloud providers may impose execution limits on the service such as code size limits, query or request size limits and execution timeout limits.

1.8.7 *Improved Economies of Scale*

Cloud computing offers economies of scale to consumers. An individual organisation may not be able to afford the upfront purchase of certain expensive computing resources. Therefore, instead of purchasing such expensive resources, an organisation may rent or lease these resources from a cloud provider and only pay for the use of such resources. For instance, an organisation may collaborate with other similar organisations and set up their own private community cloud to share costs and benefits.

1.9 Cloud Adoption Challenges

Although cloud computing offers several lucrative benefits over traditional computing, it brings new challenges as well. These challenges need to be assessed in conjunction with its benefits for effective and informed cloud adoption. Some of the challenges of cloud computing are:

- security
- privacy
- compliance
- portability
- interoperability
- social

1.9.1 *Security*

Security is one of the most important concerns of cloud adoption. Security refers to the ability of the cloud to handle security threats such as malware and denial-of-service. Cloud providers usually apply state-of-the-art security mechanisms, which are sometimes beyond the affordability of an individual consumer. An audit of cloud security mechanisms (e.g. encryption, malicious code control) needs to be conducted by certified third parties and any relevant audit security reports should be made available to concerned consumers to build a trusted relationship.

1.9.2 *Privacy*

A public cloud is a multitenant environment which can be used by multiple organisations or tenants. It is important to ensure that cloud providers have appropriate access control measures to counter any privacy breaches or unauthorised access to the information stored in the multitenant shared environment. Similar to cloud security challenges, an audit of cloud privacy or access control needs to be conducted by certified third parties and any relevant privacy audit reports should be made available to concerned consumers. Privacy is achieved in a number of ways, such as single sign-on authentication and authorization, IP-based access, organisation and role-based access etc.

1.9.3 *Compliance*

Cloud computing is a geographically distributed environment. Cloud providers may have their cloud IaaS resources housed at different facilities in different countries. It is important for a cloud provider to address local and international legal compliance requirements, if any. It is also important for a cloud consumer to have information about the location of the cloud provider's facility. Cloud consumers should be able to choose the specific cloud service facility, which can be governed through provider-consumer SLA.

1.9.4 *Portability*

There are a number of cloud environments. An application developed and deployed in one cloud environment may not be able to run or be portable in another environment. This could be due to a lack of cloud standards, an emerging area which needs more attention from cloud providers and standards development bodies.

1.9.5 *Interoperability*

Interoperability is the ability to share information between different cloud and non-cloud environments. There is limited interoperability of information between clouds. Similar to the portability challenge, there is a need to develop standards for cloud interoperability. A cloud service should have the ability to interact with a service or application running in an offline mode, if required. A cloud service should have the ability to sync back to a central service running offline, when required. Both portability and interoperability are very important requirements for cloud adoption.

1.9.6 *Social*

Cloud adoption is not all about technological adoption. Successful cloud adoption requires identifying and addressing social human-related challenges. These challenges may include human behavior, organisational culture, and the political environment of an organisation. People's mindsets and motivations are critical elements in the successful adoption of cloud computing.

1.10 Book Organisation

It will be helpful to explain the issue of adaptive cloud enterprise architecture capability with the help of a case study. To do so, a fictitious company is created, called the Super Financial Services (SFS) enterprise. The SFS enterprise operates both in local and international markets. It has over 40,000 employees working in geographically distributed locations all over the world. It offers personal, small business and corporate banking services to its customers via online and in-branch channels. The SFS enterprise already has an enterprise architecture capability but it needs to create an adaptive cloud enterprise architecture capability within the existing enterprise architecture capability to guide the systematic adoption of the cloud across the enterprise.

This book discusses the use of a meta-framework, such as The Gill Framework®: AESS metamodel and ADOMS lifecycle management approach, to adapting, defining, operating, managing and supporting the adaptive cloud enterprise architecture capability for this large fictitious SFS enterprise. The fictitious SFS enterprise case study will help to explain the establishment of the adaptive cloud enterprise architecture capability in the context of practical cloud adoption. The final chapter provides additional case study scenarios which discuss adaptive cloud enterprise architecture for different cloud adoption contexts. This book is intended for enterprise strategists, enterprise architects, domain architects, solution architects, researchers, and anyone who has an interest in enterprise architecture and cloud computing disciplines. The contents of this book are organised into ten chapters as follows.

Chapter 1 – Introduction: This chapter provides an introduction to the basic concepts of cloud computing, its evolution, its essential characteristics, service models, deployment models and stakeholders. It also highlights some of the cloud benefits and challenges. This chapter provides basic cloud knowledge as a foundation, which is necessary for understanding the topic of adaptive cloud enterprise architecture capability.

Chapter 2 – Cloud-Enabled Enterprise Adaptation: This chapter discusses modern enterprise adaptation and challenges. Further, it discusses key enterprise architecture frameworks and challenges in the context of cloud-enabled enterprise adaptation. This chapter also introduces to The Gill Framework® (AESS metamodel and ADOMS approach) for adapting, defining, operating, managing and supporting the adaptive cloud enterprise architecture capability.

Chapter 3 – The Adaptive Enterprise Service System Metamodel: This chapter provides an overview of the AESS metamodel of The Gill Framework®.

Chapter 4 – The Adaptive Enterprise Service System Lifecycle Management: This chapter describes the AESS lifecycle management approach, called ADOMS.

Chapter 5 – Adapting Cloud Enterprise Architecture Capability: This chapter describes the adapting capability of the ADOMS approach in the context of the fictitious SFS enterprise.

Chapter 6 – Defining Cloud Enterprise Architecture Capability: This chapter describes how to define an adaptive cloud enterprise architecture capability for the fictitious SFS enterprise.

Chapter 7 – Operating Cloud Enterprise Architecture Capability: This chapter describes how to operate the adaptive cloud enterprise architecture capability of the fictitious SFS enterprise to produce cloud architecture artefacts.

Chapter 8 – Managing Cloud Enterprise Architecture Capability: This chapter describes how to manage changes in the adaptive cloud enterprise architecture capability and artefacts of the fictitious SFS enterprise.

Chapter 9 – Supporting Cloud Enterprise Architecture Capability: This chapter describes how to support the adaptive cloud enterprise architecture capability of the fictitious SFS enterprise.

Chapter 10 – Case Study Examples: This chapter presents the conclusion and additional case study scenarios which discuss the adaptive cloud enterprise architecture for different cloud adoption contexts.

Bibliography: It outlines the relevant and important academic and industry sources.

1.11 Summary

Cloud computing is an emerging phenomena and organisations across the globe are showing significant interest in cloud adoption. Cloud adoption is not a simple straightforward service provisioning venture, rather it is a strategic change initiative. Organisations should develop a strategic adaptive cloud enterprise architecture capability to guide the systematic and strategic architecture-driven adoption of cloud computing. This book discusses the AESS metamodel and ADOMS approach to adapting, defining, operating, managing and supporting an adaptive cloud enterprise architecture capability to facilitate cloud adoption.

Chapter 2

Cloud-Enabled Enterprise Adaptation

2.1 Introduction

Modern enterprises operate in complex, fast-paced and highly regulated environments where technology is not a support function, rather, it is a core component of their enterprise strategy and architecture (Gill et al. 2015). Technology plays an important role in the operation, improvement, growth and transformation of an enterprise. It is important for enterprises to proactively scan their internal and external environments (e.g. local, national and internal environments), and seek any challenge or opportunity for enterprise adaptation. This necessitates the identification of the appropriate capabilities to enable consistent and smooth enterprise adaptation.

Continuous enterprise adaptation is largely dependent on an agile or flexible or adaptive enterprise architecture capability (Doucet et al. 2008). Adaptive enterprise architecture is a strategic capability that plays a pivotal role in defining and realising the enterprise adaptation strategies and roadmaps (Ross et al. 2006). An adaptive enterprise architecture capability is the ability of an entity to apply different agile architecture methods, practices, models and tools to produce an adaptive enterprise architecture design that supports enterprise adaptation (Gill 2014).

An adaptive enterprise architecture capability is responsive (scans, senses and reacts appropriately to expected and unexpected changes), flexible (adapts to expected or unexpected changes at any time), speedy (accommodates expected or unexpected changes rapidly), lean (focuses on reducing waste and cost without compromising on quality), and learning (focuses on enterprise fitness, improvement, transformation and innovation) (Qumer and Henderson-Sellers 2008). It requires the engagement of multiple enterprise capabilities (e.g. enterprise requirements, strategy, project, and service management) and stakeholder groups who may have different perspectives, objectives and conflicting priorities.

The current influx of a number of new cloud-enabled technologies and trends provide both benefits and challenges to enterprises. Business and IT executives must compare the cost savings, flexibility, scalability, readiness, technology investments, security and data confidentially issues when making decisions about adopting emerging cloud technologies. The challenge is how best to approach cloud adoption in public and private enterprises. Enterprises need to develop an adaptive cloud enterprise architecture capability to guide the systematic and strategic adoption of cloud-enabled technologies (Gill et al. 2014).

This book uses The Gill Framework® (Gill 2014) to guide the establishment of an adaptive cloud enterprise architecture capability. The use of the Gill Framework® is not limited to cloud adoption. The Gill Framework® is a generic meta-framework of integrated capabilities for assessing, designing, improving, and transforming agile or adaptive enterprises. It defines an agile enterprise as an adaptive enterprise service system (AESS). It is an open source service-oriented meta-framework and is freely available[a] to use at no cost by acknowledging the source and copyright holder. The Gill Framework® was first developed in 2006 to guide enterprise agile adoption and improvement. It then further evolved and is continuously evolving to support the design of agile enterprises. The Gill Framework® provides the AESS metamodel and the ADOMS approach.

The generic AESS metamodel incorporates design principles (design thinking), core metamodel elements, guiding elements and their relationships. The AESS metamodel can be extended and tailored to define the enterprise context-specific AESS metamodel, which can then be used to define the agile or adaptive enterprise, its capabilities and

---

[a] http://www.aqgill.com/

services. The core of the AESS metamodel is its three core conceptual elements.

- Adaptive enterprise service system (enterprise level)
- Adaptive service system (capability level)
- Adaptive service (service level)

The ADOMS approach offers the following five AESS lifecycle management capabilities.

- **A**dapting (to changes)
- **D**efining (an agile or adaptive capability)
- **O**perating (an agile or adaptive capability)
- **M**anaging (an agile or adaptive capability)
- **S**upporting (an agile or adaptive capability)

The Gill Framework® has its foundation in design thinking (Martin 2009). It incorporates agility (Qumer and Henderson-Sellers 2008), service science (Spohrer and Kwan 2009) and a living system of systems (Miller 1995; Maier 1998) principles. Design thinking is a balanced interplay of intuition and analytical thinking for the continuous design or re-design of an adaptive enterprise for innovation and efficiency. The Gill Framework® can be used as a guiding meta-framework to adapting (e.g. adaptation first approach), defining, operating, managing and supporting an adaptive cloud enterprise architecture capability. The AESS metamodel and ADOMS approach are discussed in detail in Chapter 3 and Chapter 4, respectively. This chapter provides an overview of the following basic concepts, frameworks and challenges related to cloud-enabled enterprise adaptation and architecture.

- Enterprise
- Enterprise Adaptation
- Enterprise Adaptation Challenges
- Enterprise Architecture
- Enterprise Architecture Challenges

2.2 Enterprise

An enterprise is a complex adaptive system which can be established to carry on a private or public business. An enterprise has a flat or matrix or hierarchical organisation of actors who directly or indirectly have interest in the enterprise. These actors play different roles, such as customers, suppliers, shareholders, partners, associates and regulators. These actors interact, operate, collaborate, compete, and form markets (e.g. local, national and international) to exchange services for some value or monetary benefit. Actors define their vision and related strategic business goals. Business goals are further decomposed into business objectives. Actors define priorities and strategic plans in order to employ strategies to achieve the goals and tactics to achieve the objectives. These goals and objectives are used to measure the performance of an enterprise through key performance indicators. The performance of an enterprise can be constrained by the internal and external drivers and limiting factors.

An enterprise can be decomposed into different business units, functions, departments or capabilities. An enterprise has capabilities that describe the business functions. Business value is achieved through the execution of a set of activities – a.k.a. value stream. Business policy and rules guide the execution of tactics through business processes to achieve the business objectives. A business process has events and can span across different business units. Business relies upon business information for effective operations and decision making. A business process is initiated due to some event. An event is something that causes a change in the existing state of a business. An enterprise presents a holistic view of a public or private organisation that is engaged in profit or non-profit activities. Thus, an enterprise can be defined as:

". . . an entity, regardless of its legal form . . . including partnerships or associations regularly engaged in economic activities" (European Commission 2003).

The Open Group (Harrison 2011) defines an enterprise as:

"The highest level (typically) of description of an organization and typically covers all missions and functions. An enterprise will often span multiple organizations".

An enterprise, as a whole, comprises the interconnected internal and external parts of an organisation. The internal parts represent business units and business functions. The external parts represent customers, suppliers, partners and regulators. These individual internal and external parts focus on different goals that are linked to the shared vision of an enterprise. A shared vision sets the direction for the whole enterprise. An enterprise's shared vision focuses on "What an enterprise as a whole aspires to achieve." For instance, an enterprise may have a vision to become a leader in providing information management solutions to government agencies. A vision helps to shape and set the target or goals (ends). An enterprise develops strategies (means) to achieve their goals. An enterprise's strategies are constrained and realised by the enterprise architecture, project, service and requirements management capabilities. This book presents the service-centric view of an enterprise in contrast to a traditional product-centric view and defines an enterprise as:

"an adaptive enterprise service system that emerges through the collaboration or volunteer interactions of different adaptive service systems. An adaptive enterprise service system is a complex distributed integrated supply chain network of entities or adaptive service systems that interact with each other for value co-creation" (Gill 2013).

The adaptive enterprise service system (a.k.a. AESS) view shifts the focus from the traditional service or product delivery enterprise to the service-oriented architecture and cloud service value co-creation enterprise. Hence, a cloud-enabled enterprise is an example of an AESS.

2.3 Enterprise Adaptation

Enterprise adaptation is to actively identify changes based on both intuition and analytics, and effectively respond to these changes to achieve the desired business goals. Enterprise adaptation is context-driven and occurs in response to changes in the internal and external environment of an enterprise. It is important for an enterprise to have the capability to proactively scan its environment and look for any challenges or opportunities for adaptation. While adaptation is in progress, it is important for an enterprise to keep the lights on to ensure the smooth running of the enterprise operations.

Technology plays an important role in the adaptation of an enterprise. Technology-enabled enterprise adaptation is not an option any more. It is not only mandatory and important, it is imperative for the survival of an enterprise in today's technology-dominant, competitive market. A demonstrated ability to adapt is one of the key indicators when someone evaluates the market value of an enterprise. An enterprise needs to constantly adapt to keep dominating the business within their respective sector. Technology enables enterprises to differentiate their offerings in an extremely competitive local, national and international environment. For instance, a self-service kiosk technology in a retail shop enables the customers to search and buy products without the intervention of a salesperson. This is an effective way to reduce sales costs and increase customer connectivity by providing them with an additional channel.

Technology-enabled adaptation occurs for a number of reasons. Depending on the industry sector, one reason for technology-enabled adaptation could be to reduce cost and increase revenue through automation. For instance, enterprises may use cloud services to refurbish their technology infrastructure in the anticipation of cost and carbon emission reduction. Enterprises may consider the adoption of emerging cloud-based predictive analytics and Big Data technologies to make better and more informed decisions. Technological innovations are enabling enterprises to innovate and adapt with the adoption of emerging technologies. Technology-enabled adaptation could be important for an enterprise to improve time to market of products and services. This can be achieved through the integration of a number of capabilities, such as adaptive enterprise architecture, project management (e.g. XP, Scrum, and Lean practices), and cloud technologies. Technology is moving at a fast pace, and customers are moving along with technology. Therefore, enterprises should have the ability to quickly identify and respond to the technological innovations which match customer needs. Essentially, technology-enabled adaptation should concur to continuously offer products and services in response to changing technology-acumen customer habits and lifestyle.

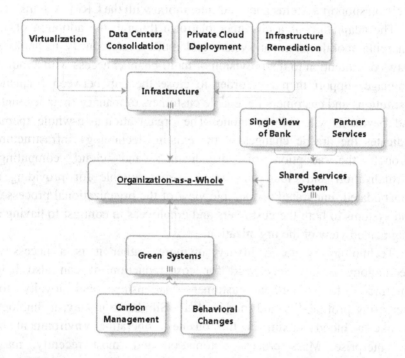

Fig. 2.1. Technology trends in the financial services industry (based on Gill et al. 2015).

The author of this book was recently engaged in a large enterprise transformation project which examined the technology-enabled adaptation themes in the financial services sector (Gill 2015). This recent research provided important insights into the emerging technology-driven adaptation themes in the financial services sector in two key areas: customer platform and organization-as-a-whole. The organization-as-a-whole theme is shown in Fig. 2.1. These adaptation themes indicate the drastic changes in technology in the financial services sector.

Technology is driving strategic advantage across the financial services sector and despite the recent economic crisis, investment in technology-enabled adaptation programs is still one of the priorities. For instance, the emerging themes related to customer platform adaptation suggest the adoption of emerging CRM (Customer Relationship Management) systems to provide a 360 degree or single view of the customer. Enterprises are currently embracing collaboration tools and decision support systems and their integration with the CRM systems.

The adaptation of a customer platform through the adoption of an emerging mobile payment system and multi-level security technology draws our attention to the provision of multi-channel access with a multi-language support theme in order to close the gap between financial institutions and customers i.e. enable customers to manage their accounts and payments via a Smartphone. The organization-as-a-whole theme indicates the drastic changes in the existing technology infrastructure through the adoption of virtualization and cloud computing. Virtualization and cloud computing seems suitable for providing a consolidated, integrated and simple view of the organizational processes and systems to both the customers and employees in contrast to having a fragmented view of the organization.

Technology is not a luxury anymore, rather it is a necessity. Technology is not only used for cost reduction, it can also help enterprises to strengthen customer relationships and loyalty for increasing profitability and market share. Similar to money, technology is like a blood stream in the business operating environment of an enterprise. Mass process automation and, most recently, mass information management regimes are showing that the adoption of technology for adaptation is not only radical but disruptive. Enterprises need to constantly adapt in response to changing business and technologies to stay or become dominant in their respective sectors, or they will get stepped over or they will be less competitive than their rivals who do adapt. Enterprises need to respond and respond very quickly, and timely adaptation should occur sooner rather later. Based on the recent advances in technology, in the next 3-5 years, there will be a large shift in the way enterprises operate, improve, grow and transform. Enterprises will move away from a traditional to more interactive, collaborative and integrated agile structure, i.e. digital and physical channel integration, mobilization, social media and cloud adoption. However, an enterprise should adopt a strategic adaptive enterprise architecture-driven approach to take on new emerging technologies, such as the cloud while ensuring full transparency in relation to investment cost, benefits and risk through informal and formal market research and partner engagement.

2.4 Enterprise Adaptation Challenges

The technological revolution is augmenting the pace of competition and globalisation. Enterprises are often challenged by the constantly changing lifestyles of individual customers (e.g. especially the adoption of the latest devices, such as Smartphone, iPads and tablets by younger customers) and market demands. Enterprises that fail to recognise the constantly changing customer and market needs will fail to achieve their enterprise mission and vision. Enterprises need to learn how to make quick changes in their existing operating environment to maintain or gain a competitive advantage. Enterprises are constantly under increasing pressure and are organically evolving as complex adaptive systems. The cloud-enabled adaptation of an organically evolving environment is not an easy task and requires a large number of stakeholders, capabilities and investment commitments. Some of the challenges to modern enterprise adaptation are as follows:

- Disintegrated project-driven engagement, governance and investments lead to local optimisation at the cost of the whole;
- Difficult to have end-to-end traceability from enterprise strategy to architecture to project and service management (operations);
- Difficult to coordinate and align multiple projects, disciplines and stakeholder groups at the enterprise level;
- Distributed and global supply chain of services impacting enterprises world-wide;
- Enterprises are inherently complex and organic;
- Enterprise-wide engagement is relatively weak or limited;
- Enterprise-wide conflicting priorities;

- Tendency to set goals, objectives and KPIs for different silos which are counter-productive to each other;
- Lack of reusability of enterprise assets;
- Mass resource coordination difficulty;
- Missing whole-of-enterprise view;
- Most enterprises operate in silos and focus on local adaptation;
- Project-focused enterprise adaptation initiatives lack a holistic view;
- Project-focused user stories/requirements often miss the holistic enterprise structure (e.g. enterprise architecture); and
- Traditional disintegrated product development view as opposed to a value co-creation service offering view.

2.5 Enterprise Architecture

Enterprise architecture is a strategic capability that can be used to deal with modern cloud technology-enabled enterprise adaptation challenges. Architecture is defined as the "fundamental concepts or properties of a system in its environment embodied in its elements, relationships, and in the principles of its design and evolution" (ISO/IEC 42010 2007). The term "system" in this definition refers to the "enterprise as a system". Enterprise architecture is a blueprint that describes the overall structural, behavioral, social, technological, and facility elements of an enterprise's operating environment which share common goals and principles. An enterprise architecture capability can be established to support the development and management of enterprise architecture artefacts (Harrison 2011). An enterprise architecture capability deals with both the domain and solution architecture artefacts. Domain architecture includes mainly business architecture and technology architecture whereas solution architecture is developed for a specific project, program or portfolio.

The development of an enterprise architecture capability is a complex task. It can be supported by the enterprise architecture frameworks, methods, practices, models and tools. There are a number of well-known architecture frameworks, such as Zachman (2008), Department of Defense Architecture Framework (DoDAF) (DoD 2010), Federal

Enterprise Architecture Framework (FEAF) (FEAF 2013), and The Open Group Architecture Framework (TOGAF) (Harrison 2011). The following sections review these well-known frameworks in the context of adaptive cloud enterprise architecture capability establishment for cloud adoption.

2.5.1 *The Zachman Framework*

The Zachman Framework is an ontology-based enterprise architecture framework for organizing enterprise architecture processes and artefacts. The Zachman Framework does not provide an enterprise architecture process for implementing and operating an enterprise architecture capability; however, it provides enterprise architecture conceptual elements and their relationships. The Zachman Framework is a structured two-dimensional matrix defining six enterprise architecture views (see Fig. 2.2): contextual, conceptual, logical, physical, detailed and

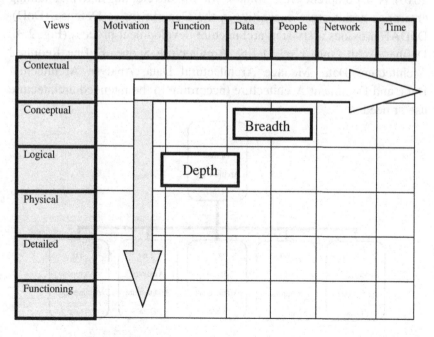

Fig. 2.2. The Zachman Framework (adapted from Zachman 2008).

functioning (Zachman 2008). The row headers of this matrix represent enterprise architecture views. The column headers of this matrix define the motivation (why), function (how), data (what), people (who), network (where) and time (when) elements.

The combination of a row (e.g. contextual) and a column (e.g. why) describes each enterprise architecture view (see arrows in Figure 2.2). For instance, the interaction of "Data" and "Contextual" view elements defines the Enterprise Contextual Data Model at a very high level. Similarly, this model is detailed as we further approach the "Functioning" view. The Zachman Framework does not provide a concrete enterprise architecture implementation methodology, however, it provides a generic and structured ontology that can be used in tailoring a situation-specific adaptive cloud enterprise architecture capability.

2.5.2 *Department of Defense Architecture Framework*

The Department of Defense Architecture Framework (DoDAF) (DoD 2010) is a comprehensive framework for developing and maintaining enterprise architecture capability in the Department of Defense (DoD). DoDAF provides a six-step architecture development process (Fig. 2.3): Define Architecture Use, Define Architecture Scope, Define Required Architecture Data, Manage Architectural Data, Analyse Architecture Data, and Document Architecture (according to the intended architecture use or needs).

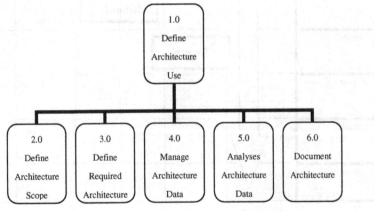

Fig. 2.3. The DoDAF Process (adapted from the DoD 2010).

The DoDAF also discusses the architecture meta-model, model, viewpoints and presentation techniques. The DoDAF meta-model is structured around the interoperability of processes and systems. It focuses on conceptual data, logical data, and physical exchange specifications. DoDAF models can be developed using a number of architecture views and presentation techniques (dashboard, graphical, reference models, etc.). DoDAF is an information-driven framework which facilities the development of enterprise architecture in accordance with the decision makers' needs in the enterprise. It supports five levels of decision making: planner, owner, designer, builders and sub-contractors. The core to the DoDAF is the viewpoint matrix. DoDAF specifies the following key viewpoints.

- Architecture Context Viewpoint
- Capability Viewpoint
- Data and Information Viewpoint
- Operational Viewpoint
- Project Viewpoint
- Service Viewpoint
- Standard Viewpoint
- Systems Viewpoint

In contrast to the Zachman Framework, DoDAF provides a concrete enterprise architecture process, a meta-model, models, viewpoints and presentation techniques. DoDAF defines the enterprise architecture capability that is developed to collect, store, manage and analyse data about the whole or part of an enterprise to address the decision makers' needs at different levels.

2.5.3 *Federal Enterprise Architecture Framework*

Similar to DoDAF, the Federal Enterprise Architecture Framework (FEAF) (FEAF 2013) is a comprehensive framework for developing and maintaining the enterprise architecture capability of the Federal Government. FEAF provides a common and standardized approach and principles to developing and sharing architecture information between agencies. The core to FEAF (Fig. 2.4) is a Collaborative Planning Methodology (CPM) and a Consolidated Reference Model (CRM). CPM and CRM provide a common language to guide agencies in the development and maintenance of enterprise architecture for planning investments.

The CPM specifies five key activities, which are organised into two iterative phases: organise and plan, and implement and measure. The organise and plan phase has three activities: identify and validate, research and leverage, and define and plan. This phase is focused on collaboratively identifying and prioritizing stakeholders' needs, researching and leveraging existing assets and need analysis initiatives, and developing a plan to address the identified needs. The implement and measure phase has two activities: invest and execute, and perform and measure. This phase is focused on actually executing the plans, measuring the performance and taking any corrective actions and making decisions.

The CRM specifies six interrelated reference models: Performance Reference Model (PRM), Business Reference Model (BRM), Data Reference Model (DRM), Application Reference Model (ARM), Infrastructure Reference Model (IRM), and Security Reference Model (SRM). PRM specifies the agency's and intra-agency's strategic goals or objectives. BRM specifies agencies, customers, partners, providers, and intra- and inter-agency shared services. DRM is focused on data standardisation and information exchange. ARM is focused on enterprise applications, integration and a service bus. IRM is focused on hardware and software infrastructure assets. SRM is focused on ensuring the security of the enterprise assets at different levels.

Similar to DoDAF, FEAF aims to establish and maintain an effective enterprise architecture capability for enabling technology-enabled government transformations, facilitating decision making, and developing roadmaps.

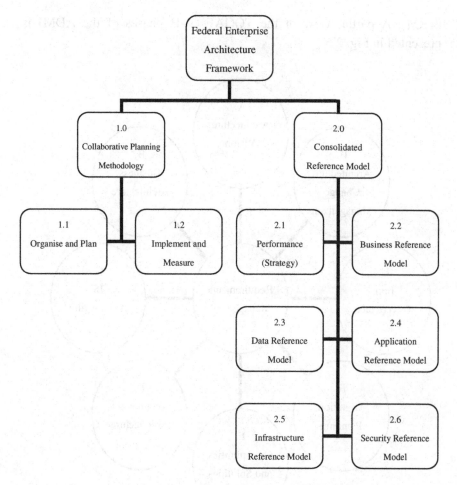

Fig. 2.4. The FEAF (adapted from the FEAF 2013).

2.5.4 *The Open Group Architecture Framework*

The Open Group Architecture Framework (TOGAF) (Harrison 2011) is a comprehensive generic framework for developing and maintaining enterprise architecture capability. TOGAF is not tied to any public or government agency. TOGAF provides the architecture development method (ADM), templates, guidelines, techniques, content meta-model (CM), templates, enterprise continuum, and a technical reference model

(TRM). A partial view of the TOGAF (A-H phases of the ADM) is presented in Fig. 2.5.

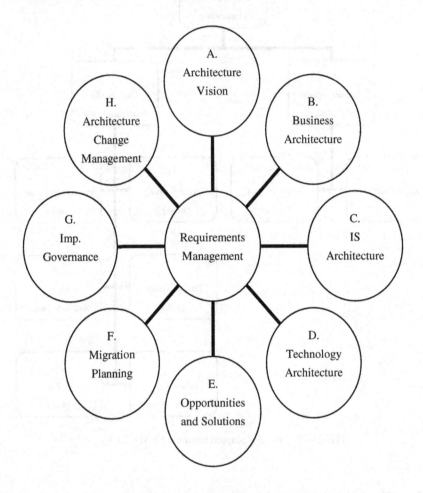

Fig. 2.5. TOGAF (based on The Open Group 2011).

The core to TOGAF is the ADM. ADM has nine phases: Preliminary, Architecture Vision, Business Architecture, Information System Architecture, Technology Architecture, Opportunities and Solutions, Migration Planning, Implementation Governance, and Architecture Change Management. These phases can be iteratively executed for establishing an enterprise architecture capability; developing the vision, business, information systems, technology and solution architectures; performing implementation and migration planning and governance; and managing changes in the enterprise architecture capability and design. In contrast to DoDAF and FEAF, TOGAF is not tied to government enterprises. It is a generic and comprehensive framework that can be tailored for the development of an effective enterprise architecture capability for technology-enabled enterprise adaptation.

2.5.5 *Review*

These enterprise architecture frameworks are based on industry best practice. These frameworks can be used to establish an adaptive cloud enterprise architecture capability. However, the challenge is that these frameworks are unlikely to be able to be used or adopted off-the-shelf for any specific enterprise. The scope of these frameworks is slightly different from each other, and their differences indicate that a standard single enterprise architecture framework may not be universally applied. It is suggested that, based on a specific enterprise cloud adoption context, the best practice of one framework can be combined or tailored into other frameworks to create a situation-specific adaptive cloud enterprise architecture capability. Hence, they all have to be tailored to suit the enterprise context and also need to be integrated with the other existing enterprise frameworks or capabilities, such as enterprise strategy, project, and service and requirements management. The situation-specific tailoring and integration of the adaptive cloud enterprise architecture capability can be guided by a meta-framework such as The Gill Framework®.

Enterprise architecture treats an enterprise's operating environment as a system or a system of systems that has sub-systems, components or parts. These components interact, influence, and adapt to achieve their goals. Enterprise architecture is designed, governed and evolved through a set of architecture principles. In order to tackle the challenges of cloud-enabled enterprise adaptation, enterprises need to harvest an adaptive cloud enterprise architecture capability and design to deal with complex cloud adoption initiatives. Some of the benefits of using an adaptive cloud enterprise architecture-driven approach for cloud-enabled enterprise adaptation are as follows:

- Provides a whole-of-enterprise view;
- Assists in the assessment of cloud adoption opportunities, risks and investment priorities;
- Develops and realises the enterprise's cloud strategy, roadmap and portfolio;
- Enables enterprise cloud adoption through projects and architecture change management; and
- Engages, coordinates, integrates and aligns cloud-enabled enterprise architecture with other enterprise management capabilities for effective enterprise-wide cloud adoption.

2.6 Enterprise Architecture Challenges

Traditional top-down approaches to enterprise architecture development and management are continuously challenged by the dynamic business environment. Enterprises are lagging behind in harvesting an agile or adaptive enterprise architecture capability. The application of traditional top-down approaches to enterprise architecture are criticized for not delivering or showing the value early, as traditional top-down approaches take a few months to a year to develop and effectively operate an enterprise architecture capability. Perhaps it is not so much about the approach itself, it is also dependent on the ability of the enterprise architecture practitioners as well. Nevertheless, an enterprise needs to establish an agile or adaptive cloud enterprise architecture capability to support and manage cloud-enabled enterprise adaptation. Most modern enterprises have managed to have well established agile or adaptive project management capabilities. Being agile or adaptive in one area and not agile in another area, such as in enterprise architecture, will cause misalignment and inconsistency in the enterprise. This misalignment will adversely impact the cloud-enabled adaptation initiatives of an enterprise. Having an adaptive cloud enterprise architecture capability is not enough; essentially, the architecture work products or enterprise architecture design should be adaptive as well.

The adaptive cloud enterprise architecture capability also needs to be integrated and aligned to the adaptive enterprise strategy, project, service and requirements management capabilities. This will enable an enterprise to plan, execute, coordinate and manage complex cloud-enabled enterprise adaptation in an effective and consistent manner. These capabilities must be integrated and aligned for traceability and smooth and consistent enterprise adaptation. One of the biggest challenges is that enterprises struggle to maintain integration and alignment between these key capabilities.

Adaptive cloud enterprise architecture requires the support of an enterprise cloud strategy capability. An enterprise cloud strategy is constrained by and realised by the cloud enterprise architecture through the development and management of a number of cloud projects. Organisations may have ambitious goals and powerful visionary slogans. However, strategic goals and slogans are not enough for complex cloud adoption. An adaptive cloud enterprise must have a clear strategy and an actionable roadmap for their cloud adoption initiatives. It is extremely important for an enterprise to have a clear strategic stance or position, identify limiting factors, strengths, weakness and opportunities and identify strategies to reduce or eliminate the limiting factors and risks through the adaptive cloud enterprise architecture-driven cloud adoption. The enterprise cloud strategy should not only be an ad-hoc pack of 20-25 PowerPoint slides. It should be a living document and should be continuously reviewed and managed and should be linked to the artifacts in the adaptive cloud enterprise architecture, project, service and requirements management capabilities for end-to-end traceability.

The challenge for enterprises is how to ensure that these capabilities are integrated and aligned for effective cloud adoption. The integration and alignment of these capabilities is critical when making decisions about the assessment, adoption or de-adoption of emerging complex technologies, such as the cloud. A lack of integration and alignment can lead to slow and inconsistent adaptation. Some of the challenges associated with enterprise architecture are as follows:

- Agile in one area and not agile in another area causes enterprise misalignment and inconsistency;
- Artificial separation between business and IT strategy;
- Enterprise architecture is perceived as a non-operational and non-outcome-oriented capability;
- Enterprise architecture is perceived as an "IT" discipline;
- Executives do not understand the value of enterprise architecture;
- Enterprise strategy is often not developed or maintained to support the enterprise architecture;
- Enterprise architecture is often not linked to other management capabilities;
- A lack of collaborative relationships between enterprise architects and senior management; and
- No single enterprise architecture framework or method can be universally applied.

2.7 Summary

Cloud technologies offer several benefits over traditional non-cloud technologies. Enterprises are keen to adopt emerging cloud technologies which suit their enterprise context. The adoption of a cloud is not merely shifting applications and workload to the cloud. Enterprises need an adaptive cloud enterprise architecture capability to developing context-specific adaptive cloud enterprise architecture to support iterative cloud-enabled enterprise adaptation. This chapter provided an introduction to the basic concepts, frameworks and challenges related to cloud-enabled enterprise adaptation and architecture. The next chapter discusses The Gill Framework® - AESS metamodel.

Chapter 3

The Adaptive Enterprise Service System Metamodel

3.1 Introduction

The Gill Framework® is a meta-framework that defines an agile or adaptive enterprise as an extended adaptive enterprise service system (AESS) (Fig. 3.1). The Gill Framework® provides a generic AESS metamodel that can be extended and tailored to define the context-specific metamodel for adaptive enterprise architecture capability (e.g. such as the adaptive cloud enterprise architecture capability).

The generic AESS metamodel incorporates design principles, core metamodel elements, guiding elements and their relationships (Fig. 3.2). The design principles include agility, a living system (system of systems) and service principles. These principles underpin the design of the AESS metamodel. These architecture design principles, at a high level, are the guiding vision or underlying ideas or statements for guiding the AESS architecture. These principles can be tailored and used as a baseline for developing the context-specific principles for a particular situation. The core of the AESS metamodel is its three core conceptual elements. These core elements describe the adaptive enterprise at three different levels: adaptive enterprise service system (enterprise level), adaptive service system (capability level) and adaptive service (service level). The AESS metamodel includes nine key guiding elements that guide the core elements. The nine key guiding elements are: strategy, architecture, policy, rule, context, model, reference, legal, and standard. The AESS metamodel can be tailored to define a context-specific metamodel for adaptive cloud enterprise architecture capability (additional elements can be added to the tailored metamodel, if required). This chapter describes the generic AESS metamodel design principles, core elements, guiding elements and their relationships.

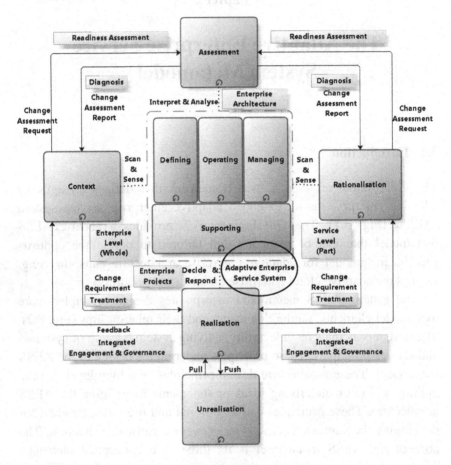

Fig. 3.1. The Gill Framework® 2.0.

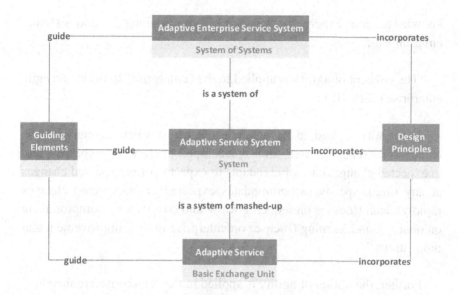

Fig. 3.2. The AESS metamodel – level 0 (core concepts).

3.2 Design Principles

This section discusses the three broad categories of the architecture design principles: agility, system and service principles.

3.2.1 *Agility*

An enterprise should have the ability to scan, sense, and adjust in response to emerging complex surrounding environments. The concept of enterprise agility or the agile enterprise can be understood and explained through the lens of an agility definition (Qumer and Henderson-Sellers 2008):

"Agility is a persistent behaviour or ability of a sensitive entity that exhibits flexibility to accommodate expected or unexpected changes rapidly, follows the shortest time span, uses economical, simple and quality instruments in a dynamic environment and applies updated prior knowledge and experience to learn from the internal and external environment."

The concept of agility is applied to the "enterprise" to define an agile enterprise (Gill 2014):

"An entity is said to be an agile enterprise when an enterprise is responsive (scans, senses and reacts appropriately to expected and unexpected changes), flexible (adapts to expected or unexpected changes at any time), speedy (accommodates expected or unexpected changes rapidly), lean (focuses on reducing waste and cost without compromising on quality), and learning (focuses on enterprise fitness, improvement and innovation)."

Further, the notion of agility is applied to the "enterprise architecture" (EA) to define an agile or adaptive EA (Gill 2014):

"An EA is said to be an agile or adaptive EA when both the EA capability and EA design are responsive (scans, senses and reacts appropriately to expected and unexpected changes), flexible (adapts to expected or unexpected changes at any time), speedy (accommodates expected or unexpected changes rapidly), lean (focuses on reducing waste and cost without compromising on quality), and learning (focuses on enterprise fitness, improvement and innovation)."

Agility (e.g. quality or non-functional requirement) is the ability of an enterprise to handle expected and unexpected internal and external changes. The architecture of the agile or adaptive enterprise, system or service can be guided by the following five agility principles.

3.2.1.1 *Responsiveness*

An agile or adaptive entity should be able to scan and sense the situation (e.g. expected or unexpected changes in the business or technology or regulatory environment) and form an appropriate response in order to deal with the changes.

3.2.1.2 *Flexibility*

An agile or adaptive entity should be able to form a flexible response (instead of a fixed response) that allows an enterprise to adapt to changing complex business demands.

3.2.1.3 *Speed*

An agile or adaptive entity should be able to form not only a flexible response but also a quick or rapid flexible response in a timely manner.

3.2.1.4 *Leanness*

An agile or adaptive entity should be able to operate with optimal or minimal resources, without compromising the quality of its outputs or offerings.

3.2.1.5 *Learning*

An agile or adaptive entity is a learning entity that demonstrates sustained continuous growth and adaptation over a period of time.

3.2.2 *System*

The traditional static view of an enterprise as a fragmented set of business units or functions is not appropriate for dealing with changes. The holistic thinking of living systems (Miller 1995) can be used to engineer and manage a modern enterprise as a living system. A system is composed of different interdependent and connected parts or sub-systems, which are managed as a whole. This means that an enterprise is a system which needs to respond to ever-changing business demands. A change in one part of the enterprise system can impact the other parts. Therefore, changes in one part of the enterprise system should not be dealt with in isolation from the other parts of the enterprise system. The architecture of an enterprise as a system can be guided by the following eight key living system principles (Gill 2014):

3.2.2.1 *System*

A system receives input. It processes the input within its constraints and produces output. System performance is impacted by the culture, norms and feedback it receives from their environment.

3.2.2.2 *Autonomous*

A system is made of other low level autonomous agent systems that consume energy or resources and responds to their environment.

3.2.2.3 *Interdependent*

A system is composed of nested parts or cells (a basic unit of function) or organs that are integrated and aligned to survive and achieve the desired business goals via different pathways.

3.2.2.4 *Integrated*

A system is an open, non-linear and integrated multi-agent system forming a whole.

3.2.2.5 *Context aware*

A context-aware system continually scans and senses its environment to identify any changes and their impact on the whole system.

3.2.2.6 *Adaptive*

An adaptive system continually strives to reduce stress and maintain a steady internal state, regardless of its external environment.

3.2.2.7 *Self-organising*

A self-organising system continually evolves toward higher levels of order for differentiation through feedback.

3.2.2.8 *Lifecycle*

A system has a lifecycle. It is created, used, maintained, transformed and retired or expired over a period of time.

3.2.3 *Service*

Service dominant logic is an emerging area in the contemporary service economy. Service is the application of physical and non-physical resources to create benefits or value for yourself and others (e.g. mutual benefits). The concept of a service can be used to describe an enterprise system as an integrated echo-system of "service systems". In the traditional enterprise context, a business capability or organisation is architected to deliver services to other service consumer organisations. In modern service-offering dominant logic, the focus is shifted to mutual voluntary interactions between service systems. These interactions are called value co-creation activities. Service systems voluntarily interact with each other, and offer or consume services (e.g. service experience) for mutual benefiters or value co-creation. A service is a fundamental element of exchange during service system interactions. The focus shifts from service delivery to service co-creation. The ten service principles (Vargo and Lusch 2008; Spohrer et al. 2008; Spohrer and Kwan 2009) can be used to guide the architecture of an enterprise system as a system of services.

3.2.3.1 *Service*

Service is the application of resources. A resource could be a financial, human, information, knowledge, competency, skill, technology (application, platform, and infrastructure) or facility resource.

3.2.3.2 *Indirect exchange*

The indirect exchange of services masks the fundamentals of the basis of exchange.

3.2.3.3 *Service provisioning*

Service provisioning refers to the sourcing of services. Goods or products offer services and are distribution mechanisms for service provisioning.

3.2.3.4 *Operant resources*

The fundamental source of competitive advantage is operant resources. An operant or active resource can act on other resources (including other operant resources) to deliver a service or change. Operant resource examples are: actors, application, and infrastructure.

3.2.3.5 *Service economy*

Service is the fundamental basis of exchange in the service economy. Services form the service economies.

3.2.3.6 *Value co-creation*

Service creation is not done in isolation of its customers. It is co-created through the active engagement of customers. Hence, the customer is always a co-creator of the value.

3.2.3.7 *Value proposition*

Service is not delivered. It can only be offered through voluntary interactions. Hence, the enterprise cannot deliver value, and value propositions can only be proposed to its intended customers.

3.2.3.8 *Customer orientation*

Customer orientation is the heart of the value co-creation-driven service economy. The customer is an active member of the service design team. This is similar to the customer-centric values and principles noted by the Agile Manifesto (2001).

3.2.3.9 *Resource integration*

Service can be co-created through the integration of service resources. All economic and social actors such as service systems, as a part of the value network (network of networks), are resource integrators.

3.2.3.10 *Value determination*

The service beneficiary determines the service value, which is always contextual.

3.3 Adaptive Enterprise Service System

The AESS metamodel has three core conceptual elements. These core elements describe the adaptive enterprise as an AESS at three different levels: adaptive enterprise service system (enterprise level), adaptive service system (capability level) and adaptive service (service level).

3.3.1 *Adaptive Enterprise Service System (Enterprise Level)*

The adaptive enterprise service system is the enterprise level conceptual element of the adaptive enterprise architecture metamodel. It is a system of different adaptive service systems that interact with each other and with their environment for value co-creation. It is also known as the ecology of different types of adaptive service systems.

It is an adaptive system of living service systems that combines the living multi-agent system of systems approach to provide the enterprise-as-a-whole view. A system of systems is different from a simple collection of large monolithic systems. A system of systems is essentially a linked-chain of different systems that operate independently, but are linked to each other to define and achieve the mutual goals. Hence, a system of adaptive service systems is a chain of inter-linked adaptive service systems. It aims to relate different adaptive service systems that participate and interact within a specific context for value co-creation.

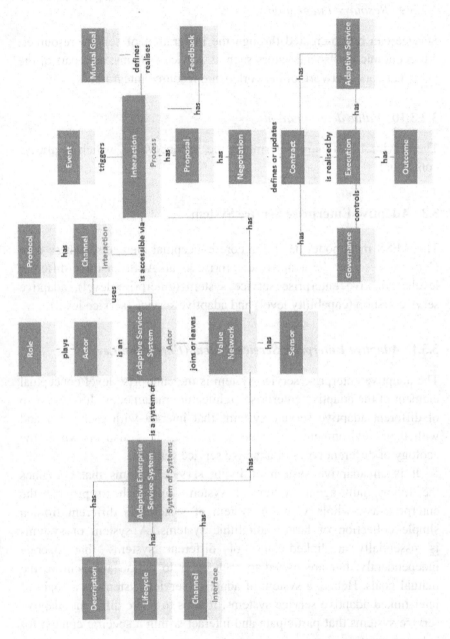

Fig. 3.3. The AESS metamodel – level 1 (adaptive enterprise service system).

In a system of adaptive service systems, desired behaviors and architecture evolve through the collaborative interactions of adaptive service systems. Fig. 3.3 shows the details of the adaptive enterprise service system level elements and their relationships. An adaptive enterprise service system is:

- a set of independent adaptive living multi-agent service systems that are integrated in the adaptive enterprise service system environment. These adaptive living multi-agent service systems can be created, acquired, operated and managed independently;
- a distributed and collaborative environment where several geographically dispersed adaptive living multi-agent service systems interact with each other for value co-creation;
- evolving in order to meet the dynamic contextual demand; based on the contextual demand, adaptive living multi-agent service systems can be added, removed, and modified in the integrated adaptive enterprise service system environment; and
- designed to exhibit emergent behavior through the interactions of adaptive living multi-agent service systems; each adaptive living multi-agent service system is independent. But a system of service systems' behavior cannot be achieved and localized to a specific single adaptive living multi-agent service system.

The AESS and its architecture, at the enterprise level, emerge through the collaboration or voluntary dynamic interactions of different adaptive living multi-agent service systems. In summary, an AESS can be defined as:

"a complex distributed integrated supply chain network of entities or adaptive living multi-agent service systems that interact with each other for value co-creation." (Gill 2014)

The AESS, at the enterprise level, is the world or ecology of different types of adaptive service systems. All adaptive service systems are resources. The AESS descriptor contains information on the resources (e.g. number of systems, types of systems, system access rights). An

AESS can be described by using different enterprise architecture models. An AESS, as a whole, is a resource which has a lifespan. An AESS, similar to living organisms, has the following common lifecycle states:

- Start or Emerge or Configure or Develop, Harvest State
- History or Past State
- Present or Current State
- Future or Target State
- End or Expire or Retire or Death State

The AESS transits from one state to another state in order to meet the changing value co-creation interaction demands. The AESS environment contains different types of adaptive service systems that are accessible via different channels. Essentially, it is a multi-channel environment. An adaptive service system offers or acquires one or many adaptive services. An adaptive service system is a concept that can be used to represent an individual, capability, function, department, unit or a group entity. Here, an adaptive service system can represent a capability, such as the adaptive cloud enterprise architecture capability.

A value network is an open and dynamic distributed demand and supply value network of uniquely identifiable adaptive service systems. A value network emerges through the joining of adaptive service systems. An adaptive service system can voluntarily join or leave the value network. A value network should allow the adaptive service systems to join, leave, discover, select and propose interaction with adaptive service systems and their services.

A demand and supply value network (e.g. human or non-human sensors) consists of sensors. Sensors monitor the internal and external environment, capture data about supply and demand events (e.g. increase or shortage in demand for specific services in the market), process it, and send it to the concerned main sensor (e.g. human or non-human) and adaptive service systems in the value network for further action (e.g. initiate interaction, source and supply additional services or service systems).

An adaptive service system is an actor or stakeholder that can join different value networks and play different roles in each value network.

A role represents an assigned or assumed responsibility. There are a number of role types such as the Service Creator, Provider, Consumer, Carrier, Partner, Auditor, Observer, Competitor, Regulator and Broker. These role types can be used as a guideline for defining situation-specific roles according to the enterprise context.

An adaptive service system can discover and select adaptive service systems from the value network and propose interactions with them by using their exposed interaction channels. An interaction channel is a point, which is made available to adaptive service systems, to propose or participate in an interaction. A channel could be a physical human (e.g. face-to-face) or technology (e.g. self-service online web, mobile, social media, API) or a mix of both types of channels. An adaptive service system can allow or restrict access to its services through interaction channels. A channel is an interface that enables interactions between adaptive service systems.

An interaction channel has an associated interaction protocol. An adaptive service system needs to follow the interaction protocol to interact with other adaptive service system. A standard interaction protocol is important for enabling interaction among heterogeneous independent adaptive service systems. For instance, a human-oriented interaction channel requires using a human-oriented interaction protocol (e.g. face-to-face communication, verbal or written communication, asynchronous and synchronous communication). A technology-oriented interaction channel may use a number of technology-oriented protocols, such as HTTPS, HTTP, SOAP (Simple Object Access Protocol), JMS (Java Message Service), REST (Representational State Transfer) etc.

The AESS emerges through the value co-creation interactions of independent adaptive service systems. A value network has one or more interactions. An adaptive service system can propose or participate in one or more interactions. An interaction is like a service demand and supply transaction. A service demand and supply lens is an appropriate way to describe the adaptive service system interactions for value co-creation. Adaptive service system interaction depends on the adaptive service demand and supply and involves at least two adaptive service systems. Adaptive service system interactions begin in response to perceived or real demand for an adaptive service. An adaptive service system may perceive that there is a demand for their service and intend to supply this service. An adaptive service system may explicitly request other adaptive service system (s) in the value network for the supply of a specific service. The demand and supply approach draws attention to the cost effective and efficient interactions for value co-creation. Each adaptive service system needs to be aware of the changing demand and supply of their services. Adaptive service systems sense demand and supply through value network sensors.

An event is a change in the state of something that triggers an interaction activity. An event could be a one-off event or a recurring event. It could be a time-driven event. An event can trigger the start of a proposal or negotiation or contract interaction activity.

A mutual goal is an interaction goal to which two or more adaptive service systems have agreed. An interaction may define or realize a mutual goal. Mutual goals do not mean that the adaptive service systems have the same goals. They could have different but mutually agreed goals.

An adaptive service system can send or receive an interaction proposal from other adaptive service systems via an interaction channel. An adaptive service system should be open to receive proposals.

A proposal is negotiated. An adaptive service system can accept or reject the proposal with the option to take no further action. If a proposal is successfully negotiated and accepted, then an existing contract is updated or a new contract is established between adaptive service systems.

A contract can be established or updated for one or more adaptive services from different adaptive service systems. A contract can also be an ongoing or fixed contract. For instance, a composite contract can be established for more than one adaptive service. A single service level contract can also be established for a specific adaptive service. Depending on the type of adaptive service, a contract can be described in different formats. It can be described both in human and machine readable format. A contract is a combination of documents that provide meta-level information about the adaptive service system and services. For example, a web services (WS) contract consists of a service description (WSDL), schema (XML), policy (WS-Policy) and a human readable service level agreement (SLA). Regardless of the nature of an adaptive service system or service, whether human or technology, a contract defines the adaptive service system and the service features, behaviors and concerns. A concern refers to the non-functional aspects of the adaptive service which could include service policy, security, privacy, performance, trust, interoperability, reliability, carbon emissions etc. An adaptive service should be viewed with its concerns and execution context. Adaptive service concerns provide the basis for a service contract.

A contract specifies a control or governance mechanism that limits or controls the execution of the contract. For instance, a control mechanism is established to track and monitor the access and use of the adaptive services (e.g. access rights). A control mechanism can allow or restrict access to specific adaptive service systems and services. Services are not generally offered for free. The demand and supply of service interactions mutually prices the services competitively. Service systems should be able to track and monitor the use of its services and bill it to the user according to the agreed contract. Services can be billed based on the monthly subscription, fixed term licenses, pay-per-use or a pay-as-you-go model (e.g. the Amazon cloud service model). An adaptive service system business model should include the guidelines for service pricing. An adaptive service system should have the ability to quickly adjust its service prices in response to changing service demand.

A contract is realised by contract execution. The execution of a contract involves the execution of one more interaction activities between relevant adaptive service systems, which may involve the creation, access or use of each other's adaptive services. Adaptive service use refers to the functional aspects of a service. It can also be interpreted as a service use case. An adaptive service system can use the services of other adaptive service systems through a value co-creation interaction channel. An adaptive service can be used in different frequencies by different adaptive service systems for different purposes. Execution has a service execution context and an adaptive service should be able to adjust according to the local execution context. An adaptive service could be a human or technology or both. A human service could be a business, information or social service type. These services can then be supported by the application, platform and infrastructure services. The adaptive service use is restricted based on the service access control and contract between the two adaptive service systems.

An adaptive service is a fundamental basis of exchange between the adaptive service systems. It is the application of resources (e.g. competency, material and machine). An adaptive service is context-aware and is continually evolving and self-adapting. It is created, used, maintained, transformed and retired or expired. An adaptive service scans and senses changes and adapts accordingly.

Adaptive service system interactions are initiated to define or realise mutual goals (e.g. outcomes). Contract execution co-creates value for achieving the mutual goals. A mutual goal is the agreed benefit for both the provider's and consumer's adaptive service systems. For instance, a shipping service system provides the transport service to other service system for some monetary benefit. Other service systems may use the shipping service system's transport service to make deliveries on time at minimal cost to other service systems i.e. their retail customers. As a result, retail customers receive their deliveries on time. In this example, all three service systems are mutually benefited (value co-creation) through service interaction.

Adaptive service system interactions achieve mutual satisfaction if the value co-creation is as per the agreed contract. Mutual satisfaction depends on the satisfaction of two or more interacting adaptive service systems. Following on from the shipping service system example, mutual satisfaction is reached if all the three interacting service systems are happy with the outcome of the interaction. The point is that all the interacting service systems are mutually benefited (value co-creation) through service interaction. This mutual satisfaction is reported via feedback interaction activities. Mutual benefits and mutual satisfaction depends on all the interacting service systems. Service system interactions result in dissatisfaction if an adaptive service system interaction outcome does not meet the agreed expectations of one or more interacting service systems. In a case where value co-creation is not as per the agreed contract, the responsible adaptive service system needs to understand and resolve the issue through feedback interactions, which may involve adjusting the mutual goals or services.

Feedback interactions enable service systems and service adaptation. The AESS is not a static system. It emerges through dynamic adaptive service system interactions. The adaptive service system provides formal or informal feedback to each other during or after interaction. An adaptive service system needs to appropriately respond to the feedback received on their services in an effective and efficient manner. The feedback and response mechanism draws attention to the adaptive nature of service systems and services. Feedback may lead to updating the adaptive service systems, services and related contracts.

This section described the AESS metamodel's enterprise level elements and its relationships. These elements and their relationships provide a holistic view of an adaptive enterprise. This top enterprise level metamodel can be tailored and used to define a context-specific AESS metamodel. The next section describes the capability level adaptive service system elements and their relationships.

3.3.2 *Adaptive Service System (Capability Level)*

The Gill Framework defines a capability (such as the adaptive cloud enterprise architecture capability) as an adaptive service system. A capability describes what an entity does and what it offers. An adaptive service system is a system of adaptive services. Adaptive service system abstraction can represent an individual human, function, business unit, department or team etc. It is a complex configuration of resources that possesses agility and offers or acquires adaptive services. These adaptive service systems are managed as a part of the whole AESS.

Individual adaptive service systems autonomously operate to achieve their goals which contribute to achieving their overall enterprise system goals. A change in one part of a system is not dealt with in isolation of the other parts of the system. This means a change in the behavior of one part can impact the behavior of other parts. The individual parts or the adaptive service system constantly exchange and update messages. An adaptive service system is context aware and is continually evolving and self-adapting. It is created, used, maintained, transformed and retired or expired. An adaptive service system scans and senses changes and adapts accordingly. An adaptive service system is the capability level conceptual element of the adaptive enterprise architecture metamodel. An adaptive service system is a system of adaptive services. This section describes the adaptive service system elements and their relationships (Fig. 3.4).

An adaptive service is a resource which has a lifespan. An adaptive service system, similar to living organisms, has lifecycle states such as:

- Start or Emerge or Configure or Develop, Harvest State
- History or Past State
- Present or Current State
- Future or Target State
- End or Expire or Retire or Death State

An adaptive service system transits from one state to another state in order to meet the changing value co-creation interaction demands. An adaptive service system is accessible via published interfaces or channels.

An adaptive service system is a configuration or organisation of actors. An actor is a human or non-human agent that supports one or more capabilities (e.g. architecture capability, business capability, information capability). A human actor could be an individual, team or organisation. An actor could be a business actor or technology actor. An actor uses adaptive services via their published service interfaces or channels. An actor produces or acquires adaptive services. An actor plays one or many assigned roles. An actor has competency. Competency refers to the knowledge, experience and skills of an individual actor. An actor has capacity. Capacity refers to the amount or volume of something (e.g. workload, storage capacity) that an actor can manage at a given point of time. One may have the competency to support some capability; however, it may not have enough capacity to do so at a given point of time. A capability is realised by one or more processes. A process involves actors, activities and tasks and uses, produces or acquires adaptive services. An event is a change in the state of something that triggers a process. An event could be a one-off event or a recurring event. It could be a time-driven event.

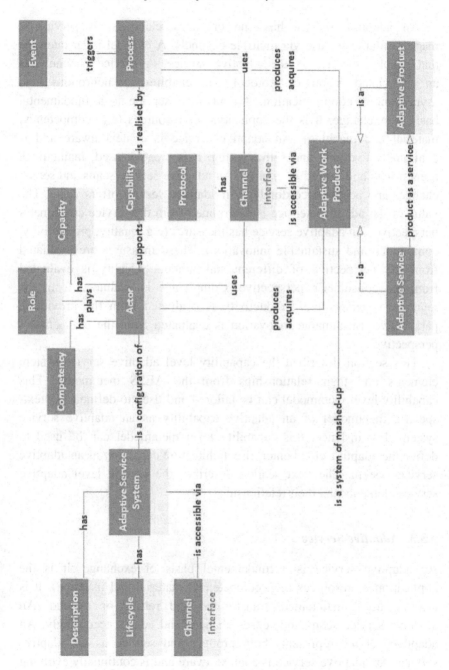

Fig. 3.4. The AESS metamodel – level 2 (adaptive service system).

An adaptive service has one or many channels. A service is made available for use via multiple channels. A channel is an interface that enables the use of the adaptive service. A service channel has an associated standard protocol for enabling asynchronous and asynchronous communication. An adaptive service is a fundamental basis of exchange. It is the application of resources (e.g. competency, material and machine). An adaptive service is context aware and is continually evolving and self-adapting. It is created, used, maintained, transformed and retired or expired. An adaptive service scans and senses changes and adapts accordingly. An adaptive service offers value. The value of the adaptive service is determined from the service consumer's perspective. An adaptive service has measures (e.g. quality, productivity, compliance and sustainable innovation). These measures are evaluated from the perspective of different stakeholders. Quality is evaluated from the consumer's perspective. Compliance is evaluated from the regulator's perspective. Productivity is evaluated from the provider's perspective. Sustainable innovation is evaluated from the competitor's perspective.

This section described the capability level adaptive service system elements and their relationships from the AESS metamodel. This capability level metamodel can be tailored and used to define a context-specific metamodel of an adaptive capability as an adaptive service system. For instance, this capability level metamodel can be used to define the adaptive cloud enterprise architecture capability as an adaptive service system. The next section describes the service level adaptive service elements and their relationships.

3.3.3 *Adaptive Service*

An adaptive service is a fundamental basis of exchange. It is the application of resources (e.g. competency, material and machine). It is created, used, maintained, transformed and retired or expired. An adaptive service scans and senses changes and adapts accordingly. An adaptive service represents both product and service as an adaptive service. An adaptive service is context aware and is continually evolving and self-adapting. An adaptive service can be classified into three major types: human, IT and facility services.

A service can be used by other services. Human services can be further classified into three types of services: business, information and social services. IT services can be further classified into three types of services: application, platform, and infrastructure services. Facility services can be further classified into three types: spatial, energy and ancillary services. All these services are realised by the relevant service components. Additional service types and relevant components can be added, if required. Fig. 3.5 shows the details of the adaptive service elements and their relationships. An adaptive service has a descriptor or description that contains information on the adaptive service and its resources. An adaptive service can be described using different service architecture models. An adaptive service description includes information about the service such as service name, short description, type, resources, operations, license, cost, value, access rights (owned, leased-contracted, shared assess, and privileged access), contract, SLA, concerns and provider.

An adaptive service transits from one state to another state. An adaptive service, similar to living organisms, has the following common lifecycle states:

- Start or Emerge or Configure or Develop, Harvest State
- History or Past State
- Present or Current State
- Future or Target State
- End or Expire or Retire or Death State

An adaptive service is accessible via published interfaces or channels. An adaptive service channel has an associated standard protocol for enabling communication. A human service is a type of adaptive service that is associated with human behavior. A human service can use other human services, facility services and IT services. As discussed earlier, a human-oriented service can be classified into business, information and social types of services.

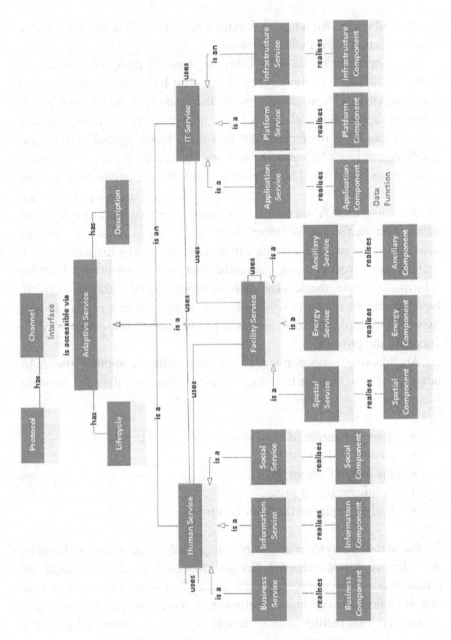

Fig. 3.5. The AESS metamodel – level 3 (adaptive service).

A business service is a human type of adaptive service that is associated with the business-oriented behavior of humans. Humans do business and provide business services. For instance, a bank teller in a bank branch is a human who provides a money transfer service to bank customers. Bank customers can use this service to transfer money from one account to another. A business service is realised or implemented by the business component. A business component refers to a business process or actor.

An information service is a human type of an adaptive service that manages information, which is required or provided during human behavior or interactions (business and social services). Human behavior or service (business or social) involves information handling. For instance, the money transfer business service example will need to use the information service to identify and know the customer's source and target bank account information to complete the money transfer. An information service is realised or implemented by an information component. An information component refers to an information management process or actor.

A social service is a human type of adaptive service that is associated with the social behavior of humans. Social behavior may include informal social interactions in addition to formal business behavior. Humans may form and join social communities of practitioners or users, and offer or acquire social services. A social service exchange or interaction involves handling social information that can be supported by information services. A social service is realised or implemented by a social component. A social component refers to a social process or actor.

An IT service is a type of adaptive service that supports human services. IT-oriented services can be classified into application, platform and infrastructure services. An application service is an IT type of adaptive service that is provided by a software application to support human and facility services. For instance, a money transfer service of a bank can be supported or automated by an online money transfer banking software application service. A software application, as a whole, can be offered as a service (e.g. Software as a Service). A behavior-driven application service supports business and social services. A data-driven application service supports information services. An application service is realised or implemented by the application component.

A platform service is an IT type of adaptive service that provides an integrated platform for an operating system, developing, testing, packaging, deploying and managing software application services. A platform, as a whole, can be offered as a service (e.g. Platform as a Service). A platform service is realised or implemented by a platform component.

An infrastructure service is an IT type of an adaptive service that provides physical and virtual infrastructure (e.g. network, storage, compute, and memory) support for software applications and platform services. Infrastructure, as a whole, can be offered as a service (e.g. Infrastructure as a Service). An infrastructure service is realised or implemented by an infrastructure component.

A facility service is a type of adaptive service that provides an environment for hosting human and IT services. A facility, as a whole, can be offered as a service (e.g. Facility as a Service). Facility-oriented services can be classified into spatial, energy and ancillary services. A spatial service is a facility type of adaptive service that provides a location or real state or space to house human and IT services. For instance, a bank can offer its business services from a bank branch facility. A bank's IT services need to be housed in a facility or location (data center). A spatial service is realised or implemented by the spatial component.

An energy service is a facility type of adaptive service that provides energy or power supply to support services housed in the facility. Energy, as a whole, can be offered as a service (e.g. Energy as a Service). An energy service is realised or implemented by an energy component. An ancillary service is a facility type of adaptive service that includes a number of facility services such as cooling, bandwidth, humidification, dehumidification, fire, safety, security, and mechanical services. An ancillary service is realised or implemented by an ancillary component.

This section described the service level adaptive service elements and their relationships with the AESS metamodel. This generic service level metamodel can be tailored and used to define a context-specific metamodel of an adaptive service. The next section describes the guiding elements.

3.3.4 *Guiding Elements*

The core elements of the AESS metamodel are influenced by the guiding elements. The Gill Framework highlights the nine key guiding elements: strategy, architecture, policy, rule, context, model, reference, legal, and standard (Fig. 3.6). Enterprises may use this element list as a guideline and may tailor it to their local needs.

Strategy describes the overall business motivation and direction. It is a whole package; it includes the mission, driver and vision. The mission supports the strategic intents. Vision refers to the aspiring statement about the future desirable state of a business. The driver triggers the change. Change could be internal or external. Changes are analysed (e.g. strength, weaknesses, opportunities and threats). Change analysis defines the goals, objectives and requirements. Goals support the vision. Strategic intents are levers that address the change in order to achieve the goals. The goal has objectives. The strategic intent has tactics. Tactics address the change in order to achieve the objectives. Goals and objectives are monitored to measure the expected and actual performance.

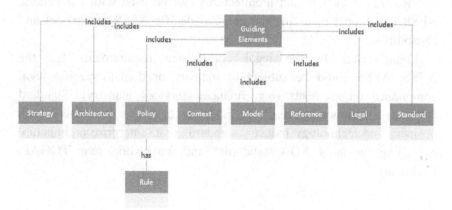

Fig. 3.6. Guiding elements.

Architecture can describe the existing architecture, capability maturity (e.g. current and target), states (e.g. current, and transition states), and scope for change (business architecture, information architecture, technology architecture etc.). Policy includes the specific rules that guide the behavior of an enterprise. Policy and rules guide the adaptive service system processes and interactions. Context awareness is important for defining, operating, managing, supporting and adapting an AESS. An AESS is context aware and continuously scans, senses, and responds to the changing enterprise context. Context can be defined by using a number of internal and external situational factors such as domain factors (e.g. industry, size, complexity, requirements, resources, stakeholders, trends), human factors (e.g. competency, capacity, culture), and technology factors (e.g. platform, infrastructure, trends).

Model refers to a number of different models such as business model, operating model, change model and lifecycle model. These models guide the AESS. For instance, a business model describes how the business makes money. The operating model describes the standardisation and integration requirements of the AESS. The change model describes how to identify and respond to changes. The lifecycle model describes the different stages of an AESS. The reference model includes a number of different industry reference models and architectures such as the information reference model for financial services, reference architecture etc. Reference models and architectures can be used with the generic AESS metamodel to define the context-specific AESS metamodel and capabilities.

Legal refers to the legal compliance requirements for the AESS. AESS could be subject to industry or domain-specific legal compliance requirements (e.g. financial services industry). Standard refers to a common approach or model or language. It includes both business and technology industry standards (e.g. enterprise architecture modelling standards, SOA standards), and frameworks (e.g. TOGAF, Zachman).

3.4 Summary

This chapter discussed the generic adaptive architecture design principles, core and guiding elements of the generic AESS metamodel. These design principles and elements provide a baseline, which can be extended, tailored and updated by the users of the generic AESS metamodel. The core of this metamodel has three core conceptual elements which describe an adaptive or agile enterprise as an AESS at three different levels: adaptive enterprise service system (enterprise level), adaptive service system (capability level) and adaptive service (service level). The adaptive service system (capability level) metamodel can be used to define the context-specific adaptive cloud enterprise architecture capability metamodel. The next chapter discusses The Gill Framework® - AESS lifecycle management approach, which is called ADOMS.

Chapter 4

The Adaptive Enterprise Service System Lifecycle Management

4.1 Introduction

The AESS lifecycle management approach is called ADOMS. It is organised into two main layers: the outer layer and the inner layer (Fig. 4.1). It starts with the adaptation (precisely adaptation first approach) outer layer, which contains the adapting (A) capability. The adapting capability offers context, rationalisation, assessment, realisation, and unrealisation services. The inner layer contains the defining (D), operating (O), managing (M) and supporting (S) capabilities. These capabilities of the AESS lifecycle management approach are referred to as ADOMS. The outer layer enables the continuous adaptation of the AESS. This chapter provides an overview of these capabilities.

4.2 Adapting

The adapting capability offers services such as context awareness, assessment, rationalisation, realisation, and unrealisation. Additional services can be included, if required, to suit the specific enterprise context. It scans and senses (monitors), interprets and analyses (assesses), decides and responds (takes action) to internal and external changes. The outer layer initially identifies the change requirements (initiatives or ideas) that may initiate one or many projects (enterprise projects). These project(s) initiatives or ideas can be further defined and handled through the inner layer of The Gill Framework®. The adapting capability provides five services that enable the continuous adaptation of the AESS capabilities and services. This capability can be extended and tailored to suit the specific enterprise context (such as the cloud adoption context). This capability can be engaged to establish and integrate the new capability or to update existing capabilities in response to changing business demands. The outer layer of the framework presents the five services of the adapting capability.

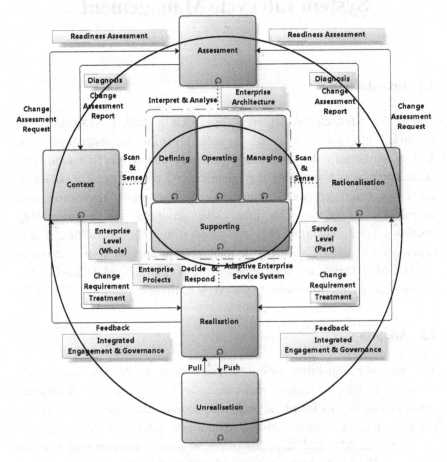

Fig. 4.1. The Gill Framework® 2.0.

The outer layer of the framework presents the five services of the adapting capability.

- Context
- Rationalisation
- Assessment
- Realisation
- Unrealisation

The Context service involves monitoring the internal and external environment to identify opportunities (e.g. trends, drivers, issues) at the enterprise level. This, along with the Assessment service, diagnoses the non-technology or technology adoption or de-adoption opportunities and treatments at the enterprise level. For instance, it can identify an opportunity to define an adaptive cloud enterprise architecture capability to guide enterprise cloud adoption. The Rationalisation service monitors the internal and external environment, and identifies opportunities for change at the individual capability service level. This service, along with the Assessment service, diagnoses technology adoption or de-adoption opportunities and treatment at the capability service level. Enterprises can use a number of human or IT monitoring tools (e.g. Nimsoft, Nagios, SmartCloud Monitoring, Splunk) to support the context and rationalisation services. Please note that this book does not endorse or promote any specific vendor or tool.

The Assessment service assesses non-technology and technology adoption (such as cloud technology) or de-adoption change readiness at an enterprise and capability service level, and provides the change assessment report (informal and formal) to the Context service. It involves the interpretation and analysis of the changes impacting the enterprise and related capabilities. For instance, the Assessment service can use the adaptive capability maturity model (ACMM – see Chapter 9) to assess the maturity of a capability, such as the adaptive enterprise architecture capability. The Realisation service decides and responds to the changes and triggers the integrated adaptive enterprise requirements, enterprise strategy, enterprise architecture, enterprise project, and enterprise service management capabilities to realise the change (e.g.

such as the cloud technology adoption change). It describes the integrated engagement and governance at the enterprise level. The Unrealisation service parks the changes that are not realised for the time being and are deferred. The deferred changes are moved to the unrealisation backlog.

4.3 Defining

The defining capability defines and integrates the adaptive enterprise architecture capability and other linked management capabilities (adaptive enterprise strategy, project, service, and requirements management). It uses the generic AESS metamodel as a guide for tailoring the enterprise context-specific AESS metamodel. The tailored AESS metamodel, along with industry best practices (e.g. distilled from industry enterprise standards, principles, reference architecture, models, frameworks), can be used to define the integrated agile or adaptive enterprise capabilities of a specific enterprise. For instance, the generic AESS metamodel (at the enterprise level) can be used to define the financial services enterprise context-specific AESS metamodel. Further, the defined AESS metamodel (at the capability level) and the enterprise architecture management industry practices (e.g. TOGAF, Zachman, NIST Cloud Reference Architecture) can be tailored to define and integrate the adaptive cloud enterprise architecture capability as an adaptive service system. Finally, the AESS metamodel (at the service level) can be used to define the adaptive cloud enterprise architecture products and services as adaptive services. A defining capability can be used to define any adaptive capability (e.g. adaptive enterprise project management, service management) by using the generic AESS metamodel.

4.4 Operating

The operating capability operates the defined adaptive enterprise architecture capability and describes the architecture for developing, testing, integrating and deploying, offering and using the cloud adaptive service systems and services in short increments. An adaptive enterprise, such as an AESS, operates in a complex, dynamic, local, global, federated, collaborated, centralized, and distributed operating environment. The AESS is a system of adaptive service systems. An adaptive service system is system of adaptive services. An adaptive service system factory continuously develops, tests, integrates, deploys and offers the adaptive service system and services for usage. Adaptive service systems interact with each other and offer or acquire adaptive services for value co-creation. An adaptive service system factory and their interactions are housed at the adaptive service system facility. The AESS operating environment is divided into three main areas (see Table 4.1).

- Adaptive service system interactions
- Adaptive service system factory
- Adaptive service system facility

Table 4.1. Operating capability.

Operating Segment	Architecture Category	Description
Adaptive Service System Interactions i.e. Cloud Interaction Architecture	Interaction Architecture	The interaction architecture can be used to describe the service demand and supply network of uniquely identifiable adaptive service systems within the context of adaptive enterprise architecture. Interaction architecture informs the requirements for other architectures e.g. Human, IT, Solution and Facility Architectures.

Table 4.1. (*Continued*)

Operating Segment	Architecture Category	Description
Adaptive Service System Factory i.e. Cloud Factory Architecture	Human Architecture	Human architecture can be used to describe the business, information, and social architectures in the context of adaptive enterprise architecture.
	IT Architecture	IT architecture can be used to describe the application, platform and infrastructure architectures in the context of adaptive architecture enterprise.
	Solution Architecture	Solution architecture can be used to describe the specific solutions within the overall context of adaptive enterprise architecture.
Adaptive Service System Facility i.e. Cloud Facility Architecture	Facility Architecture	Facility architecture includes the spatial, energy and ancillary architectures in the context of adaptive enterprise architecture.

4.5 Managing

The Gill Framework®, as an overarching meta-framework, provides an integrated adaptive approach to managing changes in the adaptive enterprise architecture capability and its architecture artefacts. The managing capability requires integrating the following management capabilities as adaptive service systems (additional capabilities can be added):

- Adaptive enterprise requirements management capability
- Adaptive enterprise strategic management capability
- Adaptive enterprise architecture management capability
- Adaptive enterprise project management capability
- Adaptive enterprise service management capability

Adaptive enterprise requirements management is required to iteratively manage the strategic, architecture, project and service change requirements. Adaptive enterprise strategic management is required to iteratively manage a robust and flexible enterprise strategy to guide the adaptive enterprise architecture capability. Adaptive enterprise project management is required to implement the adaptive enterprise architecture capability and architecture artefacts in small increments. It involves portfolio, program, project, release and iteration management. Adaptive enterprise service management is required to manage the deployed adaptive service systems and services in operation or in the pipeline.

4.6 Supporting

The supporting capability supports adapting, defining, operating and managing capabilities. This capability can be tailored to suit the specific enterprise context. This capability includes the following key components.

- Adaptive Enterprise Model
- Adaptive Enterprise Library
- Adaptive Enterprise Engineering
- Adaptive Enterprise Intelligence

The adaptive enterprise model suggests the adaptive business model, operating model, adaptive lifecycle model, adaptive change model, adaptive resource supply chain model, and adaptive capability maturity model to guide the adaptive enterprise architecture and related capabilities. Adaptive enterprise intelligence (e.g. including analytics) discusses the necessary analytics and tools support for making effective adaptation decisions. The adaptive enterprise library discusses the integrated enterprise repository to enable the management and re-usability of the enterprise assets. The adaptive enterprise engineering discusses an approach for engineering the enterprise context-specific capabilities as adaptive service systems from new and existing industry best practice stored in the adaptive enterprise library (e.g. extracted from a number of enterprise standards, reference models, and frameworks).

4.7 Application

The ADOMS is an architecture-driven approach which has been developed and is continuously updated based on current research and practice focusing on the design of agile or adaptive enterprises. The ADOMS approach with the AESS metamodel can be used by public and private organisations to deal with the following three key challenges:

- How to effectively assess, establish, integrate and continuously improve the adaptive enterprise capabilities appropriate to suit the specific enterprise context?
- How to use an adaptive enterprise architecture capability to guide the complex enterprise adaptation?
- How to ensure that enterprise-wide adaptation activities are well aligned, coordinated, linked, and tracked?

Central to this ADOMS approach is the adapting capability, which provides the context, assessment, rationalisation, realisation and unrealisation services to establish, integrate and adapt the enterprise requirements, strategy, architecture, project and service management capabilities to ensure that enterprise-wide adaptation activities are well coordinated and aligned. Effective coordination and alignment is important and can reduce waste and increase the value that is expected from the investment in enterprise adaptation. This approach will help to address coordination and alignment issues before they turn into problems. This approach can be applied to different industry verticals, and non-technological and technological contexts (e.g. cloud, mobile, social etc) to effectively manage fundamental, routine and incremental changes in the adaptive enterprise architecture capability and its artefacts.

4.8 Value

The ADOMS approach offers an adaptive, holistic and system of service systems approach to the handling the enterprise changes. This looks at the impact of the change (e.g. enterprise-wide cloud adoption impact) within the context of the enterprise-as-a-whole and not just at the individual process, system or business unit level of cloud adoption. Local isolated changes may be very successful in the short term but may have adverse impacts in the long run. Consequently, successful local change can do more harm than benefit to an enterprise, if not appropriately executed in the holistic enterprise context. Making quick changes in the local parts of an enterprise, while ignoring the bigger picture, may give the illusion of agility but may negatively impact the whole of the enterprise. The impact of both long and short term changes should be reviewed and guided through the lens of the adaptive enterprise architecture.

The ADOMS approach provides an enterprise architecture-driven mechanism to look at enterprise adaptation (e.g. such as cloud adoption) as a whole, as opposed to a piecemeal approach. It treats an enterprise as an AESS, which is a dynamic network of adaptive service systems that have mutual goals. These adaptive service systems interact with each other for value co-creation. It suggests shifting away from the traditional product-centric view of the enterprise to a contemporary service-centric view of the enterprise. It suggests looking at the impact of the adaptation (e.g. such as cloud-enabled adaptation) on all parts of the enterprise. In this way, one cannot avoid or overlook important adaptation considerations at the enterprise level, for instance, if a local business unit decides to take on a public cloud technology-driven initiative and overlook the interests of other parts of the enterprise. This approach is not a holistic or "enterprise-as-a-whole" approach. The business unit in this example is making a critical mistake and a change in the local business unit may have a devastating impact on other parts of the enterprise. A holistic approach could be difficult to achieve and can be assisted through a structured framework. A good example of an enterprise-as-a-whole thinking implementation can be seen in the recent Australian whole-of-government cloud adoption strategy. In contrast to silo cloud adoption, this strategy suggests establishing a government community cloud and using a government cloud service provider panel for sourcing public cloud services. Hence, the ADOMS approach can be used as a guide to:

- align the enterprise-wide technology and non-technology driven adaptation initiatives and investments;
- eliminate the possibilities of duplicate and inconsistent adaptation;
- foster re-usability and consolidation;
- provide a lens for emerging technology assessment and adoption; and
- take advantage of economy of scale through more cost effective enterprise adaptation contracts negotiated at the enterprise level as opposed to at the local business area or agency level.

In summary, enterprises need to define, manage, operate, support and adapt an adaptive enterprise architecture capability to guide less risky enterprise adaptation.

4.9 Summary

This chapter provided an overview of The Gill Framework® - AESS lifecycle management (ADOMS) capabilities. These capabilities can be extended, tailored and used for adapting, defining, operating, managing and supporting the context-specific adaptive enterprise architecture capability and other linked capabilities. The Gill Framework® does not replace the existing frameworks (e.g. TOGAF, Zachman). A basic stance of this framework is that no single enterprise architecture framework or method can be universally applied. They all need to be tailored, integrated and adapted to suit the enterprise context, such as the adaptive cloud enterprise architecture context. The existing enterprise architecture frameworks have their own best practices. These practices can be combined by using a meta-framework, such as The Gill Framework®, for establishing, integrating and continually improving the adaptive enterprise architecture capability to suit the specific enterprise context. The adaptive enterprise architecture capability can then be used to guide the complex enterprise adaptation. The next chapter discusses the adapting capability of the ADOMS approach, and explains how to use the adapting capability to identify the initiative for defining the adaptive cloud enterprise architecture capability for the fictional SFS enterprise.

Chapter 5

Adapting Cloud Enterprise Architecture Capability

5.1 Introduction

The ADOMS approach offers an adapting capability (the outer layer) that identifies change requirements (initiatives or ideas). A change may initiate one or many projects. The adapting capability offers five services: context awareness, assessment, rationalisation, realisation, and unrealisation. It scans and senses (monitor), interprets and analyses (assess), and decides and responds (action) to internal and external changes. Before defining the cloud architecture capability, it is important to identify the need for it. This chapter describes how the adapting capability can be used by the fictional financial services enterprise, SFS, to identify the need for establishing the adaptive cloud enterprise architecture capability (Fig. 5.1). The adapting capability can be supported by a number of models and tools, such as adaptive enterprise monitoring, assessment and intelligence tools (see Chapter 9 – Supporting capability).

5.2 The Context Service

The good health of an adaptive enterprise such as SFS requires the continuous monitoring (scanning and sensing) of enterprise-related events, emerging trends, drivers, opportunities, and pain points to identify expected or unexpected changes or limiting factors and determine their treatment. The continuous monitoring of the enterprise's health is called enterprise context awareness. Effective enterprise context awareness requires the deployment of reliable human and technology scanners and sensors to detect the actual or perceived changes (e.g. business or technology related) that could influence the adaptive enterprise or AESS. The following are the key activities for determining the enterprise context.

- Scan and sense changes at the enterprise level;
- Develop change assessment request; and
- Develop change requirements based on the change assessment report.

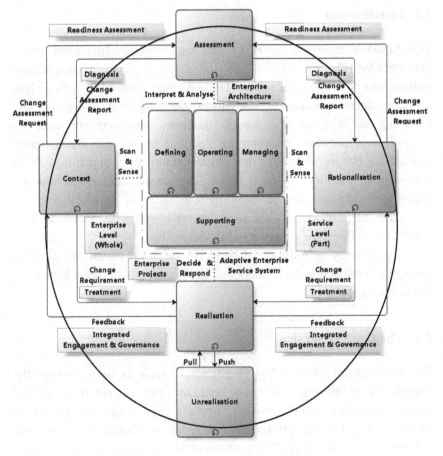

Fig. 5.1. The Gill Framework® 2.0.

SFS enterprise health context awareness is very important to identify any change initiatives. This section will help the reader to understand the following key aspects of the SFS enterprise health context awareness service.

- Context service
- Inputs to the context service
- Context service logic and outputs.

SFS is an adaptive or agile enterprise. It continuously needs to identify and resolve any health issues or limiting factors (e.g. production capacity, time) that constrain its ability to meet desired demands or performance goals and objectives to ensure a competitive advantage. It involves identifying which operating, managing and supporting elements of the SFS enterprise have limiting factors and what changes are required to deal with these limiting factors? There could be significant risks and investments that need to be identified and managed when eliminating or reducing the impact of limiting factors on SFS's enterprise health. An unresolved limiting factor would not allow the SFS enterprise to perform at an optimal level, no matter what they do. Limiting factors may result in fundamental or drastic changes in the SFS enterprise (e.g. defining enterprise architecture capability, adopting cloud technology).

Understanding the SFS enterprise health context is important to identify and treat the limiting factors or changes at the enterprise level as these influence the enterprise as a whole. However, it is not only important to identify the limiting factors or change opportunities (e.g. such as cloud adoption) in the SFS enterprise operating environment, it also requires identifying the limiting factors in the SFS enterprise capabilities that facilitate the management (e.g. strategy, architecture, projects, requirements, and service management) and support (e.g. adaptive enterprise intelligence) of the actual SFS enterprise operating environment. It also involves communicating awareness around the SFS enterprise for engaging in and preparing for the change. The SFS enterprise context service takes the enterprise from the change unawareness to change awareness stage before actually performing detailed change assessment and realisation. Therefore, it is important to communicate and spread awareness around the enterprise about the potential change(s) and their impact. The enterprise context service is critical to facilitate or pave the way for further change assessment and realisation. The context service is the application of resources (e.g. scanners, sensors, enterprise intelligence, enterprise doctor and data scientist) to identify the limiting factors or change opportunities and their treatments at the whole enterprise level. The enterprise context service can be supported by different roles such as the enterprise doctor (e.g. similar to medical doctors or professionals). The enterprise doctor can be supported by a number of other roles such as the enterprise data scientist.

In summary, the SFS enterprise context service needs to identify and resolve any enterprise health issues or limiting factors (e.g. production capacity, time) that constrain its ability to meet its goals. The context service can take the following key inputs:

- Industry reports (e.g. technology trends, events)
- Regulations
- Enterprise operating environment elements
- Enterprise management elements
- Enterprise support elements

The enterprise operating environment elements (e.g. internal and external) include:

- Adaptive service system facility architecture elements
- Adaptive service system factory architecture elements
- Adaptive service system interaction architecture elements

The enterprise management elements include:

- Adaptive enterprise requirements management frameworks, methods, tools and techniques
- Adaptive enterprise strategy management frameworks, methods, tools and techniques
- Adaptive enterprise architecture management frameworks, methods, tools and techniques

- Adaptive enterprise project management frameworks, methods, tools and techniques
- Adaptive enterprise service management frameworks, methods, tools and techniques

The enterprise support elements include:

- Adaptive enterprise models
- Adaptive Enterprise Resource Supply Chain
- Adaptive enterprise library
- Adaptive enterprise engineering
- Adaptive enterprise intelligence

The context service applies human and technological resources to continuously monitor the input elements to identify the health issues or opportunities or limiting factors at the enterprise level that may constrain its ability to meet its desired goals. It can use a number of mechanisms to identify contextual data and information, such as complex event processing and analytics. Complex event processing mechanisms can be used to identify independent events (e.g. decrease in revenue, new technology trends, regulations, new market segment) and relationships between independent events (e.g. source, time) internal and external to an enterprise for sourcing contextual information.

Context data information can be obtained from different sources, which then can be conceptualised and integrated to identify or forecast the possible limiting factors or change opportunities. The context service uses the identified possible changes (e.g. trends, drivers) or limiting factors and generates a change assessment request. The assessment request is stored in the adaptive enterprise library, which is picked up by the enterprise change assessment service to interpret and analyse the nature of the change in the adaptive enterprise architecture, any treatment options (e.g. technology or non-technology options) and risks and their acceptability at the enterprise level.

The enterprise assessment service assesses the limiting factors, change opportunities, treatment options, risks through the enterprise architecture lens, and provides the assessment report. It also involves the enterprise architecture capability assessment. The assessment report is stored in the adaptive enterprise library, which is then sent to the context service. The enterprise context service determines the different drastic changes or treatment options which are appropriate at the strategic enterprise level to address the limiting factors. Based on the assessment report, the context service develops strategic change requirements or initiatives for triggering the change realisation service. The strategic change requirements are stored in the adaptive enterprise library and are sent to the realisation service to decide and respond to the identified strategic change requirements. The strategic change requirements highlight the changes that are required at the strategic enterprise level to address the enterprise health issues or limiting factors in order to meet the target performance goals. The treatment at this level essentially defines the upstream enterprise strategic requirements, which may impact the midstream enterprise architecture and project requirements, and downstream service (operations) requirements.

The interaction between the context and assessment services is required to engage the enterprise architects and other important stakeholders to diagnose the nature of possible changes or the root causes of the limiting factors at the enterprise level. The purpose of the interaction between the context and realisation services is to develop the strategic change requirements. These interactions define the requirements for the desired healthy future state of the adaptive enterprise. The change identification and treatment could be based on intuition and analytics (e.g. standard, data and event-driven). The enterprise context and assessment services can be used to identify the strategic (enterprise future state) need to adopt cloud technology and define a new adaptive cloud enterprise architecture capability within the existing enterprise architecture capability to facilitate strategic enterprise cloud adoption.

5.3 The Assessment Service

The limiting factors or change opportunities identified at the enterprise level (e.g. whole of the enterprise) and capability service level (e.g. part of the enterprise) require assessment in order to identify the root causes and treatment options of the limiting factors. The good health of an adaptive enterprise does not only require continuous monitoring identify the expected or unexpected change opportunities, it also requires continuous interpretation and analysis of the change at a high and low detail level. The continuous interpretation and analysis of the changes is called change assessment or change readiness or capability maturity assessment. Assessment is a key service of the adapting capability. The assessment service can be supported by a number of assessment tools and models (e.g. capability maturity assessment model). The following are the key activities of the enterprise assessment service.

- Interpret and analyse change at the enterprise and service level
- Assess maturity, risks and make recommendations for risk mitigation
- Provide a change assessment report

Effective assessment service requires interaction between the context and rationalisation services. The context service was discussed in the previous section. The rationalisation service will be discussed in the next section. This section will help the reader to understand the following key aspects of the assessment service.

- Assessment service
- Inputs to the assessment service
- Assessment service logic and outputs

The SFS enterprise can assess the root causes of the identified changes (e.g. limiting factors such as performance, production capacity, time) that constrain its ability to meet its target performance goals. The assessment service performs the iterative assessment of the root causes of the identified or observed changes at two levels: enterprise level (e.g. high level assessment) and capability service level (e.g. detailed level assessment).

Assessment not only identifies the root causes of change at the context level or individual capability service level, it also involves change impact assessment. The assessment service is critical to facilitate or pave the way for developing and realising the change requirements to meet the target performance goals. The assessment service applies various resources to identify the root causes and impacts of change, and any technological and non-technological treatment options at the whole enterprise and individual capability service level. The assessment service takes the following key inputs:

- Change assessment requests
  - o Enterprise level
  - o Service level

The assessment requests specify what needs to be assessed at what level. As a minimum, an assessment request should include:

- Change description both at the enterprise or capability service levels
- Change motivations
- Change implications

The assessment service looks at the enterprise health issues, maturity, possible options, risks, mitigations and investment options at the enterprise and detailed capability service level. Consolidated assessment at a high and detailed level indicates which capabilities (existing or to be developed) in the enterprise should proceed with the adoption of a specific technology (such as cloud adoption) or a non-technology option (existing capability maturity improvement, new capability development) for smooth enterprise operations, improvement, growth and transformation.

5.3.1 *Enterprise Level Assessment*

The enterprise level assessment involves the review and identification of the adaptive enterprise capabilities within the adaptive enterprise architecture that are directly and indirectly impacted by the change opportunities or limiting factors. For instance, it can identify the candidate capabilities at the enterprise level that are appropriate for cloud adoption, without going into too much detail upfront. It is important to identify the discontinuing, demotivating and motivating factors related to the technology and non-technology opportunities at the enterprise level. Consolidated assessment at the enterprise level indicates whether the enterprise should proceed with the adoption of a specific technology or non-technology option for the TO BE adaptive enterprise (cloud) architecture state. The key point is that assessment at the enterprise level indicates how the adoption or de-adoption of the technology or non-technology options will impact the SFS enterprise architecture and strategies.

An adaptive enterprise, such as the fictional SFS enterprise, is a living AESS which requires change at different levels (whole and part level) in response to ever-changing business demands. However, prior to proceeding with the change realisation, it is important to understand and assess the current state of the enterprise architecture and identify any gaps based on the technology and non-technology options. The assessment details are stored in the adaptive enterprise library. The following key activities guide the assessment at the enterprise level through the enterprise architecture lens.

- Assess the root causes and impacts of the limiting factors at the enterprise level (e.g. enterprise architecture performance review)
- Assess the technology and non-technology opportunities with their risks to address the root causes of the limiting factors at the enterprise level
- Assess the technology and non-technology opportunities' discontinuing, motivating and demotivating factors in order to understand the enterprise change adoption readiness
- Assess how the technology and non-technology options can contribute to the success of the enterprise
- Assess which capabilities within the enterprise would be directly and indirectly impacted or defined in response to the technological and non-technology opportunities
- Assess the maturity of the capabilities such as the enterprise architecture capability maturity assessment, and identify the

opportunities for improving the existing capabilities or defining new adaptive capabilities such as the adaptive cloud enterprise architecture capability within the existing enterprise architecture capability.

5.3.2 *Service Level Assessment*

The service level assessment involves the review and identification of the capability services within the overall enterprise architecture which are directly and indirectly impacted by the change opportunities or limiting factors. For instance, it can identify the candidate services within a given capability that are appropriate for cloud adoption. Similar to enterprise level assessment, it is important to identify the discontinuing, motivating and demotivating factors related to the technology and non-technology options at a specific capability service level within the overall enterprise context. Consolidated assessment at the service level indicates whether a capability service should proceed with the adoption of a specific technology or non-technology option. The important point is that the assessment at the service level indicates how the adoption or de-adoption of technology or non-technology options impacts the enterprise architecture. The assessment details are stored in the adaptive enterprise library. The following key activities guide the assessment at a specific service level within the overall enterprise context.

- Assess the root causes and impacts of the limiting factors at the capability service level (e.g. enterprise architecture performance review at the service operations management level, service level agreement)
- Assess the technology and non-technology opportunities and risks in order to address the root causes of the limiting factors at the capability service level
- Assess the technology and non-technology opportunities' discontinuing, motivating and demotivating factors in order to understand the change adoption readiness at the service level

- Assess how the technology and non-technology options can contribute to the success of the specific service (e.g. at the service level)
- Assess which services within the capability or specific service system would be impacted by the specific technological and non-technology opportunities
- Assess and identify the opportunities for improving the existing capability services or defining new capability services such as the adaptive cloud enterprise architecture capability services within the existing enterprise architecture capability.

5.4 The Rationalisation Service

The rationalisation service involves continuous monitoring (scanning and sensing) at the capability level services. Rationalisation refers to the sense making of the enterprise level opportunities at the specific capability level services. The rationalisation service applies human and technological monitoring tools. This section will help the reader to understand the following key elements of the rationalisation service within the overall enterprise health context.

- Rationalisation service
- Inputs to the rationalisation service
- Rationalisation service logic and outputs

An enterprise needs to identify and resolve any health issues or limiting factors that constrain its ability to operate or improve at a specific capability service level in order to meet the target demand or performance goals and objectives to ensure a competitive advantage. It involves determining which enterprise operating, managing and supporting environment elements have limiting factors and what change needs to be made to the specific capability services within the overall enterprise context. There could be a need for additional investment or resources to eliminate or reduce the impact of the limiting factors on the health of the capability services. An unresolved limiting factor at the capability service level may not allow the enterprise to perform at an optimal level. The limiting factors may cause an enterprise to make minor adjustments or incremental improvements in the specific services of an individual capability.

Hence, the rationalisation service can be used to identify and treat the limiting factors at the detailed capability service level. Similar to the context service, it not only identifies the limiting factors or change opportunity in the operating environment at the capability service level, it also requires identifying the limiting factors in other relevant management capability services, such as enterprise strategy, architecture, project, requirements and service management capability services. The rationalisation service is required to facilitate detailed limiting factor assessment, change identification and realisation at the service level. The rationalisation service can take the following inputs:

- Adaptive enterprise context
- Adaptive enterprise operating environment elements
- Adaptive enterprise management elements
- Adaptive enterprise support elements

The context service provides the enterprise context to define and change the enterprise capabilities or adaptive services systems. This is important because any local changes should be in alignment with the overall enterprise context. The operating environment (e.g. internal and external) of an enterprise includes the adaptive services system facility, factory and interaction architecture elements. The adaptive enterprise management and support elements (e.g. enterprise strategy, architecture, project, requirements and service management frameworks, methods, tools and techniques) facilitate the value co-creation environment of the enterprise. The rationalisation service monitors these inputs and identifies health issues or limiting factors that constrain the health or ability of a capability service.

Similar to the context service, the rationalisation service monitors the input elements to identify the limiting factors at the detailed capability service level by using a number of approaches, such as complex event processing and analytics. The rationalisation service can use the identified limiting factors' details and generates an assessment request. The assessment request is stored in the enterprise library and is sent to the change assessment service to interpret and analyse the nature of the limiting factor or change, any treatment options, risks and their acceptability at a specific capability service level.

The assessment service assesses the limiting factors or change opportunities and produces the assessment report. The assessment report is stored in the enterprise library for the rationalisation service. The rationalisation service determines what change or treatment (e.g. growth or transformation) is appropriate to address the limiting factor at the capability service level. Based on the assessment report, it produces a service request to trigger the change realisation service. The service request is stored in the enterprise library for the realisation service for further processing (e.g. deciding and responding to the identified change). The service request includes the service requirements or changes that are required to address the service health issues or limiting factors. The treatment at this level essentially defines the downstream service requirements that could be allocated to different projects through the realisation service. Both the service and project requirements are linked to the upstream enterprise strategy and architecture requirements.

The active interactions and engagement between the rationalisation and assessment services are required for the diagnoses and treatment of the root causes and impacts of the limiting factors at a specific capability service level. The active interactions and engagement define the requirements for the desired healthy future state of the specific capability service(s). The change identification and treatment could be based on intuition and analytics. For instance, the fictional SFS enterprise rationalisation and assessment services can be used to identify the initiatives for developing the new enterprise adaptive cloud enterprise architecture capability services and cloud capability services in the overall SFS enterprise context. The identification of the most promising or lucrative change opportunities and treatments could result in resources or energy being channeled in the right direction. In summary, the rationalisation service monitors (scan and sense):

- What is impacting or limiting the adaptive capability services?
- What needs to be done in order to treat the limiting factors that influence the adaptive capability services?

In a nutshell, the rationalisation service identifies the service level requirements or change initiatives within the overall enterprise context. It can be supported by a range of service monitoring, support, incidents, problems, changes and release management roles, tools and processes.

5.5 The Realisation Service

The context and rationalisation services send the change request to the realisation service to actually realise the change requirements identified and assessed at the enterprise and capability service level. The realisation service decides and takes appropriate action in response to the requested change initiatives. It makes sure that the requested changes are appropriately identified and handled through an integrated engagement and governance mechanism. The effective realisation applies an integrated engagement and governance approach instead of local and isolated sub-optimised change management and governance. This section will help the reader to understand the following key elements of the realisation service.

- Realisation service
- Inputs to the realisation service
- Realisation service logic and outputs

The integrated engagement and governance of the enterprise strategy, architecture, projects, requirements and service management capabilities are required to make sure change initiatives are linked, aligned and governed at the whole enterprise level (e.g. systems thinking). This is because the realisation of the change requests may require a significant amount of work in the enterprise strategy, architecture, projects and services. The realisation service priorities the requirements or change initiatives and puts them in the strategic and tactical action plan. The integrated adaptive enterprise requirements management capability manages and links the strategic, architecture, service and implementation project level requirements.

The realisation service triggers and oversees changes in the strategy, architecture, projects and services based on the requirements captured in the requirements repository of the adaptive enterprise library. The realisation service engages different resources that will iteratively realise the requirements or change initiatives. The realisation could trigger the enterprise strategy, architecture and service development and management projects. The realisation details are stored in the adaptive enterprise library. Hence, the realisation service may also trigger the defining, integrating and aligning of the new or existing capabilities or services for the effective governance and management of smooth enterprise operations, improvement, growth, and transformation initiatives. For instance, the realisation service can be used to trigger a project (initiative) to define the adaptive cloud enterprise architecture capability and services for guiding SFS's enterprise cloud adoption. These initiatives are communicated across the enterprise. The realisation service applies resources for the integrated engagement and governance of the desired changes at the enterprise and capability service level. The realisation service takes the following inputs:

- Context work request
- Rationalisation work request

The context work request contains the enterprise level strategic requirements or initiatives i.e. establishing a new adaptive cloud enterprise architecture capability and enterprise cloud adoption. The rationalisation work request contains the capability service level tactical and operational requirements or changes i.e. adaptive cloud enterprise architecture capability services and cloud services. The realisation service triggers and facilitates the change implementation through effective and integrated engagement and governance. It engages relevant capabilities and allocates appropriate resources such as human and financial resources. It facilitates the integrated governance of enterprise capabilities for consistent and smooth change realisation by directing energy in the right direction. It essentially leads and tracks the changes in the underlying adaptive (cloud) enterprise architecture. It defines a road map of change. It regularly interacts with the context and rationalisation services to provide and receive feedback on change realisation. It is the responsibility of the realisation service to pick up the most promising or lucrative change opportunities to channel resources or energy in the right direction.

5.6 The Unrealisation Service

The context and rationalisation services send the service request to the realisation service to realise the change requirements identified both at the enterprise and service levels. The realisation service continuously receives work requests. It reviews and decides to accept or reject or defer the work requests. The rejected or deferred work requests are pushed to the unrealisation service for future reference. The accepted work requests are prioritised. The unrealisation service keeps track of rejected or deferred opportunities in the adaptive enterprise library – requirements repository.

5.7 Summary

This chapter described the adapting capability from the ADOMS approach. The adapting capability offers the adaptive enterprise, assessment, rationalisation, realisation and unrealisation services. The adapting capability services should have the ability to monitor, identify, evaluate, accept or embrace the change that is required in one or many capabilities within the adaptive enterprise to eliminate or reduce the impact of the limiting factors at a high enterprise level, and low detailed individual capability service level. The change assessment results at the enterprise or service level may indicate whether the change is appropriate or not. For instance, a negative cloud adoption assessment report at the enterprise level would indicate that there is not a single capability within the enterprise architecture that is suitable for cloud technology adoption. If there is at least one capability within the enterprise architecture that is suitable for cloud adoption, then a detailed assessment of cloud adoption can be performed for the specific capability in order to identify which services within the specific capability are suitable for cloud adoption. Essentially, enterprise level assessment is a first check point before committing more resources for a detailed capability service level assessment within the overall enterprise context. Positive cloud adoption assessment triggers the initiative to define the adaptive cloud enterprise architecture capability and services to support strategic enterprise architecture-driven cloud adoption. The next chapter explains how to define the adaptive cloud enterprise architecture capability in the overall context of fictional SFS enterprise cloud adoption.

Chapter 6

Defining Cloud Enterprise Architecture Capability

6.1 Introduction

The ADOMS approach offers a defining capability. This chapter describes how the defining capability can be used by the fictitious financial services enterprise, SFS, to define the adaptive cloud enterprise architecture capability as an adaptive service system (Fig. 6.1). The defining capability is concurrently used in conjunction with other capabilities, such as the adapting and supporting capabilities. The adapting capability provides the initiative for defining or updating the adaptive cloud enterprise architecture capability. The supporting capability provides the adaptive enterprise models, library, engineering and intelligence to define and update the adaptive cloud enterprise architecture capability. The defining capability can be used to define the following items for the SFS adaptive cloud enterprise architecture capability (e.g. additional items can be considered, if required).

- architecture principles
- guiding elements
- architecture capability as an adaptive service system
- architecture products and services as adaptive services
- architecture vision

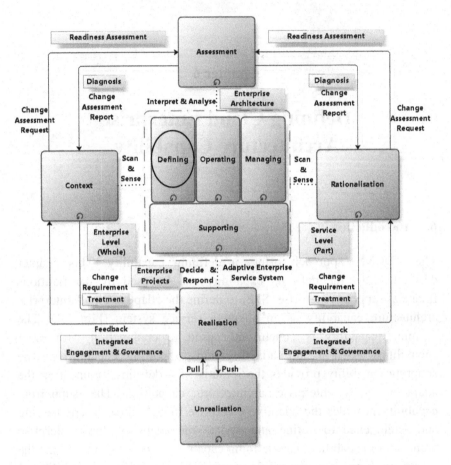

Fig. 6.1. The Gill Framework® 2.0.

6.2 Architecture Principles

The architecture principles are design constraints that influence the definition, operation, management, support and adaptation of the adaptive cloud enterprise architecture capability and its artefacts. The context-specific adaptive cloud enterprise architecture principles can be defined using the generic design principles from the AESS metamodel. The AESS metamodel provides the following three broad categories of architecture design principles (additional ones can be considered, if required):

- Agility principles
- System principles
- Service principles

Agility principles focus on the responsiveness, flexibility, speed, leanness and learning of the adaptive cloud enterprise architecture. System principles focus on the fact that the adaptive cloud enterprise architecture is composed of different interdependent and connected parts or sub-systems, and is managed as a whole living system. Service principles focus on the fact that the adaptive cloud enterprise architecture is a service-oriented architecture, where service is the fundamental unit of exchange. Table 6.1 shows the example of agility principles which can guide the adaptive cloud enterprise architecture capability and its artefacts. The adaptive cloud enterprise architecture principles can be further detailed using the architecture principles template from The Open Group i.e. cloud architecture principle statements, rationale and implications (Harrison 2011).

Table 6.1. Agility principles for the cloud.

Agility Principles	Description
Responsiveness	Cloud architecture capability and artefacts should be able to form an appropriate response in order to deal with the changes.
Flexibility	Cloud architecture capability and artefacts should be able to adapt in response to changing complex business demands.
Speed	Cloud architecture capability and artefacts should be able to operate at fast pace and deliver results quickly (e.g. quick time to market).
Leanness	Cloud architecture capability and artefacts should be able to work with optimal or minimal resources without compromising the quality of its outputs or offerings (e.g. reduced cost and waste, improved quality).

Table 6.1. (*Continued*)

Agility Principles	Description
Learning	Cloud architecture capability and artefacts should be able to learn from up-to-date knowledge and experience for sustained continuous growth and adaptation over a period of time.

6.3 Guiding Elements

The guiding elements are defined to guide the adaptive cloud enterprise architecture capability. The SFS enterprise context-specific guiding elements can be defined using the generic guiding elements from the AESS metamodel. The defining capability focuses on defining the context-specific guiding elements, such as enterprise cloud strategy, existing architecture, policy, rules, context, model, reference, legal, and standard. This book does not claim to provide an exhaustive list of guiding elements. Additional elements can be considered, if required.

6.3.1 *Enterprise Cloud Strategy*

The adaptive enterprise strategic management capability provides the adaptive cloud enterprise strategy that needs to be realised by the adaptive cloud enterprise architecture. The adaptive cloud enterprise strategy (within the overall context of enterprise strategy) describes the overall business motivation and direction for cloud adoption. It includes mission, driver and vision. Mission supports the strategic intents for cloud adoption. Vision refers to an aspiring statement about cloud-enabled enterprise architecture. Driver triggers the change in terms of cloud adoption. Cloud adoption changes are analysed (e.g. strength, weaknesses, opportunities and threats). Change analysis defines the goals, objectives and requirements for cloud adoption. Goals define the vision. Strategic intents address the cloud adoption change in order to achieve the goals. Goal has objectives related to cloud adoption. Strategic intent has tactics in the overall context cloud adoption. Tactics address the cloud adoption change in order to achieve the objectives. Goals and objectives are monitored to measure the expected and actual performance through cloud adoption.

6.3.2 *Enterprise Architecture Capability Maturity and Scope*

It is important to review the existing enterprise architecture work and architecture capability maturity. The Gill Framework® provides the adaptive capability maturity model (ACMM) to support the maturity assessment of an adaptive capability (see Chapter 9 for supporting models). The SFS enterprise can use the ACMM to formally assess their existing enterprise architecture capability and identify the target maturity level. It is assumed that the SFS enterprise has a well-defined and mature enterprise architecture capability (ACMM – Level 3: Defined). They have solution architects, domain architects and chief enterprise architects. The SFS enterprise architect team reports to the CIO. The SFS enterprise architecture capability provides architectural support to different business and IT projects across the enterprise. The SFS needs to develop an adaptive cloud enterprise architecture capability within the existing traditional enterprise architecture capability. The adaptive cloud enterprise architecture capability will provide cloud architecture support to different cloud projects across the enterprise. Cloud architecture should not only be perceived as a technology architecture. It is not appropriate to consider cloud architecture in isolation of other existing enterprise architecture layers, such as business, information, social and facility architectures. Cloud architecture should begin from business architecture. Therefore, the scope of the adaptive cloud enterprise architecture for the SFS should be considered in conjunction with the other architecture layers.

6.3.3 *Enterprise Policy and Rule*

The SFS enterprise operates in Australia, Asia, Europe and USA. Cloud services can be sourced from and hosted at different geographical locations and could be subject to local and international policy and rules.

The adaptive cloud enterprise architecture capability needs to consider the context-specific policy and rules that may constrain the to-be developed adaptive cloud enterprise architecture.

6.3.4 *Enterprise Context*

The adaptive cloud enterprise architecture capability is context aware and continuously scans, senses, and responds to the changing enterprise context. Context awareness is important for defining, operating, managing, supporting and adapting the adaptive cloud enterprise architecture capability. Context service was discussed in the adapting capability. Context service needs to monitor internal and external enterprise context factors that may affect the adaptive cloud enterprise architecture.

6.3.5 *Enterprise Model*

The supporting capability provides the adaptive enterprise models to support the adaptive cloud enterprise architecture capability. The adaptive enterprise models include enterprise business model, operating model, change model and lifecycle model. The adaptive business model describes how the business makes money in the context of cloud adoption. The adaptive operating model describes the cloud operating environment requirements, such as the standardization and integration (e.g. integration of cloud and non-cloud systems) requirements. The adaptive change model classifies the changes identified in the internal and external environment. The adaptive lifecycle model describes the different lifecycle stages of the cloud services. The details of these models are provided by the supporting capability.

6.3.6 *Enterprise Cloud Reference Architecture*

The definition of the adaptive cloud enterprise architecture capability and its artefacts, for a specific industry and enterprise, can be assisted by reviewing and selecting the relevant cloud reference architecture. There are a number of cloud reference architectures, such as the NIST cloud reference architecture (NIST 2011), Oracle reference architecture (2012), and IBM cloud reference architecture (IBM 2013). Cloud reference architecture provides a high level architecture, which specifies the main cloud actors, activities and functions. The SFS enterprise needs to review these reference architectures and define their own enterprise cloud reference architecture. The enterprise cloud reference architecture can be used to scope the adaptive cloud enterprise architecture work.

6.3.7 *Legal*

The cloud computing environment could be subject to industry- and country-specific legal compliance requirements. It is important to identify and review any such requirements in the early stages of adaptive cloud enterprise architecture capability establishment.

6.3.8 *Standard*

There are a number of architecture standards (e.g. enterprise architecture modelling standards, SOA standards) including de-facto standards, such as architecture frameworks (e.g. TOGAF, Zachman). It is important to identify, review, tailor and adopt the relevant standards to define the adaptive cloud enterprise architecture capability.

In summary, the guiding elements need to be considered when defining the adaptive cloud enterprise architecture capability.

6.4 Architecture Capability

The generic AESS metamodel provides the core elements and their relationships. The AESS metamodel is organised into three levels: enterprise, capability and service level metamodels.

- Adaptive enterprise service system (enterprise level)
- Adaptive service system (capability level)
- Adaptive service (service level) metamodels

The generic AESS metamodel can be used as a foundation to tailor an SFS enterprise context-specific AESS metamodel. The tailored metamodel should define the context-specific core AESS metamodel elements and their relationships. The defining capability focuses on defining the adaptive cloud enterprise architecture capability as an adaptive service system that incorporates architecture principles (design principles) and is guided by guiding elements. Therefore, the first step is to use the AESS metamodel (at the capability level) and define the context-specific adaptive cloud enterprise architecture capability as an adaptive service system.

The adaptive cloud enterprise architecture capability, as an adaptive service system, has a number of key elements (Fig. 6.2) (additional elements can be added, if required). It has description and lifecycle stages. The architecture capability should be accessible via channels for interaction with other capabilities or service systems. It is a configuration of actors. Actors are human or non-human agents who play different roles (e.g. cloud chief architect, cloud application architect, cloud platform architect, cloud infrastructure architect, cloud solution architecture), and have competency (cloud architecture skills, knowledge and experience) and capacity (e.g. bandwidth of work, availability) to support the adaptive cloud enterprise architecture capability.

The adaptive cloud enterprise architecture capability can include interaction, business, information, social, application, platform, infrastructure, facility and solution architecture capabilities (additional capabilities can be included, if required). These architecture capabilities can be realised by the architecture modelling, analysis, management and governance processes. These processes can be tailored by adopting specific practices, tools and techniques from the existing well-known enterprise architecture frameworks and modelling standards. For instance, the adaptive cloud enterprise architecture capability processes can be defined by selecting the architecture practices and techniques from the TOGAF, DoDAD and Zachman framework. There are a number of architecture tools (tools as adaptive services) such as Abacus, IBM Rational System Architect, and Orbus etc. Enterprises need to assess the available tools according to their local needs and context. This book does not purposely suggest any specific architecture tool.

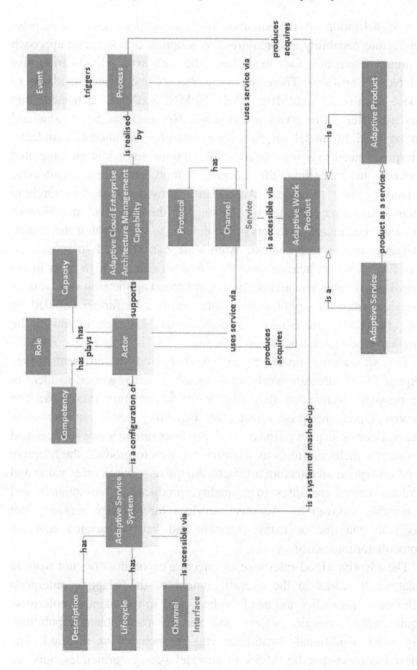

Fig. 6.2. Adaptive cloud enterprise architecture management capability.

The definition of the situation-specific adaptive cloud enterprise architecture capability also requires the adoption of a standard approach (Guiding Element) for modelling the adaptive cloud enterprise architecture artifacts. There are a number of modelling standards to choose from (e.g. ArchiMate, UML, BPMN, SoaML). Each modelling standard differs in its notation and scope. No single modelling standard can be used to model all the cloud enterprise architecture artefacts. Enterprises need to assess the available options and adopt an integrated approach to modelling the adaptive cloud enterprise architecture artifacts. For instance, ArchiMate provides an overarching comprehensive set of modelling elements for the high-level modelling of the cloud architecture artefacts at the enterprise level, within the overall enterprise architecture context. ArchiMate can be used to model the identified cloud applications and their interactions at a high level in the overall cloud enterprise architecture. Each cloud application (software as a service) from the application architecture can be further detailed by using the UML and SoaML. ArchiMate can be used to model the complete cloud infrastructure architecture.

The architecture processes can be triggered by different events (request for architecture work, assessment). There is a need to identify the possible events that may trigger the architecture processes. The adaptive cloud enterprise architecture capability actors and processes use, produce or acquire adaptive work products (architecture services and products) - including tools as adaptive services to produce the adaptive cloud enterprise architecture artefacts. Adaptive services offer value and have associated measures (e.g. quality, productivity, compliance and sustainable innovation). Adaptive services (architecture services) are accessible via one or many channels and have associated standard protocols for interaction.

The adaptive cloud enterprise architecture capability does not work in isolation. It works in the overall context of the adaptive enterprise architecture capability and needs to be linked to the adaptive enterprise requirements, strategic, project, and service management capabilities (Fig. 6.3.). Additional capabilities can be included as required. The tailored context-specific AESS metamodel (design principles, guiding elements and core metamodel) and industry best frameworks, methods, tools and techniques can be used to define and integrate these capabilities as adaptive service systems.

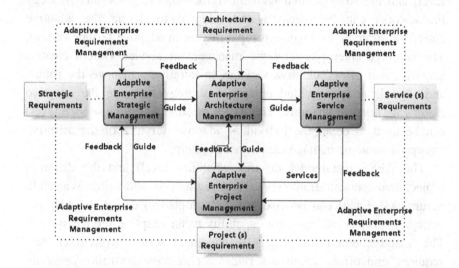

Fig. 6.3. Integrated adaptive cloud enterprise architecture management capability.

The core to the adaptive cloud enterprise architecture management capability is the adaptive enterprise requirement management capability. The AESS metamodel (at the capability level) and the different requirement engineering practices (e.g. agile and non-agile requirements elicitation, analysis, specifications and management) can be tailored and adopted to define the adaptive enterprise requirements management capability as an adaptive service system. The adaptive enterprise requirements management service system creates, acquires, and offers adaptive services to iteratively manage the strategic, architecture, project and service level requirements in the context of cloud adoption. The AESS metamodel (at the service level) can be used to detail the individual adaptive services of the adaptive enterprise requirements management service system.

The establishment of any capability is a strategic decision. A new capability is established to meet the strategic intents. Adaptive enterprise architecture management is a strategic capability that realises the adaptive enterprise strategy. The AESS metamodel (at the capability level) and the strategic management frameworks (e.g. Gartner Strategy Framework) can be assessed and adopted to define the adaptive enterprise strategic management capability as an adaptive service system. The adaptive enterprise strategic management service system creates, acquires, and offers adaptive services to iteratively manage the robust and flexible adaptive cloud enterprise strategy to guide the adaptive cloud enterprise architecture. The AESS metamodel (at the service level) can be used to detail the individual adaptive services of the adaptive enterprise strategic management service system.

The AESS metamodel (at the capability level) and the different project management frameworks (e.g. agile and non-agile: Waterfall, Scrum, XP, Lean) can be assessed and adopted to define the adaptive enterprise project management capability as an adaptive service system. The adaptive enterprise project management service system creates, acquires, and offers adaptive services for iterative portfolio, program, project, release and iteration management. The AESS metamodel (at the service level) can be used to detail the individual adaptive services of the adaptive enterprise project management service system.

The AESS metamodel (at the capability level) and the different service management frameworks (e.g. ITIL, ISO 20000) can be assessed and used to define the adaptive enterprise service management capability as an adaptive service system. The adaptive enterprise service management service system creates, acquires, and offers adaptive services to manage the cloud-enabled AESS. The AESS metamodel (at the service level) can be used to detail the individual adaptive services of the adaptive enterprise service management service system.

These adaptive capabilities, as adaptive service systems, interact with each other and with their environment, and create, offer or acquire adaptive services for value co-creation. The AESS metamodel (at the enterprise level) can be used to describe the adaptive service system interactions.

6.5 Architecture Services

The adaptive cloud enterprise architecture capability can offer, acquire and co-create adaptive services (including products). The AESS metamodel (at the service level) can be used to define the portfolio of the adaptive cloud enterprise architecture capability services.

6.6 Architecture Vision

The adaptive enterprise architecture capability as an adaptive service system is defined to realise the adaptive enterprise strategy. The adaptive cloud enterprise architecture vision describes how it will realise the adaptive cloud enterprise strategy (e.g. goals, objectives and requirements). The adaptive cloud enterprise architecture vision provides a high level description of the interaction, business, information, social, application (including data), platform, infrastructure, technology, and facility domain architecture requirements that need to be detailed to realise the adaptive cloud enterprise strategy. These domain architectures are detailed by the operating capability.

6.7 Summary

This chapter described how to define the integrated adaptive cloud enterprise architecture capability using the generic AESS metamodel and the defining capability of the ADOMS approach. The AESS metamodel and defining capability can be tailored and used to define a context-specific integrated adaptive enterprise architecture capability as an adaptive service system. The next chapter describes the operating capability of the ADOMS approach in detail. The operating capability operates the adaptive cloud enterprise architecture capability to generate cloud architecture work products.

Chapter 7

Operating Cloud Enterprise Architecture Capability

7.1 Introduction

The adaptive cloud enterprise architecture capability is operated by the operating capability as an adaptive service system. The adaptive cloud enterprise architecture capability offers cloud architecture work products (architecture products and services). This chapter describes how the adaptive cloud enterprise architecture capability can be operated by the fictitious financial services enterprise, SFS, to design the adaptive cloud enterprise architecture (Fig 7.1).

The operating capability operates the integrated adaptive cloud enterprise architecture capability in conjunction with the enterprise strategic, project, requirements and service management capabilities. Unlike a traditional isolated enterprise architecture capability resting in the ivory tower of strategic management, the operating capability puts the adaptive cloud enterprise architecture capability in the operating environment of the overall echo-system of cloud-enabled AESS. The operating capability operates the adaptive cloud enterprise architecture capability and describes the cloud architecture artefacts. The cloud-enabled operating environment (e.g. AESS) is an echo-system of adaptive service systems. An adaptive service system offers adaptive services. An adaptive service system factory continuously sources, develops, tests, integrates, deploys and offers adaptive cloud service systems and services (e.g. SaaS, PaaS, IaaS and FaaS) for usage. Adaptive cloud service systems interact with each other and exchange cloud services for value co-creation. An adaptive cloud service system factory and interactions are hosted at the adaptive cloud service system facility.

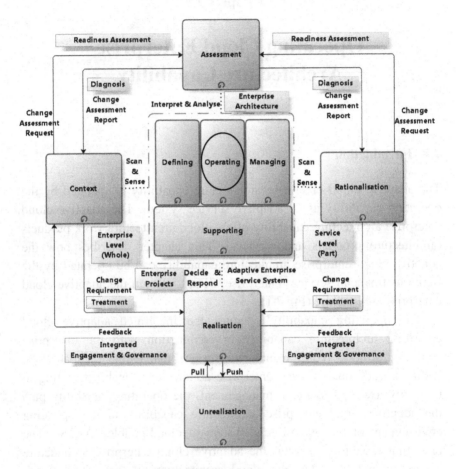

Fig. 7.1. The Gill Framework® 2.0.

The cloud-enabled operating environment is divided into three major segments (see Table 7.1):

- Adaptive (cloud) service system interactions
- Adaptive (cloud) service system factory
- Adaptive (cloud) service system facility

Table 7.1. Cloud-enabled operating environment.

Operating Segment	Architecture Category	Description
Adaptive Service System Interactions i.e. Cloud Interaction Architecture	Interaction Architecture	Interaction architecture describes the cloud service demand and supply network of uniquely identifiable adaptive service systems within the context of adaptive cloud enterprise architecture. Interaction architecture informs the requirements for other architectures e.g. human, IT, solution and facility architectures.
Adaptive Service System Factory i.e. Cloud Factory Architecture	Human Architecture i.e. Social Business Information Architecture	Human architecture can be used to describe the business, information, and social architectures in the context of adaptive cloud enterprise architecture. Human architecture as a whole refers to social business information architecture.
	IT Architecture	IT architecture can be used to describe the application, platform and infrastructure architectures in the context of the adaptive cloud architecture enterprise.
	Solution Architecture	Solution architecture can be used to describe the specific cloud solutions within the overall context of adaptive cloud enterprise architecture.

Table 7.1. (*Continued*)

Operating Segment	Architecture Category	Description
Adaptive Service System Facility i.e. Cloud Facility Architecture	Facility Architecture	Facility architecture includes the spatial, energy and ancillary architectures in the context of adaptive cloud enterprise architecture.

Adaptive cloud service system interactions are described by cloud interaction architecture. The adaptive (cloud) service system factory is described by cloud factory architecture. The adaptive cloud service system facility is described by cloud facility architecture. The operating capability uses the generic adaptive enterprise architecture conceptual model from the Gill Framework® to generate the adaptive cloud enterprise architecture conceptual model (Fig. 7.2). These conceptual models are consistent with the ISO/IEC/IEEE 42010 architecture concepts. Adaptive cloud enterprise architecture is guided by the guiding elements and incorporates design principles. Adaptive cloud enterprise architecture is developed to address stakeholders' concerns. Stakeholders' concerns can be used to construct viewpoints. A viewpoint is a template that can be used to create a view of adaptive cloud enterprise architecture for specific stakeholders. Adaptive cloud enterprise architecture contains a number of cloud architectural elements. These elements have properties and relationships. These cloud architectural elements can be represented in a matrix or catalogue. These elements can be visually represented in cloud architecture models. Visual cloud architecture models can be developed using architecture modelling languages (ArchiMate, UML, BPMN, SoaML etc.). In summary, adaptive cloud enterprise architecture elements can be organised into the following domains or layers.

- Cloud interaction architecture
- Cloud factory architecture
- Cloud facility architecture

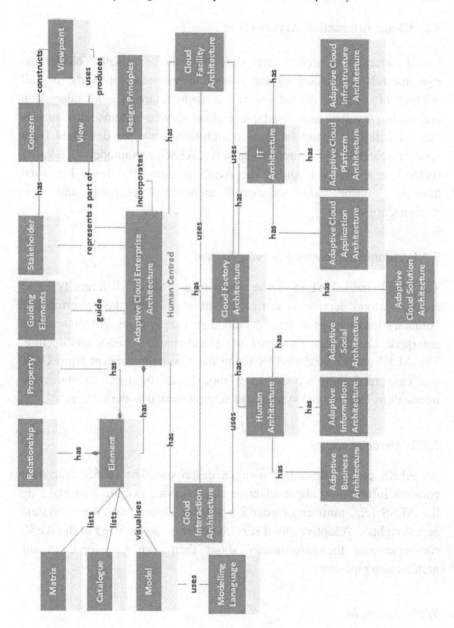

Fig. 7.2. Adaptive cloud enterprise architecture model.
(based on The Gill Framework adaptive enterprise architecture model)

7.2 Cloud Interaction Architecture

Cloud interaction architecture describes the externally observable dynamic adaptive cloud service system interactions within the overall context of adaptive cloud enterprise architecture. Cloud interaction architecture evolves as new adaptive cloud service systems leave or join the interactions. Cloud interaction architecture can be described for a specific context by using the generic AESS metamodel – level 1 (enterprise level) as a guide. The AESS metamodel – level 1 is used here to describe cloud interaction architecture elements and their relationships.

7.2.1 *Adaptive Enterprise Service System*

The cloud-enabled AESS is the world or ecology of different types of adaptive cloud service systems. It evolves through the dynamic and voluntary interactions of adaptive cloud service systems. Adaptive cloud enterprise architecture describes the cloud-enabled AESS architecture. The AESS can be modelled by using the "System" concept from UML use case modelling. A use case model can be used to show the interactions between the system and actors external to the system.

7.2.2 *Description*

An AESS can be described using a descriptor. The AESS descriptor contains information about adaptive cloud service systems that make up the AESS (e.g. number of adaptive systems, types of systems, system access rights). Adaptive cloud service systems can be listed in the AESS catalogue and the information about them can be stored in the architecture repository.

7.2.3 *Lifecycle*

An AESS has a lifespan. The AESS lifecycle model can be developed to show its current, transition and target states. The AESS lifecycle model can be developed using the UML state machine diagram.

7.2.4 *Channel*

The AESS environment contains different types of adaptive cloud service systems that are accessible via different channels. Essentially, it is a multi-channel environment. Information on these channels can be listed in the AESS catalogue and stored in the architecture repository. The AESS channels can be visually modelled by customising and using the ArchiMate "Interface" concept.

7.2.5 *Adaptive Service System*

The adaptive cloud service system offers or acquires one or many adaptive cloud services (e.g. SaaS services). It can be developed, acquired, deployed, offered and used by different actors. The adaptive cloud service system can be modelled by using the "System" concept from UML use case modelling.

7.2.6 *Value Network*

The cloud value network is an open, dynamic, distributed, demand and supply value network of uniquely identifiable adaptive cloud service systems. The cloud value network evolves through the joining or leaving of adaptive cloud service systems. The cloud value network is like an adaptive cloud service system registry that enables adaptive cloud service systems to join, leave, discover, select and propose interactions with the desired adaptive cloud service systems for cloud services. The AESS may have many public, private and hybrid cloud value networks. These cloud value networks can be modelled by customising and using the ArchiMate "Network" and related concepts.

7.2.7 *Sensor*

The cloud demand and supply value network consists of cloud sensors. These sensors monitor the internal and external cloud environment, capture data on cloud services, process it, and send it to the relevant main sensor and adaptive cloud service systems in the cloud value network for further action. The sensor can be modelled using the ArchiMate "Device" and "Node" concepts. A sensor device is physical sensor hardware. A sensor node is a combination of sensor hardware or a device and software that is capable of capturing, processing, storing and sending data. The cloud sensor network as a whole can be modelled using the ArchiMate "Network" concept.

7.2.8 *Actor*

The adaptive cloud service system is an actor or stakeholder (e.g. capability or organisations or an entity) in the AESS. An adaptive cloud service system can join different AESS cloud value networks and can play different roles in each value network. The adaptive cloud service system as an actor can be modelled by customising and using the ArchiMate "Business Actor" concept.

7.2.9 *Role*

The adaptive cloud service system, as an actor, plays different roles. A role represents an assigned or assumed responsibility. The role types could include Cloud Service Creator, Provider, Consumer, Carrier, Partner, Auditor, Observer, Competitor, Regulator and Broker. These role types can be used as a guideline for defining the situation-specific cloud roles according to the local cloud context. The adaptive cloud service system role can be modelled by customising and using the ArchiMate "Business Role" concept.

7.2.10 *Channel (Interaction)*

The adaptive cloud service system can discover and select other adaptive cloud service systems from the AESS cloud value network. It can propose interactions to other adaptive cloud service systems by using their exposed interaction channels. An interaction channel is a point which is made available to other adaptive cloud service systems to propose or participate in an interaction. An interaction channel could be

API, self-service online web, mobile or social media. The adaptive cloud service system can allow or restrict access to its adaptive cloud services through interaction channels. An interaction channel is an interface that enables interactions between adaptive cloud service systems. The interaction channels can be visually modelled by customising and using the ArchiMate "Interface" concept.

7.2.11 *Protocol*

The interaction channel has an associated interaction protocol. The adaptive cloud service system needs to follow the interaction protocol to interact with other adaptive cloud service system. A standard interaction protocol is important for enabling interaction among heterogeneous independent adaptive cloud service systems. The adaptive service system may use a number of protocols such as HTTPS, HTTP, SOAP (Simple Object Access Protocol), JMS (Java Message Service), REST (Representational State Transfer) etc. The interaction channel protocol can be visually modelled by customising and using the ArchiMate "Artifact" (e.g. protocol data object) concept.

7.2.12 *Interaction*

Adaptive cloud service system interaction depends on the adaptive cloud service demand and supply. It involves at least two adaptive cloud service systems. It is also called adaptive cloud service system choreography (multi-party interaction). The adaptive cloud service system can propose or participate in one or more interactions with other cloud service systems. Adaptive cloud service system interactions begin in response to a perceived or real demand for an adaptive cloud service. An adaptive cloud service system may perceive that there is a demand for its adaptive cloud service and may intend to supply adaptive cloud services. An adaptive cloud service system may explicitly send a request to other adaptive cloud service system (s) in the cloud value network to supply a specific cloud service. Each adaptive cloud service system needs to be aware of the changing demand and supply context of their cloud services. Adaptive cloud service systems sense demand and supply through cloud value network sensors. Note that an interaction can also be described between cloud and non-cloud adaptive service systems. The interaction can be detailed in the AESS matrix and can be visually modelled by customising and using the ArchiMate "Interaction" concept.

7.2.13 *Event*

An event is a change in the state of something that triggers an adaptive cloud service system interaction activity. An event could be a one-off event or a recurring event. It could be a time-driven event. An event can trigger the start or stop of a proposal or negotiation or contract interaction activity. An event can be visually modelled by customising and using the ArchiMate "Event" concept.

7.2.14 *Mutual Goal*

A cloud interaction may define or realise a mutually agreed goal between two or more adaptive cloud service systems. Mutual goals do not mean that the adaptive cloud service systems have the same goals. They could have different but mutually agreed goals. A mutual goal can be visually modelled by customising and using the ArchiMate "Goal" concept.

7.2.15 *Proposal*

An adaptive service system can send or receive an interaction proposal from other adaptive service systems via an interaction channel. An adaptive service system should be open to receive proposals. A proposal can be visually modelled by customising and using the ArchiMate "Artifact" concept.

7.2.16 *Negotiation*

A proposal is negotiated between adaptive cloud service systems. The negotiation activity may result in the acceptance or rejection of the proposal with the option of taking no further action. Proposal negotiation can be visually modelled by customising and using the ArchiMate "Process" and "Collaboration" concepts.

7.2.17 Contract

If a proposal is successfully negotiated and accepted, then an existing contract is updated or a new contract is established between adaptive cloud service systems. A contract can be established or updated for one or more adaptive cloud services between different adaptive cloud service systems (also non-cloud). A contract can also be an ongoing or fixed contract or sub-contract or SLA. A contract defines the functional and non-functional aspects of the adaptive cloud service system and services. The non-foundational aspects of the adaptive cloud service could include service policy, security, privacy, performance, trust, interoperability, reliability, carbon emission etc. Adaptive cloud service usage should be viewed with its concerns and execution context. The adaptive service concerns provide the basis for the service contract. The contract can be visually modelled by customising and using the ArchiMate "Contract" concept, which is a specialisation of the ArchiMate "Business Object" concept.

7.2.18 Governance

A contract specifies a control or governance mechanism that imposes governance limits and controls the execution of the cloud service contracts. The control mechanism can allow or restrict access to specific adaptive cloud service systems and their services. Cloud services are not generally offered for free. The demand and supply of cloud service interactions mutually price cloud services competitively. The adaptive cloud service system should be able to track and monitor the usage of its services and bill its users according (based on the agreed contract). Cloud services can be billed based on monthly subscriptions, fixed term licenses, pay-per-use or pay-as-you-go model (e.g. Amazon cloud service model). The adaptive cloud service system business model should include the guidelines for adaptive service pricing. An adaptive cloud service system should have the ability to quickly adjust its cloud service prices in response to changing cloud service demand. The governance process can be visually modelled by customising and using the ArchiMate "Process", "Principle" and "Constraint" concepts.

7.2.19 *Execution*

The execution of a contract involves the execution of one or more interaction activities between the relevant adaptive cloud service systems, which may involve the creation, access or use of adaptive cloud services .Adaptive cloud service usage refers to the functional aspects of a cloud service. It can also be interpreted as a cloud service use case. An adaptive cloud service system (or non-cloud) can use the services of other adaptive cloud service systems through the value co-creation interaction channel. An adaptive cloud service can be used in different times and frequencies by different adaptive cloud service systems for different purposes. The execution of a cloud service has the execution context and the adaptive cloud service should be able to adjust according to the local execution context. An adaptive cloud service could be an IT or facility service type, which is aimed at enabling or supporting human-oriented services such as business, information and social service types. The use of adaptive cloud service systems and their services is restricted based on the access control and contract between the adaptive cloud service systems (including a non-cloud). The execution process can be visually modelled by customising and using the ArchiMate "Process" concept.

7.2.20 *Adaptive Service*

An adaptive cloud service is a fundamental basis of exchange between adaptive cloud service systems (including a non-cloud). It is the application of resources. The adaptive cloud service is context aware, evolving and adapting. Adaptive cloud services can be broadly categorised as SaaS, PaaS, IaaS and FaaS. They can also be categorised as public, private and hybrid cloud services, which can be developed, acquired, deployed, offered and used by different actors (e.g. adaptive service systems). Adaptive cloud services can be modelled by customizing and using the ArchiMate "Application Service" (SaaS) and "Infrastructure Service" (IaaS) concepts. Further, the same ArchiMate concepts can be extended to model "Platform Service" (PaaS) and "Facility Service" (FaaS).

7.2.21 *Outcome*

Adaptive cloud service system interactions have some desirable outcomes. The adaptive service contract execution co-creates value to achieve mutual goals. A mutual goal is the agreed benefit between adaptive cloud service systems. Adaptive service system interactions reach mutual satisfaction or outcomes if the value co-creation is as per agreed contract. Mutual satisfaction depends on the satisfaction of two or more interacting adaptive cloud service systems (including a non-cloud). Mutual satisfaction (positive value) is established if all the interacting adaptive service systems are happy with the outcome of the interaction. It is important to note that though all the interacting adaptive service systems are mutually benefited (value co-creation) through cloud service interactions, they should also be satisfied with the resultant mutual outcome. Adaptive service system interactions will reach dissatisfaction (negative value) if the interaction outcome does not meet the agreed expectation of one or more interacting adaptive service systems. The responsible adaptive cloud service system needs to understand and resolve the outcome issue through feedback interactions, which may involve adjusting the mutual goals or services. The outcome or co-created value can be visually modelled by customising and using the ArchiMate "Value" concept.

7.2.22 *Feedback*

Mutual satisfaction or dissatisfaction is reported via feedback interaction activities. Feedback interactions enable adaptive cloud service system and cloud service adaptation. The cloud-enabled AESS is not a static system. It evolves through formal or informal feedback before, during or after the interactions. The adaptive cloud service system needs to capture and appropriately respond to the feedback received on their cloud services in an effective and timely manner. The feedback and response mechanism supports the adaptive nature of cloud service systems and services. This feedback may lead to updating the adaptive cloud service systems, services and related contracts. The feedback process can be visually modelled by customising and using the ArchiMate "Process" concept.

7.2.23 *Interaction Architecture Summary*

The cloud interaction architecture describes the externally observable evolving choreography or interactions of the adaptive cloud and non-cloud service systems. Here, we have observed how we can use the concepts from the generic AESS metamodel – level 1 (enterprise level), UML and ArchiMate to describe the cloud interaction architecture.

7.3 Cloud Factory Architecture

Earlier in this chapter, the section on cloud interaction architecture described adaptive cloud service system interactions. This section focuses on the cloud factory that sources, develops, deploys and offers adaptive cloud service systems that participate in cloud interactions. The adaptive cloud service system is a dynamic configuration or composition of adaptive cloud services for value co-creation. The adaptive cloud service system can be developed in the cloud factory by seamlessly integrating the in-house built adaptive cloud services and services sourced from partners and collaborators to meet the changing business demands. The cloud factory approach focuses on developing the adaptive cloud service systems from re-usable adaptive cloud services. In the cloud factory, an adaptive cloud service system is essentially a dynamic or on-demand configuration of internally and externally sourced reusable adaptive cloud services. The adaptive cloud service system factory approach draws our attention to the reusability of the cloud services. These cloud services contribute to the effective and efficient delivery of adaptive cloud service systems through dynamic on-demand configuration. The following key concepts related to the adaptive cloud service system factory are discussed.

- Human and IT Alignment (HIT)
- Human Architecture
  - o Adaptive Business Architecture
  - o Adaptive Information Architecture
  - o Adaptive Social Architecture
- IT Architecture
  - o Adaptive Cloud Application Architecture
  - o Adaptive Cloud Platform Architecture
  - o Adaptive Cloud Infrastructure Architecture
- Adaptive Cloud Solution Architecture

7.3.1 *Human and IT Alignment (HIT)*

The alignment of business and IT (BIT) has been the top most concern of business and technology executives. Business or IT alone cannot always offer optimum value-propositions (e.g. value to customer, value to enterprise, value to suppler). BIT alignment is the interaction of business that offers value-proposition and IT that supports business to offer optimum value-proposition. The concept of BIT is related to the adaptive business model which essentially details what IT services are required to support the business services. IT is a value added element of a business. BIT depends on a number of strategic value added factors, such as increased productivity, improved time to market, improved service quality, reduced risk and reduced cost through the use of IT. However, this traditional view of BIT misses the most important human element of an enterprise.

The Gill Framework focuses on humans, that is, the personnel involved in business who actually communicate, establish, operate and manage the business. The success of adaptive or agile enterprises depends on the effectiveness of humans, their work practices and their communication. If a human is the most important element of an adaptive or agile enterprise, then the IT (such as the cloud) value or support should also be viewed through a human perspective. Therefore, the adaptive cloud service system factory highlights the need for HIT (human-IT alignment) for real BIT (Business-IT alignment). The alignment between humans and IT (e.g. cloud services) is called HIT. It is useless to invest in cloud services that are not related to human services (e.g. the staff's job/activities, customer needs).

The adaptive service system is an instance of a specific type of service system such as human or cloud-enabled IT or a mix of both (e.g. Human-IT). The major categories of human services are: business, information and social services. The major categories of cloud-enabled IT services that are required to support human services are: cloud application (SaaS), cloud platform (PaaS) and cloud infrastructure (IaaS) services. Hence, HIT is a strategic alignment concept which focuses on what supply of cloud services is enough or required for the smooth operation, improvement, growth and transformation of human services. It is important for an enterprise to use HIT as an approach for making decisions about committing resources and investments in any enterprise operation, improvement, growth and transformation initiatives. Cloud adoption should be viewed from the human architecture perspective. Hence, adaptive cloud-enabled IT architecture cannot be discussed in isolation of human architecture. Human architecture, as a whole, describes the human-centric social business information system architecture.

Cloud factory architecture describes the cloud-enabled business, information, social, application, platform, and infrastructure architectures within the overall context of adaptive cloud enterprise architecture. These architectures and services can also be augmented by some additional support architecture such as cloud security architecture and industry reference architecture etc. Cloud factory architecture can be described for a specific context using the generic AESS metamodel – level 2 (adaptive service system - capability level) and AESS metamodel – level 3 (adaptive service - capability level).

7.3.2 *Adaptive Business Architecture*

The adoption of the cloud begins with adaptive business architecture instead of cloud IT architecture. Adaptive business architecture (Fig. 7.3) is an evolving part of the whole adaptive cloud enterprise architecture. A business can have many business types of adaptive service systems that may offer adaptive (business) services. The AESS metamodel – level 2 (capability level) and level 3 (service level) have been used to describe the business architecture elements and their relationships. These elements and relationships can be tailored to develop the context-specific adaptive business architecture. This can be further used to develop the different business architecture views. The current, transition and future states of the business architecture can be modelled by customising and using the ArchiMate "Business" layer concepts (similar to interaction architecture). A business architecture can be developed to find answers to the following types of questions.

- What are our current business capabilities (e.g. business capability model?
- Who are our key business actors and what are their roles (e.g. actors and roles model)?
- What are the key business events and processes (e.g. business process matrix and models)?
- How are these business architecture elements related to each other (e.g. matrix)?
- What are our current business services (e.g. business service catalogue)?
- What is impeding or limiting our business actors, capabilities, processes, services?
- What are the emerging business and technology trends?
- Which business actors, capabilities, processes and services need to be improved?
- What would happen if we did something or did nothing about the limiting factors?
- Which business capabilities and services can be supported through the adoption of cloud services?

Business architecture is guided by the guiding elements. Guiding elements include the business strategy that outlines the strategic business goals and objectives along with the strategic and tactical actions. Business goals and objectives are used to define key performance indicator metrics to evaluate the business performance. Business strategy, as a part of the overall adaptive enterprise strategy, is realised by the adaptive business architecture. Business strategy is also augmented by a number of supporting adaptive enterprise strategy models, such as the adaptive business model, operating model, change model, lifecycle model, strategy roadmap, business policy and rules. Business policy and rules guide the execution of tactics to achieve the business objectives. Business architecture incorporates design principles such as business principles. Business principles present the fundamental beliefs and values underpinning the adaptive business architecture. Business principles guide the development, operation, improvement, growth and transformation of an adaptive business architecture.

Adaptive business architecture is focused around the business type of adaptive service systems that transit from one state to another state in order to meet the changing value co-creation interaction demands. It is accessible via published business interfaces or channels. It is a configuration or organisation of business actors. A business actor plays one or many assigned business roles. A business actor has competency (e.g. knowledge, experience and skills). A business actor has capacity to perform the role (e.g. workload, availability). A business actor uses the adaptive work products via their published interfaces or channels. An adaptive work product can be classified as an adaptive business service and an adaptive business product. The AESS metamodel views an adaptive business product as an adaptive business service. Essentially, a business actor uses, produces or acquires adaptive business services. A business actor supports one or more business capabilities (e.g. customer relationship management capability, order management capability).

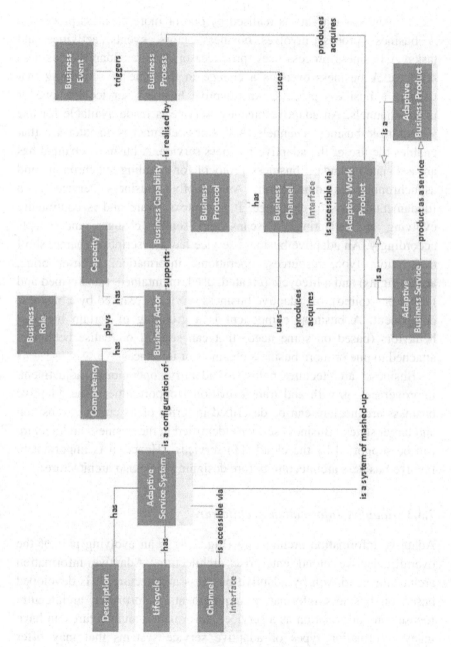

Fig. 7.3. Adaptive business architecture - capability level.
(based on The AESS metamodel – level 2)

A business capability is realised by one or more business processes. A business process involves business actors, events, activities and tasks. A business process uses, produces or acquires adaptive business services. A business event is a change in the state of something that triggers a business process. An adaptive business service has one or many channels. An adaptive business service is made available for use via multiple business channels. A business channel is an interface that enables the use of the adaptive business service. A business channel has an associated standard business protocol for enabling synchronous and asynchronous communication. An adaptive business service is a fundamental basis of exchange. It is context aware and is continually evolving and adapting. It scans and senses changes and adapts accordingly. An adaptive business service has a description (name, short description, type, resources, operations, information, license, price, access rights) and a lifecycle (created, used, maintained, transformed and retired or expired). An adaptive business service is realised by a business component. A business component is a grouping of certain business behaviors (based on some need) that can support or realise behaviors attached to one or more business channels or interfaces.

Business architecture helps to identify operational adjustment, improvement, growth and transformational opportunities. The adaptive business architecture can be described in terms of its current, transition and target states. Business services identified in the business architecture can be supported by the cloud (IT) services. Hence, it is important to involve business architecture before designing the cloud architecture.

7.3.3 *Adaptive Information Architecture*

Adaptive information architecture (Fig. 7.4) is an evolving part of the overall adaptive cloud enterprise architecture. Adaptive information architecture is driven by adaptive business architecture. It is developed based on business information requirements. Information architecture focuses on "information as a service". Information architecture can have many information types of adaptive service systems that may offer adaptive (information) services. The AESS metamodel – level 2 (capability level) and level 3 (service level) have been used to describe the information architecture elements and their relationships. These elements and relationships can be tailored to develop context-specific adaptive information architecture. This can be further used to develop different information architecture views. The current, transition and future states of the information architecture can be modelled by customising and using the ArchiMate "Business" layer concepts (similar to interaction architecture). Information architecture can be developed to find answers to the following types of questions.

- What are our current information capabilities (e.g. information capability model)?
- Who are the key information actors and what are their roles (e.g. actors and roles model)?
- What are the key information events and processes (e.g. information process matrix and models)?
- How are these information architecture elements related to each other (e.g. matrix)?
- What are our current information services (e.g. information service catalogue)?
- What is impeding or limiting our information actors, capabilities, processes, services?
- What are the emerging information and technology trends?
- Which information actors, capabilities, processes and services need to be improved?
- What would happen if we did something or did nothing about the limiting factors?
- Which information capabilities and services can be supported through the adoption of cloud services?

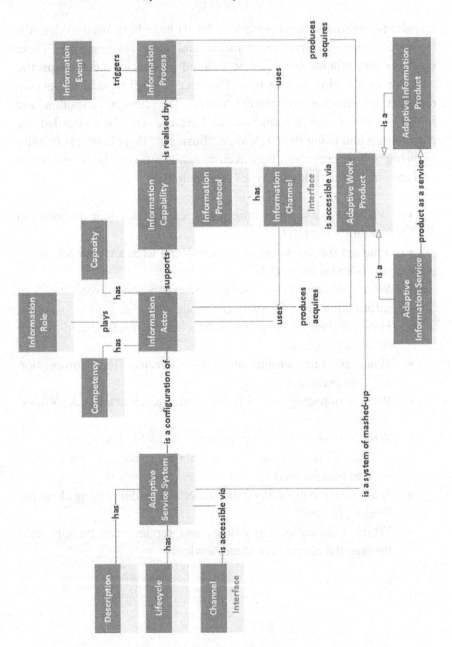

Fig. 7.4. Adaptive information architecture - capability level.
(based on The AESS metamodel – level 2)

Adaptive information architecture is guided by the guiding elements. Guiding elements include the information strategy that outlines the strategic information management goals and objectives along with the strategic and tactical actions. Information goals and objectives are used to define the key performance indicator metrics to evaluate the information management performance. Information strategy, as a part of the overall enterprise strategy, is realised by the information architecture. Information strategy is also augmented by a number of supporting enterprise strategy models, such as the business model, operating model, change model, lifecycle model, strategy roadmap, information policy and rules. Information policy and rules guide the execution of tactics to achieve information objectives. Information architecture incorporates design principles such as information principles. Information principles present the fundamental beliefs and values underpinning the information architecture. Information principles guide the development, operation, improvement, growth and transformation of information architecture.

Information architecture is focused around the information type of adaptive service systems that transit from one state to another state in order to meet the changing value co-creation interaction demands. It is accessible via published information interfaces or channels. It is a configuration or organisation of information actors.

An information actor plays one or many assigned information-related roles. An information actor has competency (e.g. information management knowledge, experience and skills). An information actor has capacity to perform the role (e.g. workload). An information actor uses adaptive work products via their published interfaces or channels. An adaptive work product can be classified as an adaptive information service and an adaptive information product (e.g. information objects). The AESS metamodel views adaptive information product as an adaptive information service. Essentially, an information actor uses, produces or acquires adaptive information services. An information actor supports one or more information capabilities (e.g. customer information management capability, product information management capability, service information management capability). Information capability is realised by one or more information processes. An information process involves information actors, event, activities and tasks. An information process uses, produces or acquires adaptive information services. An information event is a change in the state of something that triggers an information process.

An adaptive information service has one or many channels. An adaptive information service is made available for use via multiple information channels. An information channel is an interface that enables the use of the adaptive information service. An information channel has an associated standard information protocol. An adaptive information service is a fundamental basis of exchange. It is context aware and is continually evolving and adapting. It scans and senses changes and adapts accordingly. An adaptive information service has a description (name, short description, type, resources, operations, information, license, price, access rights) and a lifecycle (created, used, maintained, transformed and retired or expired). An adaptive information service is realised by the information component. An information component is a grouping of certain information-related behavior (based on some need or criteria) that can support or realise one or more information channels or interfaces.

Information architecture helps to identify operational adjustment, improvement, growth and transformational opportunities. Information architecture can be described in terms of its current, transition and target states. The information services identified in the information architecture can be supported by the cloud (IT) services. Hence, it is important to involve technology-independent information architecture to understand the business information requirements for designing cloud architecture.

7.3.4 *Adaptive Social Architecture*

Adaptive social architecture (Fig. 7.5) is an evolving part of the overall adaptive cloud enterprise architecture. Adaptive social architecture is an emerging concept. It refers to culture which influences the desired social behaviors within the operating environment of an enterprise. Social architecture is all about communities of people or social system structures (e.g. communities of users, communities of practitioners) and their behavior (e.g. conversation, collaboration, feedback, opinion, beliefs, attitudes), which play an important role in the ongoing smooth operation, improvement, growth and transformation of an enterprise. The failure or success of a change initiative (e.g. the introduction and adoption of new business or cloud services) is highly dependent on the supportive and aligned social architecture with other domain architectures. Any change in the enterprise while ignoring the social architecture is an ultimate recipe for a failure.

The Gill Framework (Gill 2014) provides the necessary concepts for social architecture. This framework defines social architecture as the "fundamental concepts or properties of a social system in its environment embodied in its elements, relationships, and in the principles of its design and evolution" (Gill 2014).

A social system is a collaborative human system, which is represented by dynamic interactions among individuals and groups (Kroeber and Parsons 1958).The key difference between a traditional static system and a social system is the dynamic nature of the social system structure and behaviours. Like any other system, it has input, output, people, process, constraints, and feedback components. Depending on the situation, a social system may emerge as a group of people or a community, which then may expand or contract over a period of time in pursuit of achieving the desired mutual goals. A social system refers to a group or organisation or society or community of practice that has the capability and capacity to create, use and share value (Wenger 1998).

Social architecture is driven by business and information architectures (a.k.a. human-centred social business information architecture) and is developed based on the social business information requirements. Social architecture focuses on social services. Social architecture can have many social types of adaptive service systems that may offer adaptive (social) services. The AESS metamodel – level 2 (capability level) and level 3 (service level) have been used to describe the social architecture elements and their relationships. These elements and relationships can be tailored to develop context-specific social architecture. This can be further used to develop the different social architecture views. The current, transition and future states of social architecture can be modelled by customising and using the ArchiMate

"Business" layer concepts (similar to interaction architecture). Social architecture can be developed to find answers to the following types of questions.

- What are our current social capabilities (e.g. social capability model)?
- Who are the key social actors and what are their roles (e.g. actors and roles model)?
- What are the key social events and processes (e.g. social process matrix and models)?
- How are these social architecture elements related to each other (e.g. matrix)?
- What are our current social services (e.g. social service catalogue)?
- What is impeding or limiting our social actors, capabilities, processes, services?
- What are emerging social and technology trends?
- Which social actors, capabilities, processes and services need to be improved?
- What would happen if we did something or did nothing about the limiting factors?
- Which social capabilities and services can be supported through the adoption of cloud services?

Adaptive social architecture is guided by the guiding elements, which include the social strategy (e.g. social goals, objectives). Social goals and objectives are used to define key performance indicator metrics to evaluate the social performance. A social strategy, as a part of the overall enterprise strategy, is realised by social architecture. A social strategy is also augmented by a number of supporting enterprise strategy models, such as the business model, operating model, change model, lifecycle model, strategy roadmap, social policy and rules. Social policy and rules guide the execution of tactics to achieve social objectives. Social architecture incorporates design principles, such as social principles. Social principles present the fundamental beliefs and values underpinning the social architecture design.

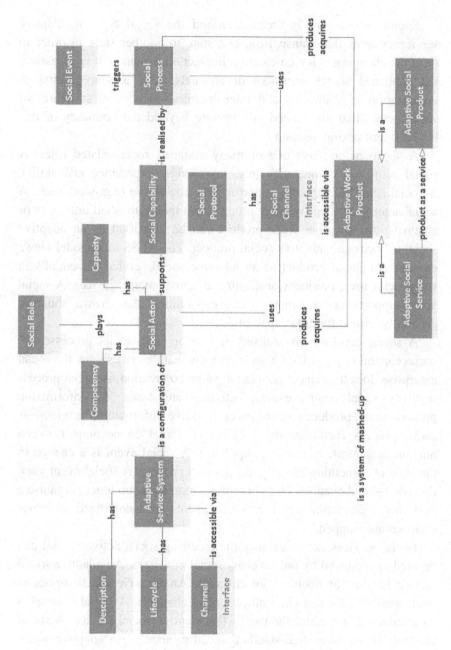

Fig. 7.5. Adaptive social architecture - capability level.
(based on The AESS metamodel – level 2)

Social architecture is focused around the social type of adaptive service systems that transit from one state to another state in order to meet the changing value co-creation interaction demands. It is accessible via published social interfaces or channels. It is a configuration or organisation (e.g. internal and inter-organisational social structure) of social actors that are related and operate beyond the boundary of one business unit or organisation.

A social actor plays one or many assigned social-related roles. A social actor has competency (e.g. knowledge, experience and skills). A social actor has capacity to perform the social role (e.g. workload). A social actor uses adaptive work products via their published interfaces or channels. An adaptive work product can be classified as an adaptive social services and adaptive social product. The AESS metamodel views an adaptive social product as an adaptive social service. Essentially, a social actor uses, produces or acquires adaptive social services. A social actor supports one or more social capabilities (e.g. crowd sourcing capability, crowd funding capability).

A social capability is realised by one or more social processes. A social capability provides a high-level view that describes what the social enterprise does to connect people i.e. value co-creation. A social process involves social actors, events, activities and tasks. An information process uses, produces or acquires adaptive information services. A social process facilitates the building of social connections between humans (e.g. staff, customers, suppliers). A social event is a change in the state of something that triggers a social process. A social event view describes social events such as organise a monthly team lunch, organise a customer appreciation day etc. Social events are categorized and their relations are mapped.

Social services are essentially the recurring social activities that can be used or produced by one or many social processes. An adaptive social service has one or many social channels. An adaptive social service is made available for use via multiple social channels. A social channel is an interface that enables the use of the adaptive social service. A social channel has an associated standard social protocol. An adaptive social service is a fundamental basis of exchange. It is context aware, evolving and adapting. It scans and senses changes and adapts accordingly. An adaptive social service has a description (name, short description, type, resources, operations, information, license, price, access rights) and a lifecycle (created, used, maintained, transformed and retired or expired). An adaptive social service is realised by the social component. A social component is a grouping of certain social-related behavior (based on some need or criteria) that can support or realise one or more social channels or interfaces.

Social architecture helps to identify operational adjustment, improvement, growth and transformational opportunities. Social architecture can be described in terms of its current, transition and target states. Social services identified in social architecture can be supported by the cloud (IT) services (e.g. cloud-based social technology such as Facebook, Twitter). Hence, it is important to involve technology-independent social architecture to understand the social requirements for designing cloud architecture.

In summary, human-centric business, information and social elements define the integrated social business information (SBI) architecture that can be supported by IT-centric cloud architecture (Human-IT alignment). IT-centric cloud architecture includes the cloud application (SaaS), platform (PaaS) and infrastructure (IaaS) architecture. Application and infrastructure architecture is based on well-known TOGAF domains. Based on recent research and projects in cloud computing, additional platform architecture has been identified and is included in the Gill Framework. The Gill Framework also suggests the separation of "Information Architecture" from "System Architecture" (as discussed in the TOGAF), because the existence of business information does not depend on the system or application. Information applications or systems actually support the information management capability. The next few sections discuss cloud IT architectures in the overall context of cloud factory architecture.

7.3.5 *Adaptive Cloud Application Architecture*

Adaptive cloud software (SaaS) application architecture (Fig. 7.6) is an evolving part of the whole adaptive cloud enterprise architecture. The AESS metamodel – level 2 (capability level) and level 3 (service level) have been used to describe the cloud application architecture elements and their relationships. These elements and relationships can be tailored to develop context-specific cloud application architecture. This can be further used to develop different cloud application architecture views. The current, transition and future states of cloud application architecture can be modelled by customising and using the ArchiMate "Application" layer concepts. Application architecture can be developed to find answers to the following types of questions.

- What are our current and future cloud application capabilities (e.g. cloud application capability model)?
- Who are the key cloud application actors and what are their roles (e.g. actors and roles model)?
- What are the key cloud application events and processes (e.g. cloud application process/function matrix and models)?
- How are cloud application architecture elements related to each other (e.g. matrix)?
- What are our current cloud application services (e.g. cloud service catalogue)?
- What is impeding or limiting our cloud application actors, capabilities, processes, services?
- What are the emerging cloud application trends?
- Which cloud application actors, capabilities, processes and services need to be improved?
- What would happen if we did something or did nothing about the limiting factors?
- Which cloud application capabilities and services can support social business information architecture and services?

Adaptive cloud application architecture is guided by the guiding elements. Guiding elements include the cloud application strategy that outlines the strategic cloud application goals and objectives along with the strategic and tactical actions. Cloud application goals and objectives are used to define key performance indicator metrics to evaluate the cloud application performance.

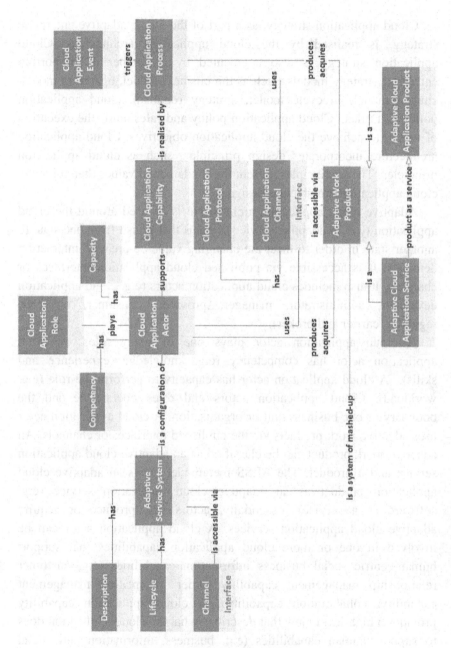

Fig. 7.6. Adaptive cloud application architecture - capability level.
(based on The AESS metamodel – level 2)

Cloud application strategy, as a part of the whole adaptive enterprise strategy, is realised by the cloud application architecture. Cloud application strategy is also augmented by a number of supporting enterprise strategy models, such as the business model, operating model, change model, lifecycle model, strategy roadmap, cloud application policy and rules. Cloud application policy and rules guide the execution of tactics to achieve the cloud application objectives. Cloud application architecture incorporates design principles, such as cloud application principles. These principles present the fundamental values that guide the cloud application architecture design.

Adaptive cloud application architecture is focused around the cloud application type of adaptive service systems that transit from one state to another state in order to meet the changing value co-creation interaction demands. It is accessible via published cloud application interfaces or channels. It also includes cloud application actors (e.g. cloud application developer, administrator, manager, provider, consumer, observer, regulator, carrier and broker).

A cloud application actor plays one or many roles. A cloud application actor has competency (e.g. knowledge, experience and skills). A cloud application actor has capacity to perform the role (e.g. workload). Cloud application actors and roles operate beyond the boundary of one business unit or organisation. A cloud application actor uses adaptive work products via the published interfaces or channels. An adaptive work product can be classified as an adaptive cloud application service and a product. The AESS metamodel views an adaptive cloud application product as an adaptive cloud application service (e.g. software as a service). Essentially, actors use, produce or acquire adaptive cloud application services. A cloud application actor can be involved in one or more cloud application capabilities that support human-centric social business information capabilities (e.g. customer relationship management capability, order information management capability, collaboration capability). A cloud application capability provides a high-level view that describes what the cloud application does to support human capabilities (e.g. business, information and social capabilities).

A cloud application capability is realised by one or more cloud application processes or functions. A cloud application process is a specific behavior which involves application actors, events, activities and tasks. A cloud application process (e.g. workflow) can be architected to support human processes (e.g. business, information and social processes). A cloud application process uses, produces or acquires adaptive cloud application services. Cloud application processes included in the cloud application architecture are further analysed and mapped to reusable cloud application services to support human services (e.g. business, information and social services) or human services can be mapped to one or many cloud application services. Cloud application services are essentially the reusable software services that can be used in more than one human process. A cloud application process uses the service-oriented architecture to link (e.g. orchestration, choreography) cloud application services for the service-oriented cloud application architecture. Adaptive cloud enterprise architecture includes the orchestration and choreography of services that can include both human and IT (cloud) services.

A cloud application event is a change in the state of something that triggers a cloud application process or function (e.g. cloud application workflow). A cloud application event can be mapped to human events (e.g. business, information and social events). An adaptive cloud application service has one or many channels. An adaptive cloud application service is made available for use via multiple cloud application channels. A cloud application channel is an interface that enables the use of the adaptive cloud application service. A cloud application channel has an associated standard cloud application protocol to enable synchronous and asynchronous communication or interaction. An adaptive cloud application service is a fundamental basis of exchange. It is context aware, evolving and adapting. It scans and senses changes and adapts accordingly. An adaptive cloud application service has a description (name, short description, type, resources, operations, information, license, price, access rights) and a lifecycle (created, used, maintained, transformed and retired or expired). An adaptive cloud application service is realised by the cloud application component. A cloud application component is a grouping of certain application functions or behavior (based on some need) that can support or realise behaviors attached to one or more cloud application channels or interfaces.

Cloud application architecture helps to identify and assess operational adjustment, improvement, growth and transformational opportunities. Cloud application architecture can be described in terms of its current, transition and target states. Cloud application services identified in the cloud application architecture can be supported by other cloud (IT) services. Adaptive cloud application architecture is designed in the overall context of adaptive cloud enterprise architecture. It is important to involve social business information architecture when designing cloud application architecture. Nevertheless, a cloud is not a technology box, rather it exists to support social business information architecture. Adaptive cloud enterprise architecture is supported by adaptive cloud application architecture.

7.3.6 *Adaptive Cloud Platform Architecture*

Adaptive cloud platform (PaaS) architecture (Fig. 7.7) is an evolving part of the whole adaptive cloud enterprise architecture. Cloud platform architecture describes the cloud factory platform as an adaptive service system. The cloud factory platform is an environment that supports the planning, analysis, architecture, design, implementation (DevOps), testing and deployment, and management of cloud services that support human-oriented service (e.g. business, information and social architecture and services). The AESS metamodel – level 2 (capability level) and level 3 (service level) have been used to describe the cloud platform architecture elements and their relationships. These elements and relationships can be tailored to develop the context-specific cloud platform architecture. This can be further used to develop the different cloud platform architecture views. The current, transition and future states of the cloud platform architecture can be modelled by customising and using concepts from the ArchiMate "Application and Technology" layers.

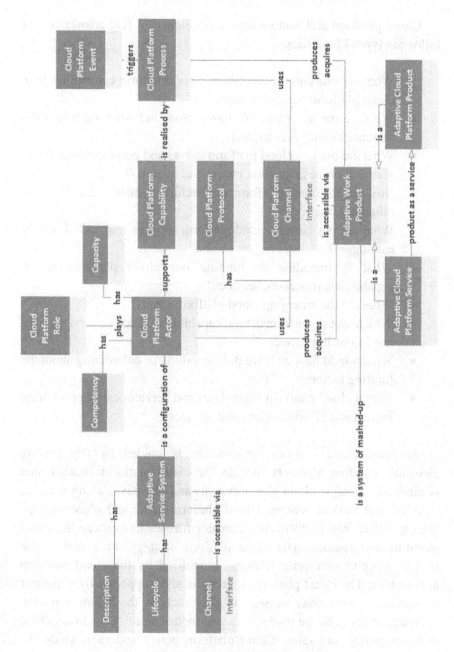

Fig. 7.7. Adaptive cloud platform architecture - capability level.
(based on The AESS metamodel – level 2)

Cloud platform architecture can be developed to find answers to the following types of questions.

- What are our current and future cloud platform capabilities (e.g. cloud platform capability model)?
- Who are the key cloud platform actors and what are their roles (e.g. actors and roles model)?
- What are the key cloud platform events and processes (e.g. cloud platform process/function matrix and models)?
- How are the cloud platform architecture elements related to each other (e.g. matrix)?
- What are our current cloud platform services (e.g. cloud service catalogue)?
- What is impeding or limiting our cloud platform actors, capabilities, processes, services?
- What are the emerging cloud platform trends?
- Which cloud platform actors, capabilities, processes and services need to be improved?
- What would happen if we did something or did nothing about the limiting factors?
- Which cloud platform capabilities and services can support other human and IT architecture and services?

Adaptive cloud platform architecture is guided by the guiding elements. Guiding elements include the cloud platform strategy that outlines the strategic cloud platform goals and objectives along with the strategic and tactical actions. Cloud platform goals and objectives are used to define key performance indicator metrics to evaluate the cloud platform performance. The cloud platform strategy, as a part of the overall adaptive enterprise strategy, is realised by the cloud platform architecture. The cloud platform strategy is also supported by a number of supporting enterprise strategy models such as the business model, operating model, change model, lifecycle model, strategy roadmap, cloud platform policy and rules. Cloud platform policy and rules guide the execution of tactics to achieve cloud platform objectives. Cloud platform architecture incorporates design principles such as cloud platform principles. These principles present the fundamental values underpinning the cloud platform architecture. These principles guide the development, operation, improvement, growth and transformation of cloud platform architecture.

Cloud platform architecture is focused around the cloud platform type of adaptive service systems that transit from one state to another state in order to meet the changing value co-creation interaction demands. It is accessible via published cloud platform interfaces or channels. It also includes cloud platform actors (e.g. cloud platform developer, administrator, manager, provider, consumer, observer, regulator, carrier and broker).

A cloud platform actor plays one or many roles. A cloud platform actor has competency (e.g. knowledge, experience and skills). A cloud platform actor has capacity to perform the role (e.g. workload). Cloud platform actors and roles operate beyond the boundary of one business unit or organisation. A cloud platform actor uses adaptive work products via their published interfaces or channels. An adaptive work product can be classified as an adaptive cloud platform service and a product. The AESS metamodel views an adaptive cloud platform product as an adaptive cloud platform service (e.g. platform as a service). Essentially, actors use, produce or acquire adaptive cloud platform services. A cloud platform actor can be involved in one or more cloud platform capabilities that support human and IT capabilities. A cloud platform capability provides a high-level view that describes what the cloud platform does to support human and IT capabilities.

A cloud platform capability is realised by one or more cloud platform processes or functions. A cloud platform process (e.g. implementation process, testing process) is a specific behavior which involves platform actors, event, activities and tasks. A cloud platform process uses, produces or acquires adaptive cloud platform services. Cloud platform processes included in the cloud platform architecture are further analysed and mapped to reusable cloud platform services. Cloud platform services are essentially the reusable platform services that can be used in more than one process.

A cloud platform event is a change in the state of something that triggers a cloud platform process or function. An adaptive cloud platform service has one or many channels. An adaptive cloud platform service is made available for use via multiple cloud platform channels. A cloud platform channel is an interface that enables the use of the adaptive cloud platform service. A cloud platform channel has an associated standard cloud platform protocol to enable interaction. It is context aware, evolving and adapting. It scans and senses changes and adapts accordingly. An adaptive cloud platform service has a description (name, short description, type, resources, operations, information, license, price, access rights) and a lifecycle (created, used, maintained, transformed and retired or expired). An adaptive cloud platform service is realised by the cloud platform component. A cloud platform component is a grouping of certain platform functions or behavior (based on some need) that can support or realise behaviors attached to one or more cloud platform channel or interface.

Cloud platform architecture helps to identify and assess operational adjustment, improvement, growth and transformational opportunities. Cloud platform architecture can be described in terms of its current, transition and target states. Cloud platform services identified in the cloud platform architecture can be supported by other cloud (IT) services. Adaptive cloud platform architecture is designed in the overall context of adaptive cloud enterprise architecture. It is important to involve human and IT architecture when designing cloud platform architecture. Adaptive cloud enterprise architecture is supported by adaptive cloud platform architecture.

7.3.7 *Adaptive Cloud Infrastructure Architecture*

Adaptive cloud infrastructure (IaaS) architecture (Fig. 7.8), with embedded loosely coupled reusable distributed cloud infrastructure hardware and software services (e.g. storage, network, processing services), is an evolving part of the whole adaptive cloud enterprise architecture. Cloud infrastructure is an environment that supports cloud application and platform services.

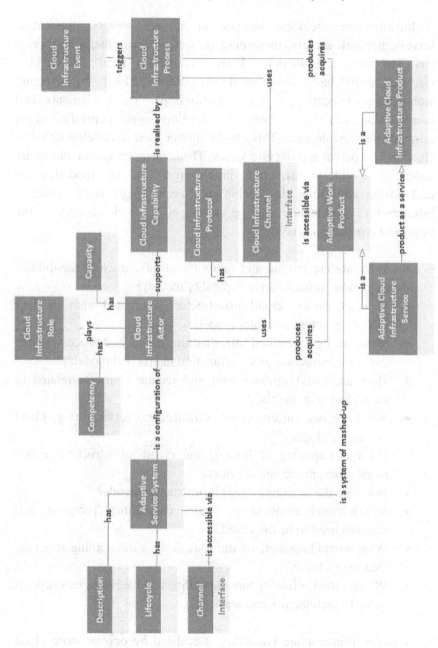

Fig. 7.8. Adaptive cloud infrastructure architecture - capability level.
(based on The AESS metamodel – level 2)

Infrastructure includes database or storage servers, application servers, network servers, messaging servers, and an enterprise service bus. The AESS metamodel – level 2 (capability level) and level 3 (service level) have been used to describe cloud infrastructure architecture elements and their relationships. These elements and relationships can be tailored to develop context-specific cloud infrastructure architecture. This can be further used to develop different cloud infrastructure architecture views. The current, transition and future states of cloud infrastructure architecture can be modelled by customising and using the ArchiMate "Technology" layer concepts. Infrastructure architecture can be developed to find answers to the following types of questions.

- What are our current and future cloud infrastructure capabilities (e.g. cloud infrastructure capability model)?
- Who are the key cloud infrastructure actors and what are their roles (e.g. actors and roles model)?
- What are the key cloud infrastructure events and processes (e.g. cloud infrastructure process/function matrix and models)?
- How are cloud infrastructure architecture elements related to each other (e.g. matrix)?
- What are our current cloud infrastructure services (e.g. cloud service catalogue)?
- What is impeding or limiting our cloud infrastructure actors, capabilities, processes, services?
- What are the emerging cloud infrastructure trends?
- Which cloud infrastructure actors, capabilities, processes and services need to be improved?
- What would happen if we did something or did nothing about the limiting factors?
- Which cloud infrastructure capabilities and services can support other IT architecture and services?

A cloud infrastructure capability is realised by one or more cloud infrastructure processes or functions. A cloud infrastructure process is a specific behavior which involves infrastructure actors, events, activities and tasks. A cloud infrastructure process can be architected to support IT processes. A cloud infrastructure process uses, produces or acquires adaptive cloud infrastructure services. Cloud infrastructure processes included in the cloud infrastructure architecture are further analysed and mapped to reusable cloud infrastructure services to support IT services. Cloud infrastructure services are essentially the reusable memory, storage, network and processing services.

A cloud infrastructure event is a change in the state of something that triggers a cloud infrastructure process or function. An adaptive cloud infrastructure service has one or many channels. An adaptive cloud infrastructure service is made available for use via multiple cloud infrastructure channels. A cloud infrastructure channel is an interface that enables the use of the adaptive cloud infrastructure service. A cloud infrastructure channel has an associated standard cloud infrastructure protocol for enabling interactions. An adaptive cloud infrastructure service is a fundamental basis of exchange. It is context aware, evolving and adapting. It scans and senses changes and adapts accordingly. An adaptive cloud infrastructure service has a description (name, short description, type, resources, operations, information, license, price, access rights) and a lifecycle (created, used, maintained, transformed and retired or expired). An adaptive cloud infrastructure service is realised by the cloud infrastructure component (e.g. device, node, and network). A cloud infrastructure component is a grouping of certain infrastructure functions or behavior (based on some need) that can support or realise behaviors attached to one or more cloud infrastructure channels or interfaces.

Cloud infrastructure architecture is intended to identify and assess operational adjustment, improvement, growth and transformational opportunities. Cloud infrastructure architecture can be described in terms of its current, transition and target states. Cloud infrastructure services identified in the cloud infrastructure architecture can be supported by other cloud (IT) services. Adaptive cloud infrastructure architecture is done in the overall context of adaptive cloud enterprise architecture. It is important to involve human and IT architectures when designing the cloud infrastructure architecture. As discussed earlier, the cloud is not a technology box, rather it exists to support the social business information and IT architectures. Adaptive cloud enterprise architecture is supported by the adaptive cloud infrastructure architecture.

7.3.8 *Adaptive Cloud Solution Architecture*

Adaptive cloud solution architecture is a mix of both human and IT layers or domain architectures. It is a sub-set of the human and IT architectures, which is done at the context-specific portfolio, program, project, release, and iteration levels to guide specific cloud solution implementation. Adaptive cloud solution architecture evolves as the cloud projects are implemented in short releases and iterations.

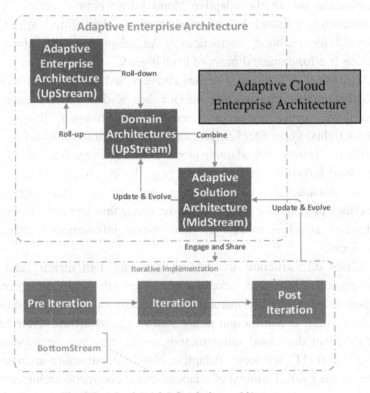

Fig. 7.9. Adaptive (cloud) solution architecture.

Adaptive cloud solution architecture, in the midstream, is an integration point between the adaptive cloud enterprise architecture capability and the adaptive enterprise project management capability (Fig. 7.9). Adaptive cloud solution architecture, as a part of the larger adaptive cloud enterprise architecture, evolves in short iterations. For instance, an initial high-level adaptive cloud solution architecture can be developed by combining both the human and cloud (IT) domain architecture elements to address the stakeholders' concerns. The domain architecture elements, such as business process models and cloud application communication diagrams, can be used to identify user stories and design the initial adaptive cloud solution architecture (e.g. pre-iteration). High-level adaptive cloud solution architecture would then evolve as the design details emerge through project implementation in short increments (e.g. iteration). Adaptive cloud solution architecture should be flexible to allow the design emergence and implementation in short iterations. It should be reviewed and be updated or re-factored after each iteration (e.g. post-iteration), if required, to reflect any changes due to implementation iteration.

The elements from the evolving adaptive cloud solution architecture should be continuously updated in the upstream domain architectures, which will then be rolled up in the overall adaptive (cloud) enterprise architecture to maintain a holistic view and integrity. It can be observed that adaptive cloud enterprise architecture evolves as agile or adaptive cloud implementation projects are executed in short iterations. Agile project teams, in practice, maintain the physical/and or virtual agile card walls to share and communicate project information (e.g. in backlog, in progress, done). Agile teams should have the relevant architecture information on their agile wall. An agile wall can display the adaptive cloud solution architecture (e.g. project-specific) diagrams or information along with the traditional agile wall contents. An agile wall with adaptive cloud solution architecture provides a shared vision for both on-site and off-site (geographically dispersed locations) agile project teams.

Adaptive cloud solution architecture can be developed at the portfolio, program, project, release, and iteration level. Adaptive cloud solution architecture can be supported by the "architecture owner" role.

The architecture owner should actively engage and share information about the adaptive cloud enterprise and solution architecture with the cloud implementation project teams. This is in contrast to defining a traditional detailed upfront solution architecture. The architecture owner should apply a participatory architecture design approach (e.g. engage an iteration manager, product owner, team etc.) to define and update adaptive cloud solution architecture. For instance, instead of working in isolation, the architecture owner can work with the product owner in identifying the user stories or requirements. Product owners' user stories need to be linked to the architecture. The impact of the user stories needs to be looked into through the lens of the relevant cloud solution architecture building blocks. The solution architecture integrated with the domain architectures in the upstream and cloud project implementation user stories in the bottom stream may help reduce the technical debt.

The architecture owner, in the down-stream, should actively engage in iteration planning, stand-up, review and retrospective meetings; and provide the required updated information on the architecture assets or building block (via adaptive cloud solution architecture) to help implementation project teams to stay focused and make just-in-time and effective informed decisions about the project planning and design in the overall context of adaptive cloud enterprise architecture. The architecture owner, in the up-stream, should actively engage with the domain and enterprise architecture owners and share the updated information regarding the architecture assets (via the evolving adaptive cloud solution architecture). In summary, the adaptive cloud enterprise architecture approach to cloud adoption requires active feedback-driven participatory architecture design (PAD) practices to keep the cloud implementation teams focused, informed and aligned across different project implementations.

7.4 Cloud Facility Architecture

Adaptive cloud enterprise architecture is a distributed network of uniquely identifiable independent adaptive cloud service systems that are hosted on geographically dispersed facilities. An adaptive cloud service system facility is a built environment that provides a place for hosting adaptive cloud service systems and services. These adaptive cloud service systems and services can be provided by the same or different adaptive cloud service system factories. Adaptive cloud service systems and their interactions could be hosted, mirrored or replicated on the same or different cloud facility. A cloud facility can be architected and built to support simple to mission-critical complex and sensitive adaptive cloud service systems and services. A cloud facility could be located in the same or different country. A cloud facility that is located outside the boundary of an enterprise and country may be required to comply with the relevant (e.g. local or global) legislative requirements and standards. The choice of interaction between two adaptive cloud service systems could be impacted by the choice of a cloud facility where these service systems are hosted. For instance, an adaptive cloud service system from one country may not like to store their data on the data center service system hosted at a different cloud facility in a different country.

The AESS metamodel – level 2 (capability level) and level 3 (service level) have been used to describe the cloud facility architecture elements and their relationships (Fig. 7.10). These elements and relationships can be used to develop context-specific cloud facility architecture. This can be further used to develop different cloud facility architecture views. The current, transition and future states of cloud facility architecture can be modelled by customising and using the ArchiMate "Business and Technology" layer concepts. Cloud facility architecture discusses the three types of facility architectures:

- adaptive spatial architecture
- adaptive energy architecture
- adaptive ancillary architecture

Spatial architecture describes locations or sites, such as the cloud datacenter or office locations, and is designed to house human and IT architecture elements. Energy architecture describes the energy supply chain that is required to run the cloud facility. Ancillary architecture can include other facility architecture elements such as cooling, fire and security.

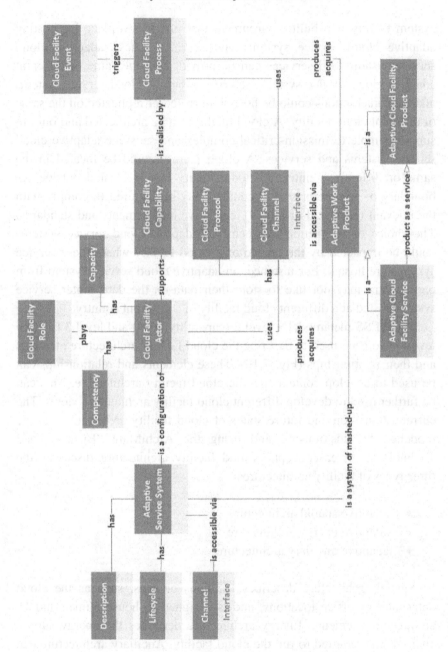

Fig. 7.10. Adaptive cloud facility architecture - capability level.
(based on The AESS metamodel – level 2)

7.4.1 *Adaptive Spatial Architecture*

Adaptive spatial architecture, with embedded reusable spatial services, is a part of the overall adaptive cloud enterprise architecture. Spatial is a location or real state or site that houses the human and IT architecture elements and services. The AESS metamodel – level 2 (capability level) and level 3 (service level) is used to describe adaptive spatial architecture elements and their relationships. These elements and relationships can be used to describe context-specific adaptive spatial architecture. This can be further used to develop different spatial architecture views. The current, transition and future states of the spatial architecture can be modelled by customising and using the ArchiMate "Business and Technology" layer concepts. Spatial architecture can be developed to find answers to the following types of questions.

- What are our current and future spatial capabilities (e.g. spatial capability model)?
- Who are the key spatial actors and what are their roles (e.g. actors and roles model)?
- What are the key spatial events and processes (e.g. spatial process/function matrix and models)?
- How are spatial architecture elements related to each other (e.g. matrix)?
- What are our current spatial services (e.g. cloud facility service catalogue)?
- What is impeding or limiting our spatial actors, capabilities, processes, services?
- What are the emerging spatial trends?
- Which spatial actors, capabilities, processes and services need to be improved?
- What would happen if we did something or did nothing about the limiting factors?
- Which spatial capabilities and services can support other human and IT architectures and services?

A spatial capability is realised by one or more spatial processes or functions. A spatial process is a specific behavior which involves spatial actors, event, activities and tasks. A spatial process can be architected to support human and IT processes. A spatial process uses, produces or acquires adaptive spatial services. Spatial processes included in the spatial architecture are further analysed and mapped to reusable spatial services to support human and IT services.

A spatial event (e.g. facility shut down) is a change in the state of something that triggers a spatial process or function. An adaptive spatial service has one or many channels. An adaptive spatial service is made available for use via multiple spatial channels. A spatial channel is an interface that enables the use of the adaptive spatial service. A spatial channel has an associated standard protocol to enable interactions.

An adaptive spatial service is context aware, evolving and adapting. It scans and senses changes and adapts accordingly. An adaptive spatial service has a description (name, short description, type, resources, operations, information, license, price, access rights) and a lifecycle (created, used, maintained, transformed and retired or expired). An adaptive spatial service is realised by the spatial component (e.g. site, building, floor, rack). A spatial component is a grouping of certain spatial functions or behavior (based on some need) that can support or realise behaviors attached to one or more spatial channels or interfaces.

Spatial architecture, as a part of the cloud facility architecture, helps to identify and assess operational adjustment, improvement, growth and transformational opportunities. Spatial architecture can be described in terms of its current, transition and target states. Spatial services identified in spatial architecture are supported by other human and cloud (IT) services. Adaptive spatial architecture is designed in the overall context of cloud facility architecture. It is important to involve human and cloud (IT) architectures when designing cloud facility architecture.

An adaptive cloud service system facility's spatial capacity and location is very important. It is important to make sure that there is sufficient space at the specific location to support the present and future needs of adaptive cloud service systems. Under- or over-capacity of a facility can become an issue. An adaptive cloud service system facility aims to operate at or near its spatial capacity. An adaptive cloud service system facility should be able to accommodate unpredictable spikes or demand in capacity to support an increasing number of adaptive cloud service systems' facility needs. The capacity of an adaptive cloud service system facility should have enough space to house the following infrastructure items (additional items can considered, if required):

- the number of information processing virtual and physical servers and their capacity
- the number of storage virtual and physical servers and their capacity
- the network and communication virtual and physical equipment and their capacity
- the power equipment and capacity
- the cooling equipment and capacity
- the fire and security equipment
- additional space to operate and manage the spatial facility itself

Spatial capacity could be owned and/or rented to support adaptive cloud service system systems and services. The capacity of an adaptive cloud service system spatial facility is different from fixed traditional capacity. Adaptive cloud service system facility architecture should have the ability to quickly adjust to the changing demands for capacity unlike a traditional facility where change in demand requires a significant time to source additional spatial capacity to support the smooth running of service systems. Under- or over-capacity can impact the effectiveness and performance of an adaptive cloud service system. In an under-capacity situation, demand is higher than the available capacity. Additional capacity may be sourced to meet a higher demand. In an over-capacity situation, demand is lower than the available capacity. Additional capacity may be outsourced to reduce waste. Spatial architecture should have the ability to accommodate expected and unexpected changes in capacity demand. It should have access to multiple facility providers, not only for flexible capacity but also for facility resilience and disaster recovery purposes. Reusable and modular spatial services can be assembled to provide an operational spatial facility at the desired location to support adaptive cloud service systems.

7.4.2 *Adaptive Energy Architecture*

Energy is one of the main enablers and key issues reported by the European Commission (European Commission 2011). Energy is required for the smooth running and usage of services installed on a spatial facility. There is an increasing demand for energy for a number of reasons, such as the emergence of new human and IT services. A shortage of power or energy supply could adversely impact the facility and consequently, dependent services. It has been reported that there is a 2.2% increase per year in energy consumption (US Energy Information Administration 2013). The per day energy usage of a typical datacenter facility of 500 square meters size is approximately 27000 kilowatt-hours, which is more than the energy usage of 2500 households (Enerdata 2011). Adaptive energy architecture is required to understand, analyse and improve the energy efficiency of the facility. The AESS metamodel – level 2 (capability level) and level 3 (service level) is used to describe the adaptive energy architecture elements and their relationships. These elements and relationships can be used to develop context-specific adaptive energy architecture. This can be further used to develop different energy architecture views. Energy architecture can be developed to find answers to the following types of questions.

- What are our current and future energy capabilities (e.g. capability model)?
- Who are the key energy actors and what are their roles (e.g. actors and roles model)?
- What are the key energy events and processes (e.g. process/function matrix and models)?
- How are energy architecture elements related to each other (e.g. matrix)?
- What are our current energy services (e.g. service catalogue)?
- What is impeding or limiting our spatial actors, capabilities, processes, services?
- What are the emerging energy trends?
- Which energy actors, capabilities, processes and services need to be improved?

- What would happen if we did something or did nothing about the limiting factors?
- Which energy capabilities and services can support other human and IT architectures and services?

An energy capability is realised by one or more energy processes or functions. An energy process is a specific behavior which involves energy actors, event, activities and tasks. An energy process or supply chain can be architected to support human and IT processes. An energy process uses, produces or acquires adaptive energy services. Energy processes included in the energy architecture are further analysed and mapped to reusable energy services to support human and IT services.

An energy event (e.g. power outage) is a change in the state of something that triggers an energy process or function (e.g. turn on generator, switch to alternate energy). Adaptive energy services are essentially reusable, modular, flexible ready to deploy on-demand energy cells or servers (e.g. bloom fuel cells). An adaptive energy service has one or many channels. An adaptive energy service is made available for use via multiple energy channels. An energy channel is an interface that enables the use of the adaptive energy service. An energy channel has an associated standard protocol for energy consumption. It is context aware, evolving and adapting. It scans and senses changes and adapts accordingly. An adaptive energy service has a description (name, short description, type, resources, operations, information, price, access rights) and a lifecycle (created, used, maintained, transformed and retired or expired). An adaptive energy service is realised by the energy component (e.g. generator, UPS, fuel cells).

Adaptive energy architecture, as a part of cloud facility architecture, helps to identify and assess operational adjustment, improvement, growth and transformational opportunities. Energy architecture can be described in terms of its current, transition and target states. Energy services identified in the energy architecture can be supported by other human and cloud (IT) services. It is important to involve human and cloud (IT) architectures when designing cloud facility energy architecture.

The energy capacity of an adaptive cloud service system facility is very important. It is important to ensure that there is sufficient energy available at a specific facility to support the needs of adaptive cloud service systems. Under- or extra-energy capacity can become an issue. An adaptive cloud service system facility aims to operate at or near its energy capacity. An adaptive cloud service system facility should be able to accommodate unpredictable spikes or demand for energy to support an increasing number of adaptive cloud service systems. The energy capacity of an adaptive cloud service system facility should have enough supply to support the following items (additional items can be considered, if required):

- information processing virtual and physical servers and their capacity
- storage virtual and physical servers
- network and communication virtual and physical equipment
- power equipment
- cooling equipment
- fire and security equipment
- additional energy to operate and manage the facility itself (e.g. lift operations)

The energy capacity of an adaptive cloud service system facility is different from fixed traditional capacity. Adaptive cloud service system facility energy architecture should have the ability to quickly adjust to changing energy demands, unlike a traditional facility where a change in demand requires significant time to source the additional energy to support the smooth running of the adaptive cloud service system. Under- or over-capacity can impact the effectiveness and performance of an adaptive cloud service system. In an under-energy situation, demand is higher than the available energy. Additional energy may be sourced to meet the higher demand. In an over-capacity situation, demand is lower than the available energy. Additional energy may be outsourced to reduce waste. Adaptive energy architecture should have the ability to accommodate expected and unexpected changes in energy demand. Similar to spatial architecture, it should have access to multiple energy providers not only for flexible capacity but also for resilience and disaster recovery purposes. Renewable and modular energy services can be assembled to provide sufficient energy or power at the desired facility to support adaptive cloud service systems.

7.4.3 *Adaptive Ancillary Architecture*

Adaptive ancillary architecture supports the overall facility architecture. Ancillary architecture includes a number of services, such as cooling, humidification, dehumidification, fire, safety, security, and mechanical services. The AESS metamodel – level 2 (capability level) and level 3 (service level) can be used to describe the different ancillary architecture(s) elements and their relationships.

It is important to make sure that there is sufficient cooling available at a specific facility to support the needs of adaptive cloud service systems. An under- or over-cooling capacity of a facility can become an issue. An adaptive cloud service system facility aims to operate at or near its optimal cooling demands. An adaptive cloud service system facility should be able to accommodate unpredictable spikes in cooling demand. An adaptive cloud service system facility should have enough cooling capacity to support the facility. The cooling capacity of an adaptive cloud service system facility is different from a fixed traditional capacity. Adaptive cloud service system facility ancillary architecture should have the ability to quickly adjust to changing demands. Under- or over-capacity can impact the effectiveness and performance of an adaptive enterprise service system. For instance, reusable and modular cooling services can be assembled to provide an operational facility with sufficient cooling at the desired location to support adaptive cloud service systems. Similar to cooling ancillary architecture, other ancillary architectures such as humidification, dehumidification, fire, safety, security, and mechanical services etc. can be created by using the AESS metamodel – level 2 (capability level) and level 3 (service level).

7.5 Modelling Languages

The adaptive cloud enterprise architecture capability requires modelling language support. The adaptive cloud enterprise architecture elements or artefacts can be modelled and analysed using a range of modelling languages. There are a number of modelling languages and tools to choose from. There are at least over twenty modelling languages. A single modelling language usually does not provide end-to-end modelling support, as is required by the adaptive cloud enterprise architecture capability (Gill and Qureshi 2015). As noted earlier, this book proposes to use a hybrid modelling approach to model the adaptive cloud enterprise architecture artifacts, both at the high and low detailed level for a particular context. A hybrid approach combines multiple languages appropriate to a particular modelling context, such as combining ArchiMate, BPMN and UML.

7.5.1 *ArchiMate*

ArchiMate (The Open Group, 2013) is a high-level architecture modelling language. It provides a meta-model and graphical notation for modelling the three business, application and technology layers of the enterprise architecture. It also provides two extensions. ArchiMate is organised into active, behavioural and passive structures.

The business layer offers modelling constructs to model the business architecture elements and their relationships. As noted earlier in this chapter, the business layer of ArchiMate can be extended to model the information and social architecture elements and their relationships. The application layer offers modelling constructs to model the software application architecture elements and their relationships. The application layer of ArchiMate can be extended to model the cloud software (SaaS) application architecture elements and their relationships. The technology or infrastructure layer offers modelling constructs to model the infrastructure architecture elements and their relationships. The technology layer of ArchiMate can be extended to model the cloud platform (PaaS), infrastructure (IaaS) and facility (FaaS) elements and their relationships.

ArchiMate also includes the motivation extension, and implementation and migration extension modelling constructs. The motivation extension can be used to model the context or reasons behind the adaptive cloud enterprise architecture work. The implementation and migration extension offers modelling constructs that can be used to model the adaptive cloud enterprise architecture portfolio, program, project (implementation), and plateau (migration). ArchiMate provides an overarching high-level modelling language which can be used to model adaptive cloud enterprise architecture artifacts at a high-level. An enterprise may use ArchiMate to model at a high-level and BPMN and UML for low-level detailed modelling.

7.5.2 BPMN

BPMN (OMG, 2013) is a business process modelling language. It provides a notation for modelling business processes in detail. The scope of BPMN is to support the modelling of business processes in detail. Enterprises can identify and model business processes at a high level using ArchiMate. Then BPMN can be used to detail business processes just-in-time, if and when required. The business strategy, organizational structure, functional breakdowns, data, information and rule models are considered to be beyond the scope of BPMN.

7.5.3 UML

UML (OMG, 2011) is a software application modelling language. UML specifications are organised in two parts: UML infrastructure and superstructure. UML infrastructure describes the fundamental constructs that are required to create the UML. UML superstructure describes UML from a user perspective, which aims at using UML to model software applications in detail. The UML meta-model offers three types of key diagrams: behaviour, interaction, and structure diagrams to model software applications. Business processes can be modelled using UML activity diagrams; however, BPMN provides a much richer set of modelling constructs and detail in the modelling of business processes. Therefore, it is not generally recommended to use UML as the sole or specialized modelling language for business processes.

Hence, it is recommended to use and extend ArchiMate as a baseline language to model the business, information, social, SaaS, PaaS, IaaS and FaaS architectures at a high level in the overall context of adaptive cloud enterprise architecture modelling. The details of business, information and social processes can then be modelled using BPMN. The details of the SaaS application can be modelled by using UML. Other modelling languages can be reviewed and considered for modelling the desired artifacts. ArchiMate, BPMN and UML layers and their elements are mapped in Table 7.2. These layers and elements can be extended and used to model adaptive cloud enterprise architecture.

Table 7.2. Modelling elements.

Layers	ArchiMate	BPMN	UML
Business Layer	**Active Structure:** Business Actor Business Role Business Collaboration Business Interface Location	Pool Swimlane	Actor Swimlane Collaboration
	Behavioral: Business Process Business Function Business Interaction Business Event Business Service	Activity Task Gateway Sequence Events Pool Swimlane	Ativitiy Use Case Event Swimlane
	Passive Struture: Business Object Representation Meaning Value Product Contract	Data Object Data Store	Object
Application Layer	**Active Structure:** Application Component Application Collaboration Application Interface	-	Class Component Collaboration Interface
	Behavioral: Application Function Application Interaction Application Service	-	Method Interaction
	Passive Struture: Data Object	-	Object

Table 7.2. (*Continued*)

Layers	ArchiMate	BPMN	UML
Technology Layer	**Active Structure:** Node Device System Software Infrastructure Interface Network Communication Path	-	Node
	Behavioral: Infrastructure Function Infrastructure Service	-	Method
	Passive Struture: Artifact	-	Artifact
Extension	**Motivational Concepts:** Stakeholder Driver Assessment Goal Requirement Constraint Principle	-	-
	Implementation and Migration Concepts: Work Package Deliverable Plateau Gap	-	-

7.6 Summary

This chapter described the operating capability of the ADOMS approach in the context of adaptive cloud enterprise architecture capability. The operating capability can be tailored and used for a specific context. The operating capability involves a number of cloud architectures and services in the context of adaptive cloud enterprise architecture. These architectures include cloud interaction architecture, cloud factory architecture and cloud facility architecture. Interaction architecture describes the dynamic interactions between adaptive cloud service systems. Cloud factory architecture describes human, IT (cloud) and solution architectures. Human architecture describes business, information and social architectures. IT (cloud) architecture supports human architecture. It describes the adaptive cloud application, platform and infrastructure architectures. Adaptive solution architecture is a subset and mix of human and IT architecture elements. Finally, cloud facility architecture describes the spatial, energy and ancillary architectures. Essentially, cloud facility architecture supports interaction and factory architectures. In summary, these all integrated architectures describe adaptive cloud enterprise architecture. The next chapter describes the managing capability of adaptive cloud enterprise architecture in detail.

Chapter 8

Managing Cloud Enterprise Architecture Capability

8.1 Introduction

The adapting capability continuously monitors, assesses, engages, governs and feeds the change initiatives to the managing capability. The adaptive cloud enterprise architecture capability and architecture evolve in response to change initiatives. This chapter describes how the managing capability can be used by the fictitious financial services enterprise, SFS, to effectively handle changes in the adaptive cloud enterprise architecture capability and architecture. The managing capability offers an integrated approach to handling changes through the integration of adaptive enterprise strategy, architecture, requirements, project, and service management capabilities (Fig. 8.1).

The cloud-enabled operating environment is a living complex adaptive echo-system of adaptive service systems and requires the integration and alignment of various key capabilities such as adaptive cloud enterprise strategy, enterprise architecture, enterprise requirements management, enterprise project management and enterprise service management. The managing capability facilitates managing changes in the adaptive cloud enterprise architecture capability and architecture in conjunction with other related capabilities. The lack of integration and alignment of these key capabilities would lead to inconsistent changes in the cloud-enabled operating environment.

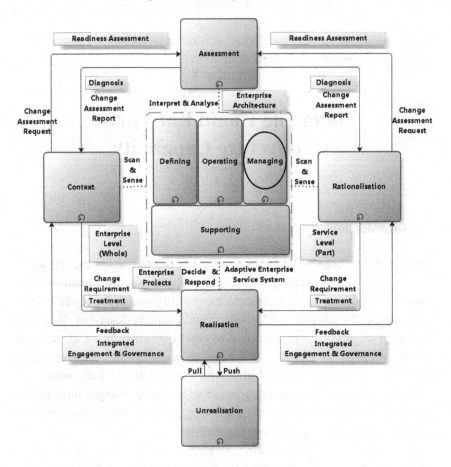

Fig. 8.1. The Gill Framework® 2.0.

This book describes an integrated approach to managing (see Fig. 8.2) changes in the adaptive cloud enterprise architecture capability and architecture to meet the constantly changing business demands. A change requirement or request for change can be identified through the adapting capability. A change is a requirement that can be classified as an operational (e.g. bug fixing, keeping the lights on), continuous improvement (e.g. incremental implementation of the architecture), growth (e.g. enhancement) or transformational change (e.g.

reengineering). A change requirement identified for the adaptive cloud enterprise architecture capability and architecture may trigger strategic, project and service management requirements. The linking of change requirements is one way to integrate adaptive cloud enterprise strategy, architecture, project, and service management capabilities for the effective and consistent management of changes in the adaptive cloud enterprise architecture capability and architecture. Hence, the managing capability requires integrating and aligning the following key management capabilities when handling cloud changes:

- adaptive (cloud) enterprise requirements management capability
- adaptive (cloud) enterprise strategic management capability
- adaptive (cloud) enterprise architecture management capability
- adaptive (cloud) enterprise project management capability
- adaptive (cloud) enterprise service management capability

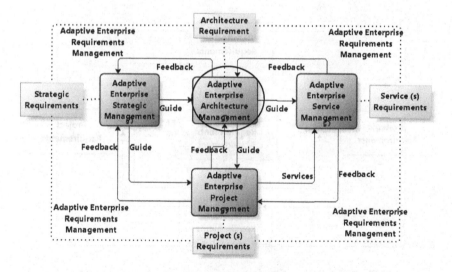

Fig. 8.2. Managing capability – integrated adaptive enterprise architecture management.

8.2 Adaptive Enterprise Requirements Management

Changes in the adaptive cloud enterprise architecture capability and architecture should not be handled in isolation of other related changes. As discussed earlier, a change in cloud architecture may lead to changes in other areas. An integrated adaptive (cloud) enterprise requirements management capability is required for tracking and managing the strategic, architecture, project and service change requirements or initiatives (see Fig. 8.3) as a whole. Hence, it is required to integrate and align enterprise-wide change initiatives or requirements. It should provide an end-to-end 360° degree view of the change requirements. The adaptive (cloud) enterprise requirements management capability can be established by using the capability and service level AESS metamodels (as discussed earlier). Agile and non-agile requirements management practices, roles and tools can be used to support the adaptive (cloud) enterprise requirements management capability.

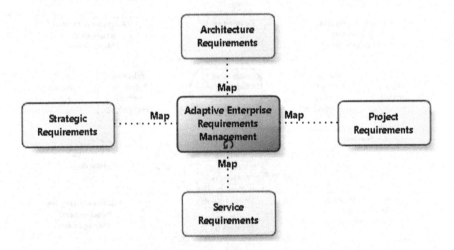

Fig. 8.3. Adaptive (Cloud) enterprise requirements management.

It is important to establish a shared cloud enterprise requirements management repository where all the change requirements are linked and traceable. For instance, strategic cloud requirements or initiatives should be linked to the adaptive cloud enterprise architecture, service and project level requirements for traceability. Project level requirements can be linked to strategic initiatives at the program and portfolio level in the upstream and can be linked to release and iteration level requirements in the downstream. The requirements-based linking will enable traceability from the adaptive cloud enterprise strategy to other related capabilities. Traceability is critical to ensure that the change initiatives or requirements are not handled or implemented in isolation and are effectively handled as a whole. The adaptive (cloud) enterprise requirements management capability is essential to ensure that the whole enterprise is moving in the right direction.

8.3 Adaptive Enterprise Strategic Management

Adaptive cloud enterprise architecture changes may trigger changes in the enterprise strategy or vice versa. The adaptive (cloud) enterprise strategic management capability is required to manage changes in the strategy (see Fig. 8.4). The adaptive enterprise strategy presents the overall direction of the cloud-enabled operating environment. It is critical to develop a robust and adaptive cloud enterprise strategy. An adaptive cloud enterprise strategy is more than just airy-fairy business goals and actions. It should offer a means to respond to the most pressing operational, improvement, growth and transformational limiting factors and changes.

The adaptive (cloud) enterprise strategy consists of an integrated business strategy, information strategy, social strategy, cloud application strategy (SaaS), platform strategy (PaaS), infrastructure strategy (IaaS), facility strategy (FaaS) etc. The adaptive (cloud) enterprise strategic management capability can be established by using the capability and service level AESS metamodels (as discussed earlier). Agile and non-agile strategic management practices, roles and tools can be used to support the adaptive (cloud) enterprise strategic management capability. Fig. 8.4 presents the adaptive enterprise strategic management, which is tailored using the well-known business motivation model (BMM) of OMG (2014). It highlights different aspects of the enterprise strategy.

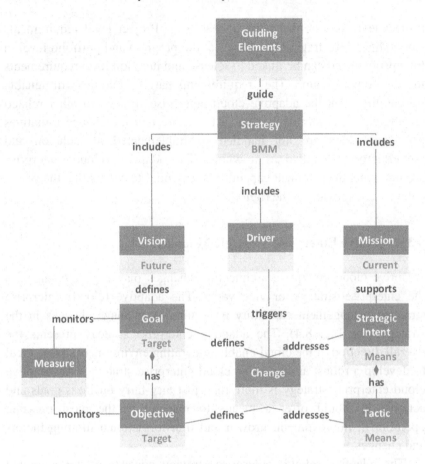

Fig. 8.4. Adaptive (Cloud) enterprise strategic management.

The ArchiMate motivation extension can also be used to model the strategic concepts. As discussed earlier, guiding elements such as business rules, policy, and principles need to be considered to guide the adaptive cloud enterprise strategy (e.g. strategic choices). Strategy includes the mission, vision and drivers of the cloud-enabled operating environment. Mission defines the current state of play. Vision defines the future state of play. Drivers trigger the change. The potential change can be analysed by using SWOT analysis (strengths, weaknesses, opportunities, and threats) to define the goals which are linked to the vision in the upstream and objectives in the downstream. Strategic intent defines the strategic choice statements in response to change, which is required to achieve the desired goals and objectives. Goals are also derived from the vision, and objectives are derived from goals. Goals and objective can be monitored to measure the strategic performance.

Strategic cloud-related intents or change initiatives alone are not enough. Strategic intents can be supported by strategic model(s) and strategic plan(s). Strategic models may include a cloud-enabled business model, operating model, lifecycle model and change model. The current state of these models needs to be reviewed in order to define the future state of these models in response to the identified change(s). The gap analysis between the current and future state will essentially support the defining of the strategic intents or requirements. Strategic action plans with a specific timeframe and resources need to be developed to put the strategic intents or requirements into practice. Adaptive enterprise requirements management is needed to iteratively establish and update the strategic cloud initiatives or requirements backlog. Hence, the adaptive (cloud) enterprise strategy is a set of strategic cloud requirements that can be further linked to adaptive (cloud) enterprise architecture, service and project requirements for traceability. This traceability from adaptive enterprise strategy to other capabilities is critical in order to ensure that the enterprise strategy is correctly realised by the other capabilities, such as adaptive enterprise architecture, project and service management.

8.4 Adaptive Enterprise Architecture Management

Adaptive (cloud) enterprise architecture management (see Fig. 8.5) is a core capability in integrated change management. The managing capability manages changes related to both the adaptive cloud enterprise architecture capability and architecture in conjunction with the enterprise strategic, project, requirements and service management capabilities. The linking of adaptive enterprise architecture capability to and from other upstream (adaptive enterprise strategy) and downstream (adaptive enterprise project and service management) capabilities is very critical to ensure that the architecture changes are not handled in isolation.

Adaptive cloud enterprise architecture does not merely consider the architecture changes, rather it can trigger changes in the adaptive cloud enterprise strategy and roadmap via a two-way feedback loop mechanism. Hence, it is not always the case that the enterprise strategy will influence enterprise architecture but it is very likely that enterprise architecture may also influence enterprise strategy development. For instance, enterprise architecture vision, developed during phase A of the TOGAF, is linked to enterprise strategy. The SFS enterprise may review and use architecture change management practices from different frameworks (e.g. such as TOGAF -phase H) to handle changes in the adaptive cloud enterprise architecture capability and architecture. Furthermore, it is important to note here that adaptive cloud enterprise architecture is not confined to only growth and transformational change initiatives or programs. It is also important to engage an enterprise architecture capability (if necessary) to handle operational changes and continuous improvement programs. Hence, it is not practical to manage changes in adaptive cloud enterprise architecture in isolation of other key capabilities, such as adaptive cloud enterprise strategic, project and service management.

The combined layers of adaptive cloud enterprise architecture and project management, in between adaptive enterprise strategic and service management layers, facilitate strategy design to strategy implementation. Adaptive cloud enterprise architecture is the glue between different silo capabilities for effective human and IT alignment. The integrated change management approach will help enable the enterprise-wide consistent operational, improvement, growth and transformational changes. Adaptive cloud enterprise architecture is essential for consistent technology adoption and coherent integrated cloud-enabled AESS lifecycle management. As discussed earlier in this book, the adaptive (cloud) enterprise architecture management capability can be established by using the capability and service level AESS metamodels (as discussed earlier). Agile and non-agile enterprise architecture management practices, roles and tools can be reviewed, selected and used from different frameworks (such as TOGAF, DoDAF, FEAF etc.) to support the adaptive cloud enterprise architecture capability.

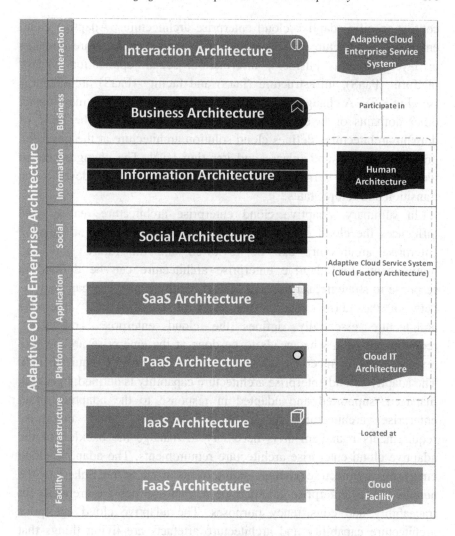

Fig. 8.5. Adaptive (Cloud) enterprise architecture.

As noted earlier, adaptive cloud enterprise architecture can be described from different perspectives, such as cloud reference architecture, enterprise architecture, domain architecture and solution architecture. Cloud reference architecture (e.g. NIST cloud reference architecture, IBM cloud reference architecture) is a generic architecture or industry standard that can be used as a guide for the development of context-specific adaptive cloud enterprise architecture. Adaptive cloud enterprise architecture has a number of integrated architecture domains or layers such as business, information, social, application (SaaS), platform (PaaS), infrastructure (IaaS) and facility (FaaS) architectures (see Fig 8.5). A change in one architecture domain or layer may impact other domains or layers. The integrated organisation of the logic of domain architectures defines cloud solution architecture at the portfolio, program, project, and release and iteration level. The changes can be identified in the current state of these architectures to develop the transition and future states.

In summary, adaptive cloud enterprise architecture realises and influences the cloud enterprise strategy. The current state of adaptive enterprise architecture can be reviewed and the future state and requirements for adaptive enterprise architecture can be defined in response to strategic, service and project requirements. The gap analysis between the current and future state of cloud-enabled enterprise architecture essentially defines the cloud enterprise architecture requirements (e.g. what needs to be done at the enterprise architecture level in order to meet the strategic, service and project requirements). The adaptive cloud enterprise architecture capability is defined, operated, managed, supported and adapted in response to the adaptive cloud enterprise architecture requirements. Adaptive cloud enterprise requirements management is necessary to manage the backlog of the adaptive cloud enterprise architecture requirements. The adaptive cloud enterprise architecture change requirements need to be linked to the adaptive cloud enterprise strategic, project and service requirements for traceability and consistency purposes. The adaptive cloud enterprise architecture capability and architecture artefacts are living things that evolve in response to changes.

8.5 Adaptive Enterprise Project Management

The adaptive cloud enterprise architecture capability and architecture (e.g. cloud SaaS application architecture) can be implemented through one or many projects. The adaptive (cloud) enterprise project management capability is also required for the implementation of any changes, both in the capability and architecture. Adaptive (cloud) enterprise project management can be achieved through active integrated engagement and governance (e.g. COBIT). The linking of the adaptive enterprise project management capability to and from other upstream (Enterprise Strategy and Architecture) and downstream (Enterprise Service Management) capabilities is very critical for consistent and effective change implementation through the execution and management of a number of projects organised into programs and portfolios.

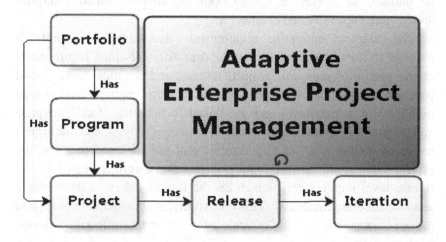

Fig. 8.6. Adaptive (Cloud) enterprise project management.

As discussed earlier, adaptive enterprise project management, strategy, architecture and service management capabilities complement each other and are linked via a two-way feedback loop mechanism. For instance, the adaptive cloud enterprise architecture is not confined to a single project, rather it provides an overview of the entire enterprise cloud service landscape and compliance requirements and can be used to guide different cloud projects. It is not practical to manage cloud projects as an independent and isolated program of works, rather it should be linked with the cloud enterprise strategy, enterprise architecture and enterprise service management.

Adaptive cloud enterprise project management can be organised into adaptive portfolio, program, project, release, and iteration management (Fig. 8.6). A cloud portfolio can include cloud programs and individual cloud projects that are required to implement the cloud architecture or change initiatives. Each program is a set of individual cloud projects that can simultaneously run to implement the cloud adoption change initiatives. The adaptive cloud enterprise architecture is not specific to a single cloud project but provides an overall cloud strategic context and platform to guide the consistent and aligned management of a number of cloud projects occurring at the same time. Several cloud projects could be initiated to deliver or update both the adaptive cloud enterprise architecture capability and architecture.

The adaptive enterprise requirements management capability is required to iteratively establish and update different cloud requirements at the portfolio, program, project, release, and iteration level. Cloud portfolio and program level requirement backlogs capture cloud change initiatives at a high level and are linked to adaptive cloud enterprise architecture and strategic requirements for traceability. The cloud project requirements are a set of requirements that are allocated to a specific project. The cloud project requirements can be further linked to the release level requirements, which can be further linked to the iteration level detailed requirements. This traceability, within adaptive enterprise project management, is critical to coordinate effective change implementation.

In summary, adaptive (cloud) enterprise project management is about managing a set of cloud implementation projects that are iteratively planned and executed for effective enterprise-wide cloud adoption and change management. The adaptive (cloud) enterprise project management capability can be established by using the capability and service level AESS metamodels, as discussed earlier, and the adaptive enterprise project management capability reference model (Fig. 8.7). The Gill Framework offers the adaptive enterprise project management capability reference model. It shows the adaptive enterprise project management capability services that are organized into five layers: portfolio, program, project, release, and iteration.

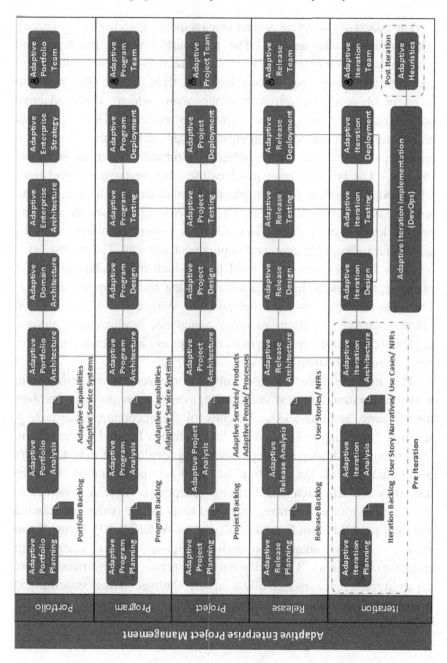

Fig. 8.7. Adaptive enterprise project management capability reference model.

The adaptive enterprise project management capability layers specify relevant teams and services. The relationship within the layer and between layers is bidirectional with horizontal (top-down and bottom-up) and vertical slicing (e.g. left-to-right and right-to-left). The portfolio layer involves the adaptive portfolio team which offers adaptive portfolio planning, analysis and architecture services. Adaptive portfolio architecture is linked to the adaptive domain architectures of adaptive (cloud) enterprise architecture, which is ultimately linked to enterprise strategy. The program layer involves the adaptive program level team which offers adaptive program planning, analysis, architecture, design, testing, and deployment services. The project layer involves the adaptive project level team which offers adaptive project planning, analysis, architecture, design, testing, and deployment services. The release layer involves the adaptive release level team which offers adaptive release planning, analysis, architecture, design, testing and deployment services. The iteration layer involves the adaptive iteration level team which offers adaptive iteration planning, analysis, architecture, design, implementation (DevOps: integrated development and operation), testing, deployment and heuristics services.

The iteration layer is also further organized into pre-iteration, iteration, iteration and post iteration segments. A pre-iteration involves the planning, analysis and architecture of the upcoming iteration (e.g. iteration 2 planning in iteration 1). An iteration is focused on the design, implementation, testing and deployment (e.g. deployment in test, staging or production) of the iteration in hand. A post-iteration involves heuristics for reflection and learning (adapting). Agile and non-agile project management practices, roles and tools can be reviewed, selected and used from different frameworks (such as Waterfall, XP, Scrum, Lean etc.) to support adaptive (cloud) enterprise project management capability services. The adaptive enterprise project management capability reference model offers agility, holistic living systems and design thinking that can be used to steer the changes through portfolios, programs, projects, releases and iterations.

8.6 Adaptive Enterprise Service Management

The implementation of the changes involves both development and operations (DevOps). Cloud operations and management are handled by the adaptive enterprise service management capability. The linking of adaptive enterprise service management to and from other capabilities is very critical for consistent and effective cloud operations in the context of overall change management. Adaptive enterprise service management is not confined to only cloud service operations and management, it can also trigger change requirements that may impact the adaptive cloud enterprise architecture capability and architecture, and consequently, cloud project and strategic management. Therefore, the change requirements need to be evaluated as a whole to determine the change impact and necessary changes in the cloud enterprise strategy, architecture, projects and service management. Hence, it is not practical to handle the adaptive enterprise cloud architecture capability and architecture changes in isolation of the adaptive enterprise service management capability.

Adaptive enterprise service management is concerned with the smooth operation and management of the overall cloud-enabled AESS, service systems and services. The adaptive (cloud) enterprise service management capability can be established by using the capability and service level AESS metamodels, as discussed earlier. Service management practices, roles and tools can be adopted from different industry standards and frameworks (such as ISO standards, ITIL) to support the adaptive (cloud) enterprise service management capability. In practice, service management is concerned with both the ongoing cloud service business support and operational support. The integrated organising logic or configuration of adaptive services forms the adaptive service system. The cloud-enabled AESS refers to the living system of systems that is evolved through the interaction of different independent adaptive cloud service systems. The adaptive services, service systems and enterprise service systems can be described in terms of current, transition and future states. The gap between the current and future state essentially defines the service requirements (e.g. what needs to be done at the adaptive service, service system and enterprise service system level?).

Adaptive enterprise service management provides a set of cloud service requirements that can be linked to cloud enterprise strategy, architecture and project requirements for traceability and consistency purposes. For instance, a cloud service change request can be traced from adaptive enterprise service management to adaptive cloud enterprise strategy (e.g. understand impact on enterprise strategy), adaptive cloud enterprise architecture (e.g. understand impact on enterprise architecture) and adaptive cloud enterprise project management (e.g. understand impact on the existing and upcoming new projects) for end-to-end impact analysis and change management. Such traceability is critical to ensure that the whole cloud-enabled enterprise is moving in the right direction.

8.7 Summary

Integrated management capability for the cloud leads to an integrated or connected cloud-enabled adaptive or agile enterprise. The management capability involves a number of integrated management capabilities. The adaptive enterprise requirements management capability provides support for managing enterprise-wide change requirements. Adaptive cloud enterprise architecture realises the adaptive enterprise cloud strategy change requirements. The adaptive cloud enterprise architecture capability can be used to iteratively architect the cloud service systems and services that need to be implemented and deployed for value co-creation interactions. Adaptive enterprise project management iteratively implements the adaptive cloud enterprise architecture capability, architecture and any relevant changes. Adaptive enterprise service management is responsible for the ongoing support and management of the deployed cloud service systems and services. Adaptive cloud enterprise service management manages the cloud value co-creation interactions and provides any feedback or changes to the adaptive cloud enterprise architecture, project and service management capabilities. The next chapter discusses the supporting capability of the ADOMS approach.

Chapter 9

Supporting Cloud Enterprise Architecture Capability

9.1 Introduction

The supporting capability provides items such as the adaptive enterprise model, library, engineering, and intelligence to support adapting, defining, operating and managing other capabilities. Additional items can be included, if required, to suit the specific enterprise context. This chapter describes how the supporting capability can be used by the fictitious financial services enterprise, SFS, to support the adaptive cloud enterprise architecture capability and architecture (Fig. 9.1).

9.2 Adaptive Enterprise Model

The adaptive enterprise model defines the way the cloud-enabled adaptive enterprise operates or intends to operate for value co-creation. It is a manifestation of the adaptive enterprise strategy. It evolves in response to a constantly changing competitive situation. There is at least one-to-one mapping between the adaptive enterprise strategy and model. The adaptive enterprise model includes the following key models, to which others can be added, if required:

- Adaptive business model
- Adaptive operating model
- Adaptive lifecycle model

- Adaptive change model
- Adaptive resource supply chain model
- Adaptive capability maturity model

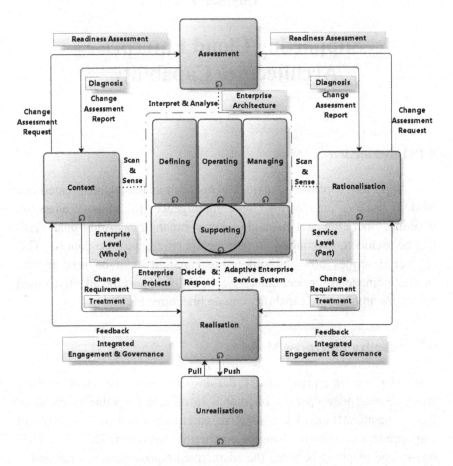

Fig. 9.1. The Gill Framework® 2.0.

9.2.1 *Adaptive Business Model*

Cloud adoption is not only concerned with technology adoption. It is important to define a context-specific cloud-enabled adaptive business model (Fig. 9.2) and use the business model to guide strategic cloud adoption. The cloud-enabled business model can be developed by the

SFS, based on the desired cloud value proposition and value co-creation. The cloud business model describes how cloud service systems and services will take position, collaborate, compete and co-create value (e.g. make money) through dynamic interactions. It describes the unique value propositions that are the foundation of all cloud interactions for value co-creation.

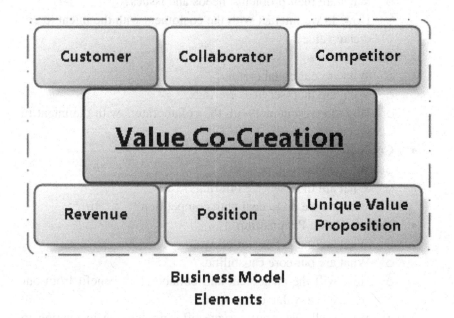

Business Model Elements

Fig. 9.2. Business model.

The value propositions (e.g. a cloud service offering to target internal and external service customers) are vital to value co-creation interactions. A cloud service offering should be coupled with strong value propositions. A value proposition relates to how the cloud service system offerings will benefit the involved parties. For instance, a cloud service offering may benefit in terms of increasing revenue, reducing collaborators' production cost, or meeting customers' dynamic data storage needs. For instance, a current state business model can be defined by the SFS enterprise to understand and analyse what they do and how they co-create value. The SFS enterprise cloud business model can be described from the following six business elements. However, these elements can be modified or additional elements can be added to the business model.

- **Customers**
  - Who are our customers?
  - What are their problems, needs and issues?
  - How do we interact with the customers with the intent to co-create value?
- **Collaborators**
  - Who are our collaborators?
  - What are their service offerings?
  - How do we interact with the collaborators with the intent to co-create value?
- **Competitors**
  - Who are our competitors?
  - What are their service offerings?
  - What do we do to deal with competition?
- **Unique Value Proposition**
  - What are our service offerings?
  - What are our core capabilities?
  - How will the customers and collaborators benefit from our services i.e. value co-creation?
  - What will make our service offerings unique in relation to other services in the market?
- **Revenue**
  - What is our cost structure?
  - How do we make money?
- **Position**
  - What is our strategic stance in the market?
  - How do we position ourselves and approach the market?

A business model is the translation of an enterprise strategy for value co-creation. The SFS enterprise may have more than one business model describing its current, transition and target states. It is imperative to define and clarify business models before committing any investment in the cloud initiatives. Further, business models can be put into practice by defining the SFS enterprise cloud operating model.

9.2.2 Adaptive Operating Model

The adaptive cloud enterprise strategy needs to be supported through the definition of a clear adaptive cloud operating model. The cloud operating model provides the strategic level direction for architecting and operating adaptive cloud enterprise architecture. A cloud operating model defines how cloud architecture needs to be designed for value co-creation. A cloud operating model is a way to reflect strategic cloud initiatives. The choice of an operating model is an important strategic decision, which indicates how the SFS enterprise intends to implement its cloud enterprise strategy (e.g. business and technology strategy perspectives). The cloud operating model provides the operating picture of the cloud-enabled enterprise.

Ross et al. 2006 define two key elements of the operating model: standardisation and integration. Building on their valuable work, this book describes an additional eight elements for the cloud operating model. The SFS enterprise can assign a low to high ranking to each operating model element, as per their local context: Collaboration, Consolidation, Customisation, Pre-determination, Globalisation, Integration, Localisation, Modularisation, Standardisation and Virtualisation.

The SFS enterprise needs to strategically position and select a combination of the above-mentioned operating model elements for the right balance and a competitive advantage. The SFS enterprise can adopt a balanced approach when strategically choosing elements for the cloud operating model, and making investment decisions to implement the chosen cloud operating model. The cloud operating model elements and the following key question can be used as a guideline when making decisions about the cloud operating model.

- To what extent will the enterprise gain value through investments in choosing the specific operating model element or a combination of operating model elements with a specific high to low ranking?

9.2.2.1 *Collaboration*

This refers to the adaptive enterprise strategy that requires collaborations of independently managed cloud service systems or services for value co-creation. A service system can propose value-proposition collaboration to another service system that may accept or reject the value-proposition. The interaction or collaboration emerges based on the mutual agreement for value co-creation. The adaptive cloud enterprise strategy needs to include initiatives on collaboration.

9.2.2.2 *Consolidation*

This refers to the adaptive enterprise strategy that requires consolidation of service systems or services for value co-creation. This may involve the consolidation of business and technology (e.g. applications, platforms, and infrastructure) services of the various service systems that exist in the enterprise operating environment. The adaptive cloud enterprise strategy needs to include initiatives on consolidation.

9.2.2.3 *Customisation*

This refers to the enterprise strategy initiatives that require customisation of the part or whole of the cloud service system. This may involve the customisation of business and technology (e.g. applications, platforms, and infrastructure) services that exist in the enterprise operating environment. Customisation may help to enhance service flexibility, which is required to support the business. The adaptive enterprise strategy may include initiatives about the customisation of some customisable special business and technology services. The SFS enterprise needs to make a choice about how much and which services need to be customised in the cloud adoption context.

9.2.2.4 *Pre-determination*

This refers to the adaptive enterprise strategy that focuses on the deliberate design strategy for value co-creation. In deliberate design, the interactions between independent and centrally managed service systems are most likely predetermined (e.g. less emergent behaviour) and agreed to fulfil the specific purpose. The SFS enterprise needs to make a choice about how much and which services need to be deliberately designed in the cloud adoption context.

9.2.2.5 *Globalisation*

This refers to the adaptive enterprise strategy that focuses on the global design strategy for value co-creation. In globalisation, a part or the whole of the cloud architecture is designed with a view to provide global business support (e.g. multi-currency support). In a global environment, independent cloud service systems from different countries or geo-restriction territories interact with each other for value co-creation. The SFS enterprise needs to make a choice about how much and which services need to be designed with a view to support global business operations.

9.2.2.6 *Integration*

Consideration of the seamless integration between cloud and non-cloud adaptive service systems and their services is fundamental to successful cloud adoption. A part or the whole of the adaptive cloud service system can be integrated with other systems for value co-creation. This may involve the integration of business and technology (e.g. applications, platforms, and infrastructure) services. The SFS enterprise strategy needs to include initiatives on cloud integration.

9.2.2.7 *Localisation*

This refers to the enterprise strategy that focuses on the local design strategy for value co-creation. In localisation, a part or the whole of the cloud architecture is designed with the view to serve only local business operations. In a local environment, independent service systems from local to region or country interact with each other for value co-creation. The SFS enterprise needs to make a choice about how much and which services need to be designed with a view to support local business operations. The SFS enterprise may choose to take on a hybrid cloud approach involving both global and local opportunities.

9.2.2.8 *Modularisation*

The cloud-enabled environment depends on reusable services. The foundational unit of the cloud-enabled environment is the modular and loosely coupled reusable business and technology services. These reusable services can be used to generate different on-demand configurations of cloud service systems for value co-creation. A modular and loosely coupled cloud service system has the ability to adapt to changing business needs. The SFS enterprise strategy may include initiatives on modular business design.

9.2.2.9 *Standardisation*

This refers to the enterprise strategy that focuses on service standardisation for value co-creation. In standardisation, a part or the whole of the service system is focused on standardisation. This may involve the standardisation of business and technology (e.g. applications, platforms, and infrastructure) services. Standardisation may help to reduce the number of services and resources required to do business. For instance, the SFS enterprise may focus on the standardisation of most of the business services (e.g. degree of standardisation: low to high) and the maximisation of the deployment of global service system solutions to support global or standardised services. The enterprise strategy needs to make a choice about how much and which services need to be standardised (e.g. 80% common standardised global services, 20% local market-specific services). The SFS enterprise may not be able to standardise everything and may decide to take on both a partial standardisation and partial customisation approach for a competitive advantage.

9.2.2.10 *Virtualisation*

This refers to the enterprise strategy that focuses on the virtualisation of technology services (e.g. fundamental to cloud computing) for optimal value co-creation. In virtualisation, a part or the whole of the service system is focused on creating a virtual environment. This may involve the virtualisation of technology (e.g. applications, platforms, and infrastructure) services. Virtualisation may help to reduce the cost of technology services to support the business services. The SFS enterprise needs to make a choice about how much and which technology services need to be virtualised (e.g. degree of virtualisation: low to high).

9.2.3 *Adaptive Lifecycle Model*

The AESS is a living system of systems comprising many cloud and non-cloud service systems with embedded services (e.g. business and technology services). An adaptive cloud enterprise architecture, similar to a living organism, has adaptive lifecycle stages (see below for the typical lifecycle stages). A lifecycle model needs to be defined for adaptive cloud enterprise architecture.

- Start or Emerge or Configure or Develop, Harvest State
- History or Past State
- Present or Current State
- Future or Target State
- End or Expire or Retire or Death State

Adaptive cloud enterprise architecture is initiated or emerges through the interaction of service systems for value co-creation. An individual cloud service system can be configured by using the reusable cloud services that participate in value co-creation interactions. An individual reusable cloud service is developed, deployed and used in configuring many cloud service systems.

An adaptive cloud enterprise architecture changes from one state to another state to meet the changing value co-creation interaction demands. Changing from one state to another state creates history or past or transition states. The past state refers to the previous state. The present (transition) state refers to the current operating state. The future state refers to the target operating state. The service systems and services in adaptive cloud enterprise architecture will not live forever and will eventually pass away or be retired when they are no longer required or when it is appropriate to end or abandon their use. The end or death state marks the retirement of the adaptive cloud enterprise architecture service systems or services.

9.2.4 *Adaptive Change Model*

The change model is based on design thinking (Martin 2009). A change can be identified through the balanced interplay of both intuition (e.g. creativity) and analytics (e.g. standard driven, data driven and event driven). A vision based on intuition could lead to a change initiative. A change can be initiated to implement a specific standard or maturity model, which is called a deliberate standard driven change. A change that is initiated in response to the data received from the environment is called a data-driven change. A change that is initiated in response to an event received from the environment is called an event-driven change. A change can lead to adaptation. A change can be classified as an operational, continuous improvement, growth or transformational change (Fig. 9.3). Adaptive cloud enterprise architecture comprising of many service systems with embedded services (e.g. business and technology services) constantly evolves from one state to another state. The change model classifies the changes into four categories, which are shown in the change model.

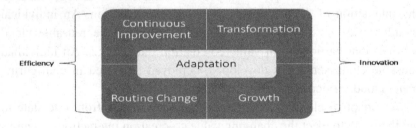

Fig. 9.3. Change model (based on design thinking).

The change model has four quadrants (see Fig. 9.3), which are described below.

9.2.4.1 *Operational routine change (low efficiency)*

This refers to changes that focus on internal consistency and compliance through mandatory routine changes. A round change can be a simple fix to keep the lights on. An operational change may be a simple change request, which may require the initiation of a project to address the change.

9.2.4.2 *Continuous improvement (high efficiency)*

This refers to incremental changes. An incremental change can be implemented through the initiation of a continuous improvement program of works, which may involve a number of stakeholders and projects.

9.2.4.3 *Growth (low innovation)*

This refers to the enterprise growth-related strategic change initiatives that do not require drastic changes in the existing state of an adaptive enterprise architecture. A change could be triggered to introduce an existing product or service in another market.

9.2.4.4 *Transformation (high innovation):*

This refers to the initiatives that require drastic changes in the existing state of an adaptive enterprise architecture. The SFS enterprise's initiative to adopt the cloud is a transformational change. This means that moving from an existing non-cloud computing environment to the cloud computing environment is a transformational change. Transformational changes and a relevant program of works could be initiated with the view to enhance business innovation.

The SFS enterprise needs to strategically position and choose the combination of these quadrants for the right balance of adaptation. If the

SFS enterprise chooses to focus too much on operational "efficiency" through small routine changes and incremental improvements in the core competencies, they may lose their competitive edge. If they tend to focus too much on "innovation", they may fall into the trap of becoming less efficient. The SFS enterprise may adopt a balanced approach when committing resources to efficiency and innovation change-related initiatives. The SFS cloud adoption initiative is classified here as transformational change (innovation category). The change model can be used as a guideline when identifying change initiatives or requirements.

- To what extent will the enterprise receive vale through investments in running the operations smoothly?
- To what extent will the enterprise receive value through investments in continuous improvement initiatives?
- To what extent will the enterprise receive value through investments in continuous growth initiatives?
- To what extent will the enterprise receive value through investments in continuous transformation initiatives?

Operational routine change, continuous improvement, growth and transformation example scenarios for the fictitious financial service, SFS, are depicted in the following table (Table 9.1).

Table 9.1. Change scenarios.

Change Classification	Project Scenarios
Operation (Minor Adjustments)	- Make changes in the existing operating environment in order to meet the mandatory changing financial services industry regulatory requirements - Adjust investment product to meet the mandatory changing financial service services industry regulatory requirements

Table 9.1. (*Continued*)

Change Classification	Project Scenarios
Improvement (Major Adjustments)	• Add investment report generation and export features to existing online banking website • Implement continuous improvement program
Growth (Addition)	• Develop new capabilities • Offer new investment product through existing online website • Make no or minor changes to the existing online banking website to support new investment product
Transformation (Evolution)	• Change in the genetic structure or fundamental state • Offer existing and new investment products through existing online banking website and also through a new mobile and self-service kiosk channel. • Install self-service kiosk in bank branches to search for and buy products • Use mobile apps to capture customer leads • Use cloud-based social media tools to increase brand awareness and customer loyalty

Table 9.1. (*Continued*)

Change Classification	Project Scenarios
	• Use cloud-based social media tools to increase staff communication and productivity
	• Re-engineer customer business processes

Changes in the adaptive enterprise architecture due to regulatory and compliance requirements fall under the category of operation. The provision of additional features (e.g. export, email or print report) on the existing online website or service system is not a transformative change, rather, it is a routine change, which is focused on continuous improvement. The addition of a new financial product or service in the existing portfolio is not a transformational change in the above case. Transformation is clearly dissimilar to continuous operation, improvement and growth. Transformation tends to be more abrupt when it first occurs, and then any changes in the transformed state may lead to routine or continuous improvement or growth. Any changes due to business growth may lead to transformation or routine or continuous improvement. The SFS enterprise needs to operate, continuously improve, grow and transform; however the biggest challenge is, given the limited resources, to find the right balance of changes in order to ensure the smooth running of the business for a competitive advantage.

9.2.5 *Adaptive Resource Supply Chain Model*

The changing business landscape is always pushing the boundaries of what an individual system or organisation or enterprise is capable of. The SFS enterprise needs to look beyond its internal structure and analyse itself as a part of the large distributed supply chain. A distributed integrated adaptive enterprise resource supply chain comprises distributed networks of legally separated entities (e.g. producers, suppliers, testers, distributors, and customers) that offer (and consume) adaptive cloud service systems and cloud services to (and from) each other. The adaptive enterprise resource supply chain, unlike traditional historical data and forecast-based supply chains, requires the monitoring of the cloud operating environment and forms an appropriate response to ever-changing business demands.

The adaptive cloud operating environment needs to be architected, operated and managed like an integrated adaptive supply chain network to develop and source reusable and configurable cloud services and cloud service systems for value co-creation interactions. The value co-creation interactions (in the interaction architecture) determine the demand and drive the integrated adaptive supply chain network. The end customers, along with other interested parties, are the members of the adaptive supply chain network. The traditional service network focuses on the one-way delivery of services to customers, whereas the adaptive supply chain network focuses on service co-creation through the engagement of end customers and resources to drive mutual benefits.

A cloud service is the application of resources (e.g. human, financial or intellectual resources) and it is also a resource as well. It is not created in isolation of the other items, rather, it is co-created for value co-creation. The cloud factory can develop adaptive cloud service systems from in-house reusable services (resources) and services sourced from the supply chain network. An integrated supply chain is a competitive network that prices resources and services, based on their demand and supply. An enterprise-as-a-whole can make strategic decisions about who should and should not be in their cloud service supply chain network. The Australian whole of government cloud services panel initiative is an example of such a cloud supply chain network. This approach can help enterprises to strategically take advantage of economies-of-scale while having a single panel or view of the integrated supply chain for a competitive advantage. The integrated supply chain network can be classified into three main streams (Fig. 9.4):

- upstream
- midstream
- downstream

The cloud factory midstream pulls services from the upstream. The cloud factory upstream sources services from internal and external service supply chain networks or panels. The upstream pushes the required services to the midstream. The midstream assembles, integrates and packages services into adaptive cloud service systems. The downstream pulls adaptive cloud service systems from the midstream and offers them for value co-creation interactions. The midstream pushes the required adaptive cloud service systems to the downstream for deployment and offering. The adaptive cloud service system factory houses cloud services and cloud service systems in the adaptive cloud service system facility. In summary, the adaptive cloud service system factory offers cloud service systems for value co-creation interactions.

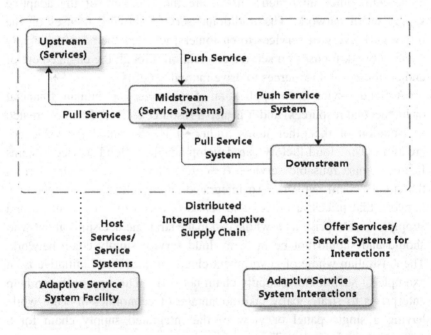

Fig. 9.4. Adaptive enterprise resource supply chain.

It is important to model the integrated supply chain network streams to effectively analyse, establish, operate, improve and transform the adaptive cloud service system factory. The integrated supply chain network describes how services flow from the upstream to the downstream. The adaptive cloud service system factory approach enables the examination of the whole of the integrated supply chain network when developing cloud sourcing strategies and architecture. The cloud service factory applies resources (e.g. intellectual, financial, competencies, skills, knowledge) for the development, acquisition, testing, deployment and offering of adaptive cloud service systems and services.

9.2.6 *Adaptive Capability Maturity Model*

The adaptive capability maturity model (ACMM) provides a systematic approach to assessing the maturity of an adaptive capability. The generic ACMM can be tailored and used to assess the maturity of an adaptive capability, such as the adaptive enterprise architecture capability, to identify the target maturity level. The ACMM is organised into the following six stages or levels (0-5), corresponding to the ADOMS approach.

- Level 0: Infancy
- Level 1: Initial
- Level 2: Transition
- Level 3: Defined
- Level 4: Managed
- Level 5: Adapting

These levels are tailored and discussed here in the context of adaptive enterprise architecture capability maturity.

9.2.6.1 *Level 0: Infancy*

This level suggests that an enterprise is operating (ADOMS – Operating) at the infancy level where the local solution architecture processes are mainly used to support the individual (cloud) projects. There is no holistic defined adaptive (cloud) enterprise architecture capability. There is no support (ADOMS – Supporting) for establishing an adaptive (cloud) enterprise architecture capability.

9.2.6.2 *Level 1: Initial*

This level suggests that an enterprise is operating (ADOMS – Operating) ad-hoc local and informal enterprise architecture processes to support the individual (cloud) projects. There is a lack of integrated engagement and governance. There is a missing link and alignment between enterprise architecture and other capabilities, such as enterprise strategic, project and service management. There is limited support (ADOMS – Supporting) for establishing an adaptive (cloud) enterprise architecture capability.

9.2.6.3 *Level 2: Transition*

This level suggests that an enterprise has started defining (ADOMS – Defining) the formal adaptive (cloud) enterprise architecture capability. There is limited integrated engagement and governance. There is growing support (ADOMS – Supporting) for establishing an adaptive (cloud) enterprise architecture capability.

9.2.6.4 *Level 3: Defined*

This level suggests that an enterprise is effectively operating (ADOMS – Operating) a formally defined (ADOMS – Defining) adaptive (cloud) enterprise architecture capability. There is integrated engagement and governance. There is a clear linking and alignment between the enterprise architecture and other capabilities such as enterprise strategic, project and service management. There is good support (ADOMS – Supporting) for operating a formal adaptive (cloud) enterprise architecture capability.

9.2.6.5 *Level 4: Managed*

This level suggests that the changes are effectively managed (ADOMS – Managing) in the adaptive (cloud) enterprise architecture capability (including architecture artefacts). There is an integrated engagement and governance for handling changes. There is a good support (ADOMS –

Supporting) for handling changes in the adaptive (cloud) enterprise architecture capability.

9.2.6.6 *Level 5: Adapting*

This level suggests that an enterprise is monitoring, assessing, and responding to changes for continuous adaptations (ADOMS – Adapting) in the adaptive (cloud) enterprise architecture capability. There is integrated engagement and governance for adaptations. There is good support (ADOMS – Supporting) for the adaptive (cloud) enterprise architecture capability adaptation efforts.

9.3 Adaptive Enterprise Library

The AESS metamodel and the adaptive enterprise library can be used to define adaptive (cloud) enterprise architecture management and related capabilities. The AESS metamodel is supported by the adaptive enterprise library model (Fig. 9.5), which extends the TOGAF architecture repository approach. The adaptive enterprise library model can be used to establish an integrated adaptive enterprise library to store and manage the fragments or practices to define the enterprise context-specific capabilities, such as the adaptive cloud enterprise architecture capability. It should also have the ability to store and manage the artefacts (e.g. models, requirements) produced by the capabilities. The adaptive enterprise library is a brain or memory of an adaptive enterprise and should be developed and managed like any other adaptive service system.

The adaptive enterprise library provides an integrated mechanism for storing and linking the artefacts of adaptive enterprise strategy, architecture, project, service and requirements management capabilities and services. The adaptive enterprise library can be described in terms of the following key components.

The AESS metamodel can be tailored to a specific enterprise context, based on the reference metamodels stored in the reference library. The tailored AESS metamodel can be used to define the enterprise capabilities (e.g. strategy, architecture, project, service and requirement management).

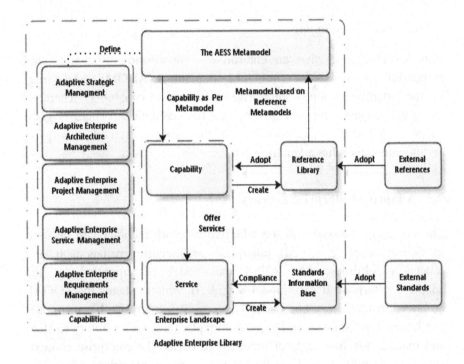

Fig. 9.5. Adaptive enterprise library.

A capability and related service offering can be created by using the AESS capability and service level metamodels. A capability can be supported by the specific fragments or practices stored in the reference library. A capability offers services that produce artefacts (e.g. requirements, architecture models). The enterprise landscape presents a snapshot of the adaptive enterprise capabilities and services, and their artefacts.

The reference library provides resources that can be used to develop and tailor a situation-specific AESS metamodel, capabilities and services. The capabilities, services and artefacts that are not in use can be pushed back into the reference library. The reference library can import and adopt external reference models. The standards information base stores the industry standards to which a capability or service or artefact must comply. The capability or service or artefact that can be used as a standard can be pushed back into the standards information base for later use. The standards information base can import and adopt external standards. The adaptive enterprise library can be further classified into the following repositories, which are discussed in the subsequent sections:

- Strategy repository
- Architecture repository
- Project repository
- Service repository
- Requirements repository

9.3.1 *Strategy Repository*

The strategy repository, as a part of the integrated adaptive enterprise library, can be established to support the adaptive (cloud) enterprise strategic management capability, services and related artifacts. The strategy repository can be described in terms of the following key components (Fig. 9.6).

The adaptive (cloud) enterprise strategic management capability can be tailored using the AESS metamodel and related strategy fragments or practices (e.g. BMM) stored in the strategy repository (e.g. reference library). The strategy landscape presents a snapshot of the adaptive (cloud) enterprise strategic management capability assets currently in use at a specific point of time. The reference library provides resources that can be used to develop the situation-specific adaptive (cloud) enterprise strategic management capability. The adaptive (cloud) enterprise strategic management capability assets that are not in use can be pushed back into the reference library for later use. The reference library can import and adopt external strategy-related reference models. The standards information base stores the industry standards to which a strategic management capability must comply. The adaptive (cloud) enterprise strategic management capability assets that can be used as a standard can be pushed back into the standards information base for later use. The standards information base can import and adopt external standards related to strategies.

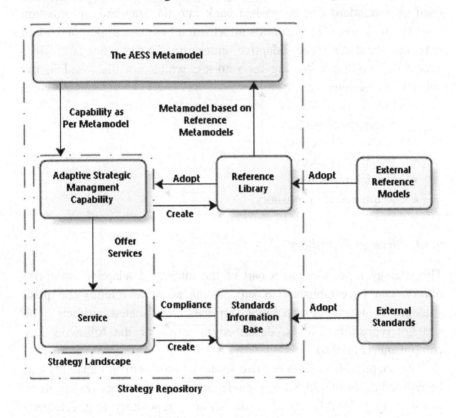

Fig. 9.6. Strategy repository.

9.3.2 *Architecture Repository*

The architecture repository, as a part of the integrated adaptive enterprise library, can be established to support the adaptive (cloud) enterprise architecture management capability, services and related artifacts. The architecture repository can be described in terms of the following key components (Fig. 9.7). The adaptive (cloud) enterprise architecture management capability is tailored using the AESS metamodel and related architecture fragments or practices (e.g. TOGAF, FEAF. DoDAF) stored in the architecture repository reference library.

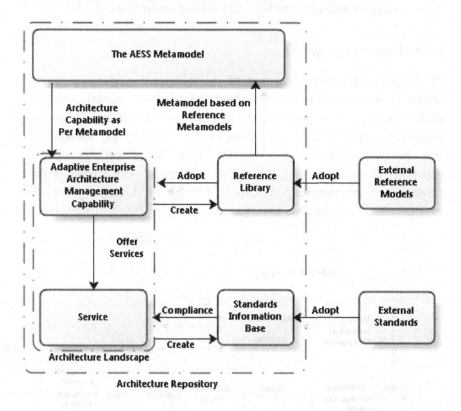

Fig. 9.7. Architecture repository.

The architecture landscape presents a snapshot of the adaptive (cloud) enterprise architecture management capability assets. The reference library provides resources that can be used to develop the situation-specific adaptive (cloud) enterprise architecture management capability. The adaptive (cloud) enterprise architecture management capability assets that are not in use can be pushed back into the reference library for later use. The reference library can import and adopt external reference models. The standards information base stores the industry standards to which an adaptive (cloud) enterprise architecture management capability must comply. The adaptive (cloud) enterprise architecture management capability assets that can be used as a standard can be pushed back into the standards information base for later use. The standards information base can import and adopt architecture-related external standards.

9.3.3 *Project Repository*

The project repository, as a part of the integrated adaptive enterprise library, can be established to support the adaptive (cloud) enterprise project management capability, services and related artifacts. The project repository can be described in terms of the following key components (see Fig. 9.8). The adaptive (cloud) enterprise project management capability is tailored using the AESS metamodel and related project fragments or practices (e.g. Waterfall, XP, Scrum, Lean) stored in the project repository reference library.

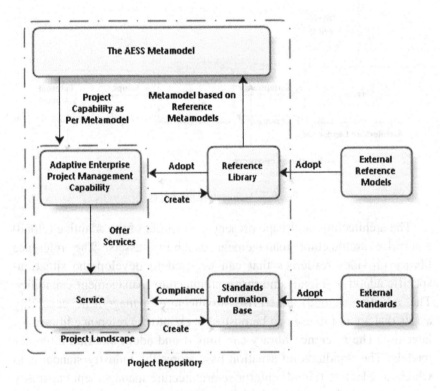

Fig. 9.8. Project repository.

The project landscape presents a snapshot of the adaptive (cloud) enterprise project management capability assets. The reference library provides resources that can be used to develop the situation-specific adaptive (cloud) enterprise project management capability. The adaptive (cloud) enterprise project management capability assets that are not in use can be pushed back into the reference library for later use. The reference library can import and adopt external reference models. The standards information base stores the industry standards to which an adaptive (cloud) enterprise project management capability must comply. The adaptive (cloud) enterprise project management capability assets that can be used as a standard can be pushed back into the standards information base for later use. The standards information base can import and adopt project management-related external standards.

9.3.4 *Service Repository*

The service repository, as a part of the integrated adaptive enterprise library, can be established to support the adaptive (cloud) enterprise service management capability, services and related artifacts. The service repository can be described in terms of the following key components (Fig. 9.9).

The adaptive (cloud) enterprise service management capability is tailored using the AESS metamodel and related service fragments or practices (e.g. ISO 20000, ITIL) stored in the service repository reference library. The service landscape presents a snapshot of the adaptive (cloud) enterprise service management capability assets. The reference library provides resources that can be used to develop the situation-specific adaptive (cloud) enterprise service management capability. The adaptive (cloud) enterprise service management capability assets that are not in use can be pushed back into the reference library for later use. The reference library can import and adopt external reference models. The standards information base stores the industry standards to which an adaptive (cloud) enterprise service management capability must comply. The adaptive (cloud) enterprise service management capability assets that can be used as a standard can be pushed back into the standards information base for later use. The standards information base can import and adopt service management-related external standards.

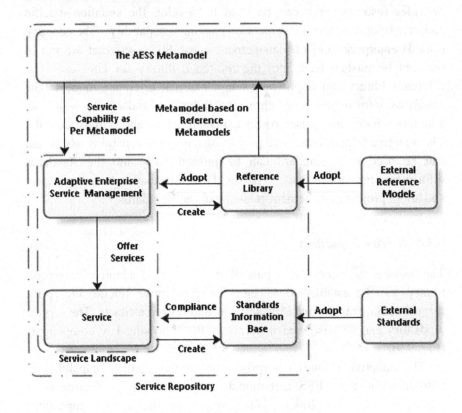

Fig. 9.9. Service repository.

9.3.5 *Requirements Repository*

The requirements repository, as a part of the integrated adaptive enterprise library, can be established to support the adaptive (cloud) enterprise requirements management capability, services and related artifacts. The requirements repository can be described in terms of the following key components (Fig. 9.10).

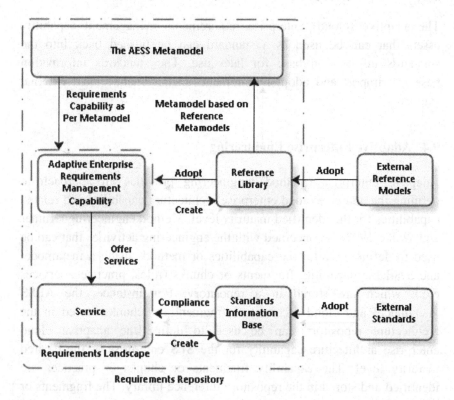

Fig. 9.10. Requirements repository.

The adaptive (cloud) enterprise requirements management capability is tailored by using the AESS metamodel and related requirement fragments or practices (e.g. epics, user stories, use cases) stored in the requirements repository reference library. The requirements landscape presents a snapshot of the adaptive (cloud) enterprise requirements management capability assets. The reference library provides resources that can be used to develop the situation-specific adaptive (cloud) enterprise requirements management capability. The adaptive (cloud) enterprise requirements management capability assets that are not in use can be pushed back into the reference library for later use. The reference library can import and adopt external reference models. The standards information base stores the industry standards to which an adaptive (cloud) enterprise requirements management capability must comply.

The adaptive (cloud) enterprise requirements management capability assets that can be used as a standard can be pushed back into the standards information base for later use. The standards information base can import and adopt requirements management-related external standards.

9.4 Adaptive Enterprise Engineering

Adaptive enterprise (method) engineering provides an approach to defining the adaptive cloud enterprise architecture capability and related capabilities for the identified maturity level. Method engineering (Kumar and Welke 1992) is concerned with the engineering activities that can be used to define or tailor the capabilities or methods using a metamodel and available capability fragments or chunks (roles, practices, services etc.), which are stored in a repository. For instance, the AESS metamodel and cloud architecture fragments or chunks stored in the architecture repository can be used to define the adaptive cloud enterprise architecture capability for the SFS enterprise at the desired maturity level. The capability fragments or chunks or practices are identified and stored in the repository reference library. The fragments or chunks can be created or extracted from other existing cloud frameworks or methods or instantiated from a standardised metamodel. A fragment or chunk in the repository should be conformant with a concept in the metamodel. The AESS metamodel can be used to describe and specify a family of capabilities in terms of concepts, rules and relationships. A capability is thus "defined" or engineered from its fragment or parts in such a way that only relevant fragments are incorporated into the defined capability and those not useful can be safely ignored. The following steps of the method engineering approach can be followed to define a capability:

- Assessing the current and target capability maturity level (e.g. ACMM)
- Defining a metamodel (e.g. AESS metamodel)

- Identifying or defining the capability fragments (e.g. cloud enterprise architecture capability)
- Storing the fragments into the repository (e.g. cloud enterprise architecture repository)
- Selecting appropriate fragments from the repository (e.g. cloud architecture fragments)
- Defining the context-specific capability for the target maturity level from the fragments stored in the repository (e.g. cloud enterprise architecture capability)
- Operating, managing, supporting and adapting the capability (e.g. cloud enterprise architecture capability).

In a nutshell, the ACMM, AESS metamodel, adaptive enterprise library and the engineering approach can be used by the SFS enterprise to assess and define the adaptive cloud enterprise architecture capability and services.

9.5 Adaptive Enterprise Intelligence

Core to adaptive enterprise architecture is its services. The adaptive enterprise service information system (SiS) can be established to support adaptive enterprise intelligence (e.g. business intelligence, analytics) needs. The adaptive enterprise SiS can provide the ability to continuously identify, source and correlate data from both internal and external sources (e.g. architecture tools, monitoring tools, CMDBs, social media, libraries); and being able to perform service lifecycle, impact, root cause, trend, cost, value, and usages analysis. The analysis should provide deeper insights into the services and underlying components. The adaptive enterprise should be able to action these insights for smooth enterprise operations, continuous improvement, growth and transformation. The following are the elements of the adaptive enterprise intelligence:

- Monitor (e.g. scan and sense) internal and external environment to identify data

- Turn data (e.g. interpret and analyse) into insights (e.g. information and knowledge)
- Turn insights (e.g. decide and respond) into actions or change initiatives.

Adaptive cloud enterprise architecture is not only a collection of diagrams and models. Essentially, it is a large set of data, information and knowledge about the adaptive services, configurations and their relations. For instance, data about the human, IT or facility service configurations and their relationships can be stored in the SiS. Fig 9.11 shows the service mapping which can be done to understand the different types of relationships between services. Table 9.2 outlines the different types of relationships which can be tailored to the local enterprise

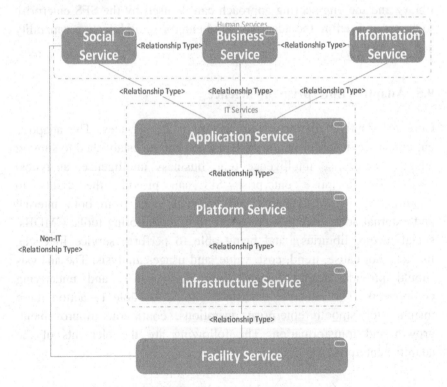

Fig. 9.11. Service mapping (external view).

Table 9.2. Relationship types.

#	Dependent-to-Provider	Provider-to-Dependent
1	depends on	supports
2	uses	is used by
3	is provided by	provides
4	is managed by	manages
5	is owned by	owns
6	is supplied by	supplies
7	is triggered by	triggers
8	is administered by	administers
9	is administered by	administers
10	is manufactured by	manufactures
11	is triggered by	triggers
12	is assigned by	assigns
13	is run by	runs
14	is virtualised by	virtualises
15	is realised by	realises
16	is contained by	contains
17	is comprised of	comprises

context. Such relationship mapping shows the external view or mapping of the services, which is useful for performing change impact analysis or root cause analysis. For instance, change in one service can impact other services. Further, an internal view or configuration of a service can also be mapped and stored in the SiS. Fig. 9.12 shows the internal view of a business service which can be developed for a specific business service (e.g. payment service). The adaptive enterprise SiS adopts a service-oriented approach to store data, information and knowledge about the adaptive cloud enterprise architecture elements.

The adaptive enterprise SiS can be supported by a number of tools for storing, analysing, reporting, monitoring, modelling and visualizing the data about the adaptive cloud enterprise architecture elements. There are a number of options to architect and implement the adaptive enterprise SiS. This book provides examples of two key options: federated SiS and centralised SiS.

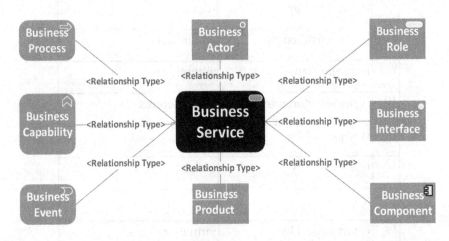

Fig. 9.12. Business architecture – business service configuration (internal view).

9.5.1 *Federated SiS*

The federated adaptive enterprise SiS (see Fig. 9.13) can consist of many application clients that can send their requests to SiS application servers. The SiS application server can send the data request via SQL or API or Service call to the SiS federated DB server. The federated SiS DB server can be deployed to connect to one or more data sources (e.g. CMDBs, monitoring systems).

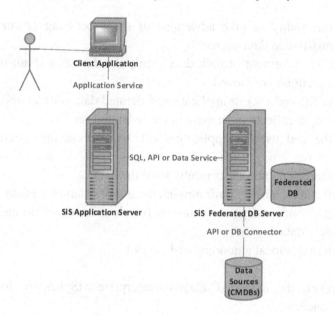

Fig. 9.13. Federated SiS.

The SiS federated DB server can send data requests to distributed multiple data sources via a single SQL statement or API or Service call. The federated SiS DB server can have local data, local and remote metadata (e.g. tables, column names, data types, and indexes), information about data sources and their connections, federated user authorization mapping to data source user authorization, and wrappers (e.g. connecting and retrieving data from distributed sources). The SiS federated DB can also cache the data sourced from multiple sources. The SiS federated DB cache can be synchronized with distributed data sources through periodic updates. The federated SiS option has the following benefits:

- the ability to join data from local and remote data sources (relational and non-relational) as if all the data is locally stored in the federated CMDB server.
- the ability to use and push down the full or partial data request to existing independent distributed data sources

- the ability to take advantage of the processing power of the distributed data sources
- less movement of bulk data – only the data as a result of query execution are moved
- to the end user or application, federated data sources appear as a single collective database in the federated server
- the end user or application can still access the specific data source
- there is no need to centrally store the data
- it can be quickly built through the use of established data sources
- it provides access to real-time (or close to real-time) and up-to-date data
- it offers local autonomy and control

However, the federated adaptive enterprise SiS has the following several concerns:

- complex interfaces to collect the data from distributed sources
- some of the data and relationships may have to be manually federated
- maintenance cost of interfaces between the federated and distributed data sources
- maintenance cost of different distributed data sources
- need to map the federated user to data sources' user authorization
- less central control on data quality

The federation of the SiS DB can be domain-specific. For instance, a federated SiS DB server can be deployed to connect to one or more adaptive enterprise architecture domain-specific (e.g. business, application domain, infrastructure domain, and facility domains) data sources.

9.5.2 *Centralised SiS*

The centralised adaptive enterprise SiS (see Fig. 9.14) options can be adopted to store and manage data at one place. The applications can directly access the data from the central SiS DB server as a single source of truth.

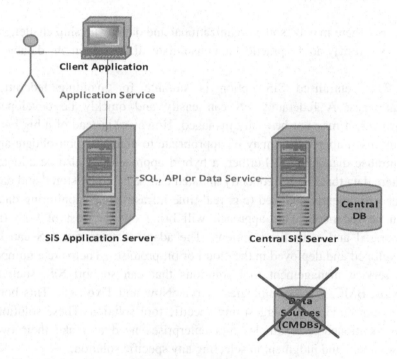

Fig. 9.14. Centralised SiS.

The centralised SiS option has the following benefits:

- there is more control over the quality of the data
- it avoids the maintenance of complex federated database and source database interfaces
- there is a consolidated single source of truth
- There is less trafficking of data
- it enables fast execution

- standardisation
- there is no need to do complex mapping between federated and source database user authorization

However, the centralised adaptive enterprise SiS has the following several concerns:

- there may be some organizational and data ownership challenges
- it may not be practical to consolidate all the data in one database

The centralised SiS option is suitable for avoiding federation challenges. A federated SiS can easily and quickly be developed, however, it may not be easily managed. However, instead of a big bang centralised approach, it may be appropriate to gradually consolidate and centralise data sources. Further, a hybrid approach can also be adopted where data that is not frequently updated can be centrally stored and data that is frequently changed (e.g. real-time infrastructure monitoring data) can be federated. This approach will bring out the best of both the federated and centralised options. The adaptive enterprise SiS can be developed and deployed in the cloud or on-premises. There are a number of service management tool solutions that can support SiS, such as Axios, BMC, CA Technologies, ServiceNow and Tivoli etc. This book does not endorse or suggest any specific tool solution. These solutions are mentioned as examples and enterprises need to make their own assessment and judgment in selecting any specific solution.

9.6 Summary

This chapter described the supporting capability. The supporting capability discussed the adaptive enterprise models, the library, engineering, and intelligence. The adaptive enterprise models include adaptive business, operating, lifecycle, change, resource supply chain and adaptive capability maturity models. The integrated adaptive enterprise library discussed a set of repositories to support managing the assets of adaptive cloud enterprise architecture and related capabilities.

The integrated adaptive enterprise library can be developed, managed and governed like any other adaptive cloud service system. Adaptive enterprise engineering discussed an approach to define the context-specific capability (e.g. adaptive cloud enterprise architecture) using the AESS metamodel and the capability fragments or practices (e.g. distilled from different frameworks) stored in the adaptive enterprise library. Adaptive enterprise intelligence discussed the ability of an adaptive enterprise to gather and act on intelligence sourced from the internal and external environment. The supporting capability discussed a number of supporting items, however, additional items can be added as required to support the adaptive cloud enterprise architecture capability. The final chapter concludes and presents additional example case study scenarios which discuss adaptive cloud enterprise architecture for different cloud adoption contexts.

Chapter 10

Case Study Examples

10.1 Introduction

This book described how to apply a meta-framework, such as The Gill Framework®, to adapting, defining, operating, managing and supporting an adaptive cloud enterprise architecture capability of a fictitious SFS enterprise. This chapter presents an additional four fictitious case study examples or scenarios, which are drawn from the commercial experience in cloud adoption projects. In order to provide diversity, each scenario discusses a different business and industrial context. The one common context to all these example scenarios is cloud adoption. The case study examples discuss adaptive cloud enterprise architecture in the practical cloud adoption context. The following fictitious case study examples are presented in this chapter:

- Government Cloud Adoption (GCA)
- Social CRM SaaS (SCS)
- Agile Development PaaS (ADP)
- Web Hosting IaaS (WHI)

10.2 The GCA Case Study

Government enterprises across the globe (e.g. Australia, Canada, UK, and U.S.A) are showing strong interest in adopting cloud technology. Canada has initiatives to use cloud SaaS for internal collaborations, PaaS for Web hosting, and IaaS for virtual computing and storage. The U.K. has a "Cloud First" approach to the government-wide adoption of cloud technology. Similarly, USA has a "Cloud First" approach to enable flexibility and interoperability between the silo systems of the different agencies. Australia (2011) has a low risk and high value driven government-as-a-whole approach to cloud adoption. Here, we discuss the GCA scenario in a fictitious Australian government agency pursuing the adoption of a private cloud. This scenario illustrates how to apply the AESS metamodel and ADOMS approach of The Gill Framework® to GCA (see Fig. 10.1).

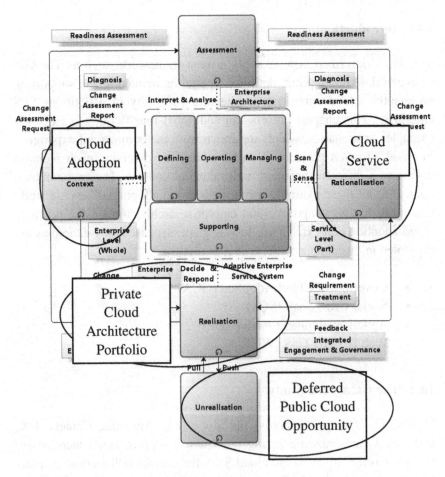

Fig. 10.1. The Gill Framework® 2.0 – GCA case.

10.2.1 *Adapting*

It is important to first identify cloud opportunities from the business perspective rather than kicking off technology-oriented cloud adoption. The outer layer of The Gill Framework® presents the five services of the adapting capability which support the identification of cloud opportunities. The five services are: context, assessment, rationalisation, realisation and unrealisation.

10.2.1.1 *Context*

The agency applies the context service and monitors and identifies the cloud as a new emerging technology for adoption at the enterprise or agency level.

10.2.1.2 *Rationalisation*

The agency applies the rationalisation service and monitors and identifies the cloud service(s) as a new emerging technology for adoption at the individual agency capability service level.

10.2.1.3 *Assessment*

The cloud adoption opportunities, identified at the government agency and capability service levels, need to be assessed. The assessment service involves the adaptive enterprise architecture capability of the agency to assess the cloud adoption opportunities (e.g. cloud technology capabilities and models) against the existing business architecture, information architecture and social architecture of the government enterprise. The adaptive enterprise architecture capability performs the assessment and identifies the agency business, information and social capabilities and services suitable for private cloud adoption. The assessment identifies cloud opportunity risks, value and impacts on existing initiatives. The assessment also involves cloud architecture capability assessment and identifies the need for establishing the adaptive cloud enterprise architecture capability, within the existing enterprise architecture capability, to guide private cloud adoption.

10.2.1.4 *Realisation*

The realisation service, based on the assessment, establishes the integrated engagement and governance, cloud adoption strategy, roadmap and portfolio to realise the identified private cloud adoption opportunities from technological, risk and value perspectives. It also triggers the initiatives related to establishing the adaptive cloud enterprise architecture capability, consolidation of the local and legacy government agency IT systems, and the integration of the private cloud to the existing capabilities.

10.2.1.5 *Unrealisation*

The unrealisation service captures the deferred cloud (e.g. public cloud in this case) opportunities, which could be reconsidered in the future. The adapting capability highlighted the need to define the adaptive cloud enterprise architecture capability to facilitate cloud adoption in the fictitious government agency. The inner layer of The Gill Framework® specifies the four capabilities for defining, operating, managing and supporting the adaptive cloud enterprise architecture capability.

10.2.2 *Defining*

The defining capability is used to define the adaptive enterprise architecture capability and integrate it to the project, requirement and service management capabilities of the fictitious agency. It uses the AESS metamodel (capability and service level), and supporting adaptive enterprise engineering approach and enterprise library to define the adaptive cloud architecture capability within the existing adaptive enterprise architecture capability. It involves reviewing and selecting industry best cloud architecture principles, practices, roles, tools and reference architecture to establish the adaptive cloud enterprise architecture capability. Rather than boiling the ocean, it focuses on defining the vision and scope of the private cloud architecture work.

10.2.3 *Operating*

This capability is not so much about designing full perfectly detailed cloud architecture upfront without its implementation. Instead of a traditional waterfall approach to architecture design and the implementation approach, the fictitious agency operates the adaptive cloud enterprise architecture capability along with the adaptive cloud enterprise project, requirements and service management capabilities to iteratively design and implement the private adaptive cloud enterprise architecture in the production or production-like environment according to the adaptive cloud enterprise strategy and roadmap. It includes defining the architecture layers (see Fig. 10.2): interaction, business, information and social architecture, and supporting SaaS, PaaS and Facility architectures. The details within these architecture layers evolve through incremental cloud architecture implementation in short iterations and releases. The factory architecture includes designing business, information and social architectures; and supporting cloud application (SaaS), platform (PaaS), infrastructure (IaaS) and facility (FaaS) architectures. It is operated as a private cloud factory to seamlessly mash-up and integrate the reusable and non-reusable cloud services to develop adaptive cloud service system solutions. The interaction architecture can be visually modelled to show the run-time complex dynamic interactions between adaptive cloud service systems.

10.2.4 *Managing*

The fictitious agency manages change to allow the adaptive cloud enterprise architecture capability and resultant architectures to evolve in small increments. It also involves the integration and engagement of the adaptive enterprise cloud requirements, strategy, architecture, and project and service management capabilities. The adaptive cloud enterprise requirements management capability is operated to iteratively define and manage the requirements for cloud services in the adaptive enterprise library – requirements repository.

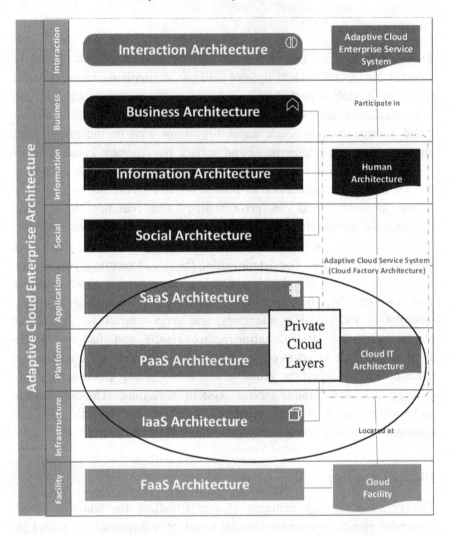

Fig. 10.2. The adaptive cloud enterprise architecture layers - GCA private cloud case.

The adaptive cloud enterprise strategic management capability is operated to provide the overall cloud strategic direction. The adaptive cloud enterprise architecture management capability is operated to design the evolving (current, transition and future states) adaptive cloud enterprise architecture of the fictitious agency. As discussed earlier, the adaptive enterprise cloud project management capability is operated (cloud portfolio, programs, projects and iterations) to iteratively implement (develop and operate - DevOps) the adaptive cloud enterprise architecture in cloud production or a production-like environment. The adaptive cloud enterprise service management capability is operated to provide ongoing operational support and management (e.g. cloud incident management, problem management, release management, change management).

10.2.5 *Supporting*

The supporting capability provides the adaptive enterprise models (cloud adoption strategy), enterprise intelligence (cloud adoption opportunities), enterprise library (architecture repository, requirements repository) and adaptive enterprise engineering support to adapting, defining, operating and managing the adaptive cloud enterprise architecture and related capabilities.

10.3 The SCS Case Study

The SCS case study discusses a scenario in which a fictitious financial services organisation (FSO) already has an established adaptive cloud enterprise architecture capability. The FSO adapting capability has identified the cloud adoption opportunity. The adaptive cloud enterprise architecture capability assesses the cloud opportunity against the human-centric business, information and social architectures (Fig. 10.3). The architecture assessment along with the context and rationalisation services identified the following FSO life insurance-related business, information and social capabilities, processes and services suitable for the public cloud Social CRM SaaS adoption.

- Business Architecture
  - CRM business capability
    - Contract management business process
    - Contract management business service

- Information Architecture
  - o Records management capability
    - Contract document management process
    - Contract document service
- Social Architecture
  - o Collaboration management capability
    - Social process
    - Social service

The realisation service triggers the cloud Social CRM SaaS application architecture update project. The unrealisation service captures the deferred private cloud CRM SaaS opportunity. A high-level layered view of the updated cloud Social CRM SaaS application architecture within the overall context of the adaptive cloud enterprise architecture is highlighted in Fig. 10.4. For simplicity and readability reasons, relationships across the layers are not shown. Further, the architecture can also show the cloud Social CRM SaaS application and its integration with other non-cloud applications. The purpose here is not to specify all the architecture details, rather the purpose is to demonstrate the use of enterprise architecture in cloud adoption.

The business architecture layer highlights the CRM business capability. The scope of the architecture is limited to life insurance and contract management. Therefore, the life insurance contract management business process and business service related to the CRM business capability are shown as an example in the business architecture layer. Similarly, the information architecture layer shows the records management capability that offers the life insurance contract document management process and service. The social architecture layer shows the collaboration management capability that offers the social process and service to support collaboration between the FSO life insurance staff and customers. Finally, the Social CRM SaaS application architecture, supporting business, information and social architecture is shown in the application architecture layer.

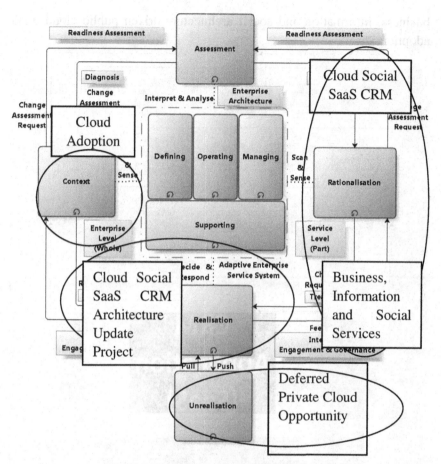

Fig. 10.3. The Gill Framework® 2.0 – SCS case.

The underlying platform (PaaS), infrastructure (IaaS) and facility (FaaS) layers of the public cloud Social CRM SaaS are not visible to the FSO, therefore, they are not shown in Fig. 10.4. The Social CRM SaaS uses the email service of the email SaaS application (ESaaS) to send contract-related notifications (e.g. contract renewal, expiry). It also uses the document service of the document SaaS application (DSaaS) to store and manage life insurance contract-related documents. The Social CRM SaaS architecture will evolve through its iterative implementation in small iterations. This example clearly shows the relevance and importance of adaptive cloud enterprise architecture in the context of business, information and social architecture-driven public cloud SaaS adoption.

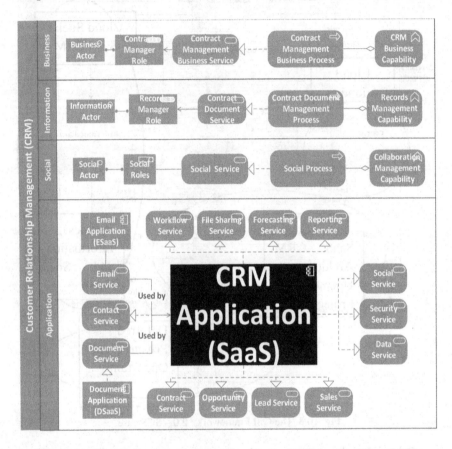

Fig. 10.4. The adaptive cloud enterprise architecture –SaaS CRM application architecture.

10.4 The ADP Case Study

The ADP case study illustrates a scenario in which the adapting capability of the fictitious software development organisation (SDO) identifies the cloud adoption opportunity. The adaptive cloud enterprise architecture capability of the SDO assesses the cloud adoption opportunity (Fig. 10.5).

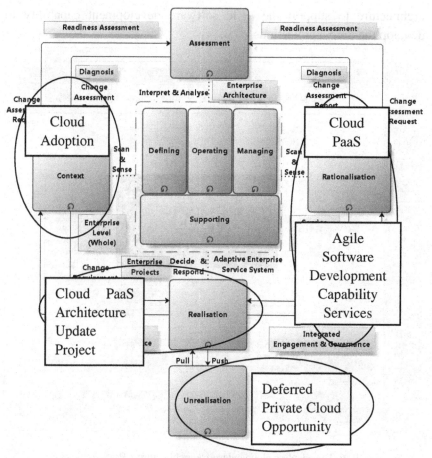

Fig. 10.5. The Gill Framework® 2.0 – SDO case.

The architecture assessment, along with the context and rationalisation services, identified the agile software development capability services suitable for the public cloud PaaS adoption. The agile software development capability offers services to the development of SaaS applications. The realisation service triggers the cloud PaaS architecture update project. The unrealisation service captures the deferred private cloud PaaS opportunity. The existing adaptive cloud enterprise architecture capability is operated to design the cloud PaaS architecture to support the agile software development capability to develop the SaaS applications.

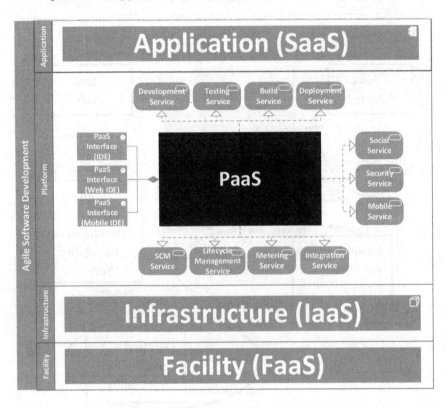

Fig. 10.6. The adaptive cloud enterprise architecture – PaaS architecture.

A high-level layered view of the cloud PaaS architecture is given in Fig. 10.6. Similar to the previous case, for simplicity and readability reasons, relationships across the layers are not shown. The scope of the architecture is limited to the PaaS. Therefore, other architecture layers are not shown or detailed. The PaaS includes the operating system and the development services. The PaaS is accessible via PaaS interfaces for agile development, testing, building, and the continuous deployment of the SaaS applications.

10.5 The WHI Case Study

The WHI case study presents a scenario in which a fictitious educational services organisation (ESO) identifies a cloud adoption opportunity. The adaptive cloud enterprise architecture capability of the ESO assesses the cloud adoption opportunity (Fig. 10.7). The architecture assessment, along with the context and rationalisation services, identifies the web hosting infrastructure capability services suitable for the public cloud IaaS adoption. The web hosting infrastructure capability offers hosting services for deploying PaaS and SaaS applications.

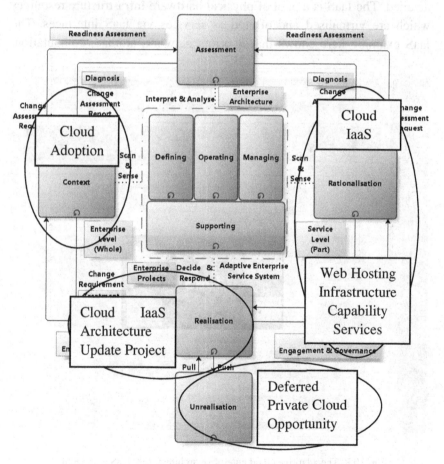

Fig. 10.7. The Gill Framework® 2.0 – WHI case

The realisation service triggers the public cloud IaaS architecture update project. The unrealisation service captures the deferred private cloud IaaS opportunity. The existing adaptive cloud enterprise architecture capability is operated to design the cloud IaaS architecture to support PaaS and SaaS applications.

A high-level layered view of the cloud IaaS architecture is provided in Fig. 10.8. Similar to previous cases, for simplicity and readability reasons, relationships across the layers are not shown. The scope of the case study example is limited to the illustration of the IaaS architecture. Therefore, other architecture layers are not shown or detailed. The IaaS is a pool of physical hardware infrastructure resources which are virtualised and offered as services via IaaS interfaces. The IaaS example here shows that it offers network, storage, computation,

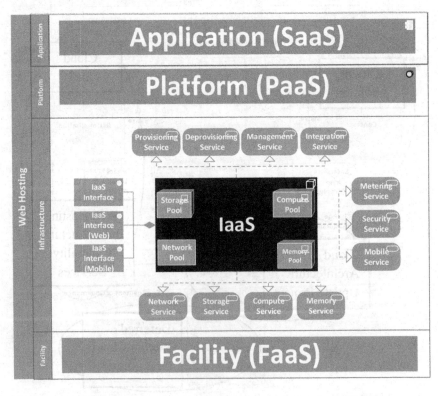

Fig. 10.8. The adaptive cloud enterprise architecture – IaaS architecture.

and memory services along with other administration and management services. The IaaS architecture seems useful for showing the required infrastructure services for web hosting. These services can be provisioned, deprovisioned, managed and integrated to create a context-specific, on-demand web hosting infrastructure for PaaS and SaaS applications.

10.6 Summary

This chapter demonstrated how an adaptive cloud enterprise architecture capability and architecture can be helpful and used to guide cloud adoption in different contexts. This chapter illustrated the use of The Gill Framework® components with the help of four fictitious case study example scenarios. These fictitious scenarios are based on the author's experience in cloud architecture and implementation projects. The first case illustrated the establishment and use of the adaptive cloud enterprise architecture capability for a private government cloud adoption scenario. The remaining three cases highlighted the use of the adaptive cloud enterprise architecture approach to guide the adoption of specific cloud services such as Social CRM SaaS, agile development PaaS, and web hosting IaaS. These all cases highlighted that one may source the public cloud service from a cloud provider, however, before jumping on the cloud bandwagon, the consumer organisation still needs the enterprise architecture capability to assess the cloud service offerings, deployment models and their suitability from a business perspective. In a nutshell, human-centric social business information architecture drives the underlying cloud technology and facility architectures, and supporting cloud services and deployment models. This book presented an adaptive cloud enterprise-driven approach to guide strategic cloud adoption.

Bibliography

Armbrust, M., Fox, A., Griffith, R., Joseph, A.D., Katz, R., Konwinski, A., Lee, G., Patterson, D., Rabkin, A., Stoica, I., Zaharia, M. (2009). "Above the clouds: A Berkeley view of Cloud Computing, UC Berkeley EECS".
http://www.eecs.berkeley.edu/Pubs/TechRpts/2009/EECS-2009-28.pdf, 2009.

Arsanjani, A. (2004). "Service-Oriented Modeling & Architecture". IBM Online article.

Australia Government. (2011). Cloud Computing Strategic Direction Paper: Opportunities and applicability for use by the Australian Government, Version 1.0.

Berzins, V., Gray, M. & Naumann, D. (1986). Abstraction-based software development, Communication of the ACM, (29:5), pp. 402-415.

Burback, R. (1998). Software Engineering Methodology: The Watersluice. PhD Thesis, University of Stanford.

Callaghan, J. (2002). Inside Intranets & Extranets: Knowledge Management and the Struggle for Power. Palgrave Macmillan. ISBN 0-333-98743-8.

Carraro, G., and Chong, F. (2006). Software as a Service (SaaS): An Enterprise Perspective. https://msdn.microsoft.com/en-us/library/aa905332.aspx.

Chalem. (2000). What Ever Happened to Client/Server?
http://www.chalem.com/html/articles/clientserver.htm (accessed on November 2011).

COBIT. http://www.isaca.org/cobit/pages/default.aspx.

Commonwealth of Australia (2012). A Guide to Implementing Cloud Services.

Dehaan, M. (2008). Methods and Systems for Provisioning Software.
http://www.google.com.au/patents/US8185891.

Doucet, G., Gotze, J., Saha, P., Bernard, S. (2008). Coherency Management: Using Enterprise Architecture for Alignment, Agility, and Assurance, Journal of Enterprise Architecture, May 2008.

DoD. (2010). The DoDAF Architecture Framework.
http://dodcio.defense.gov/TodayinCIO/DoDArchitectureFramework.aspx.

European Commission. (2010). European Commission Report: The Future of Cloud Computing, Opportunities for European Cloud computing Beyond 2010".

European Commission. (2011). Energy Efficiency Plan 2011. Technical Report.

Enerdata. (2011). Average Electricity Consumption per Electrified Household.

FEAF. (2013). Federal Enterprise Architecture.
https://www.whitehouse.gov/omb/e-gov/fea.

Forrester. (2015). Cloud Computing. https://www.forrester.com/Cloud-Computing. 2015.

Garfinkel, S.L. (1999). Architects of the Information Society, Thirty-Five Years of the Laboratory for Computer Science at MIT. MIT Press. ISBN 978-0-262-07196-3.

Gill, A.Q. (2015). The Gill Framework. www.aqgill.com.

Gill, A.Q., Alam, S.L. & Eustace, J. (2015). Social Architecture: An Emergency Management Case Study. Australasian Journal of Information Systems.

Gill, A. Q. (2015). Distributed Agile Development: Applying a Coverage Analysis Approach to the Evaluation of a Communication Technology Assessment Tool. International Journal of e-Collaboration (IJeC), 11(1), 57-76.

Gill, A.Q. (2015). Social Architecture Considerations in Assessing Social Media for Emergency Information Management Applications. The Australian Journal of Emergency Management, Vol. 30, No. 1, Jan 2015: 17-21.

Gill, A.Q. and Qureshi, M.A. (2015). Adaptive Enterprise Architecture Modelling. Journal of Software.

Gill, A.Q., Bunker, D., and Seltsikas, P. (2015). "Moving Forward: Emerging Themes in Financial Services Technologies' Adoption," Communications of the Association for Information Systems: Vol. 36, Article 12.

Gill, A.Q. (2014). Hybrid Adaptive Software Development Capability: An Empirical Study. Journal of Software.

Gill, A.Q. (2014). Applying Agility and Living Service Systems Thinking to Enterprise Architecture. International Journal of Intelligent Information Technologies (IJIIT), IGI Global.

Gill, A.Q., Smith, S., Beydoun, G., & Sugumaran, V. (2014). Agile Enterprise Architecture: A Case of a Cloud Technology-Enabled Government Enterprise Transformation. PACIS 2014, China.

Gill, A., Alam, S., & Eustace, J. (2014). Using Social Architecture to Analyzing Online Social Network Use in Emergency Management. AMCIS 2014, USA.

Busch, P., Smith, S., Gill, A.Q., Harris, P., Fakieh, B., and Blount, Y. (2014). A Study of Government Cloud Adoption: The Australian Context. ACIS 2013, New Zealand.

Gill, A.Q. (2013). Towards the Development of an Adaptive Enterprise Service System Model. AMCIS 2013, USA.

Smith, S., Gill, A. Q., Hasan, H., & Ghobadi, S. (2013). An Enterprise Architecture Driven Approach to Virtualisation. In PACIS (p. 50).

Gill, A. Q., & Bunker, D. (2012). SaaS Requirements Engineering for Agile Development. Agile and Lean Service-Oriented Development: Foundations, Theory, and Practice: Foundations, Theory, and Practice, 64.

Gill, A., & Bunker, D. (2012). Crowd Sourcing Challenges Assessment Index for Disaster Management.

Gill, A. Q., Bunker, D., & Seltsikas, P. (2012). Evaluating a Communication Technology Assessment Tool (Ctat): A Case of a Cloud Based Communication Tool. In PACIS (p. 88).

Gill, A. Q. (2012). A Decision to Adopt. CIO, (Sep/Oct 2012), 32.

Gill, A. Q., & Livingstone, R. (2012). Demanding Times.

Gill, A. Q., Bunker, D., & Seltsikas, P. (2011). An Empirical Analysis of Cloud, Mobile, Social and Green Computing: Financial Services IT Strategy and Enterprise Architecture. In Dependable, Autonomic and Secure Computing (DASC), 2011 IEEE Ninth International Conference on (pp. 697-704). IEEE.

Gill, A. Q., & Bunker, D. (2011). Conceptualization of a Context Aware Cloud Adaptation (CACA) Framework. In Dependable, Autonomic and Secure Computing (DASC), 2011 IEEE Ninth International Conference on (pp. 760-767). IEEE.

Gov.UK. (2013). Government Adopts 'Cloud First' Policy for Public Sector IT. Cabinet Office, UK. Available at: https://www.gov.uk/government/news/government-adopts-cloud-first-policy-for-public-sector-it.

Hammer, M. (1996). Beyond Reengineering: How the Process-Centered Organization is Changing Our Work and Our Lives. New York, NY: HarperCollins Publishers, Inc.

Harrison, R. (2011). TOGAF Foundation, The Open Group.

Himmelsbach, V. (2010). Canada Clears up its Cloud Strategy. ITWorldCanada.com, Available at: http://www.networkworld.com/news/2010/021610-canada-clears-up-its-cloud.html?page=1.

IBM. (2013). IBM Cloud Computing Reference Architecture 3.0.

ITIL. https://www.itsmf.org.au/best-practice/itil/.

ISO 20000. Information technology - Service management. http://www.iso.org/iso/catalogue_detail?csnumber=51986.

ISO/IEC/IEEE 42010 2007. Systems and software engineering — Architecture description. http://www.iso-architecture.org/ieee-1471/.

Jackson, M.A. (1975). Principles of Program Design, Academic.

Kern, T., and Kreijger, J. (2001). An Exploration of the Application Service Provision Outsourcing Option. Proceedings of the 34th Hawaii International Conference on System Sciences – 2001.

Kern, T., Lacity, M., Willcocks. L., Zuiderwijk, R. & Teunissen, W. (2001). ASP Market Space Report 2001. Mastering the Customers Expectations, GMG report.

Kroeber, A. L. and Parsons, T. (1958). "The Concepts of Culture and of Social System", The American Sociological Review, 23(1958), 582-3.

Krogdahl, P., Gottfried L., and Christoph, S. (2005). "Service-Oriented Agility: An Initial Analysis for the use of Agile methods for SOA Development." Services Computing, 2005 IEEE International Conference on. Vol. 2. IEEE, 2005.

Kundra, V. (2011). Federal Cloud Computing Strategy. Available at: http://www.whitehouse.gov/sites/default/files/omb/assets/egov_docs/federal-cloud-computing-strategy.pdf.

Larman, C. (2004). Applying UML and Patterns: An Introduction to Object-Oriented Analysis and Design and Iterative Development, Third Edition, Prentice Hall, 2004

Martin, R. 2009. The Design of Business: Why Design Thinking is the Next Competitive
    Advantage. Harvard Business Review Press; Third Edition.

Marshall, R. (2012). Government Launches G-Cloud Store with 257 Cloud Computing
    Suppliers. Available at: http://www.v3.co.uk/v3-uk/news/2153551/government-
    launches-cloud-store-257-cloud-computing-suppliers.

Maier, M. W. (1998). Architecting Principles for Systems-of-Systems. Syst. Engin., 1:
    267–284.

Miller, J.G. (1995). Living systems. University Press of Colorado.

NIST (2011). NIST Cloud Computing Reference Architecture.
    http://www.nist.gov/customcf/get_pdf.cfm?pub_id=909505

Nickull, D. (2005). "Service Oriented Architecture Whitepaper," Adobe Systems, Inc.

Open Cloud Manifesto. http://www.opencloudmanifesto.org/, 2009.

Odiyo, B., and Dwarkanath, M. (2011). Virtual Private Network, Uppsala universitet
    (accessed on November 2011).

Orfali, R., Edwards, J., and Harkey, D. (1994). Essential Client/Server Survival Guide.
    John Wiley & Sons, Inc. New York, NY, USA ©1994. ISBN: 0471131199.

O'Reilly (2004). History of Programming Languages, O'Reilly Media, Inc., 2004.

Oracle (2013). Oracle Reference Architecture. http://www.oracle.com/technetwork/
    architect/archday-rws-2013-krishnaswamy-1966514.pdf.

Perepa, S. (2013). Why the U.S. Government is Moving to Cloud Computing. Wired
    Innovation Insights, available:
    http://wirednext.ning.com/xn/detail/6544125:BlogPost:58430#axzz318naDO60.

Plummer, D.C., Bittman, T.J., Austin, T., Cearley, D.W., Smith, D.M. (2008). Cloud
    Computing: Defining and Describing an Emerging Phenomenon.

Qumer, A. and Henderson-Sellers, B. (2008). "An Evaluation of the Degree of Agility in
    Six Agile Methods and its Applicability for Method Engineering", Journal of
    Information and Software Technology (IST), 50(4), pp. 280-295.

Qumer, A., & Henderson-Sellers, B. (2007). ASOP: An Agile Service-Oriented Process.
    Frontiers in Artificial Intelligence and Applications, 161, 83.

Ross, J.W., Weill, P., and Robertson, D.C. (2006). Enterprise Architecture as Strategy:
    Creating a Foundation for Business Execution, Harvard Business Review Press,
    pages 256.

Hai, H., and Sakoda, S. (2009). SaaS and Integration Best Practices. FUJITSU Sci.
    Tech. J., Vol. 45, No. 3, pp. 257–264.
    http://192.240.0.102/downloads/MAG/vol45-3/paper03.pdf.

Salesforce (2008). http://www.salesforce.com/au/

Spohrer, J. and Kwan, S. K. (2009). "Service Science, Management, Engineering, and
    Design (SSMED): An Emerging Discipline - Outline & References", International
    Journal of Information Systems in the Service Sector, 1(3).

Spohrer, J., Vargo, S., Caswell, N., Maglio, P. (2008). The Service System is the Basic
    Abstraction of Service Science. 41st Annual HICSS Conference Proceedings.

Tsai, W.T., Malek, M., Chen, Y. & Bastani, F. (2006). 'Perspectives on Service-Oriented Computing and Service-Oriented System Engineering', Proceedings of the Second IEEE International Symposium on Service-Oriented System Engineering (SOSE'06), IEEE, pp. 3-10.

Theodorakis, M., Analyti, A., Constantopoulos, P., & Spyratos, N. (1999). 'Contextualization as an Abstraction Mechanism for Conceptual Modelling', International Conference on Conceptual Modeling, Paris, France, Springer Berlin/ Heidelberg, Vol. 1728.

US Energy Information Administration 2013. International Energy Outlook 2013 with Projections to 2040. Technical Report.

Vargo, S., Maglio, P., and Akaka. M. A. (2008). On Value and Value Co-creation: A Service Systems and Service Logic Perspective. European Management Journal 26 145-152.

Wenger, E. (1998). "Communities of Practice: Learning as a Social System", Systems Thinker.

Zachman, J.A. (1987). "A Framework for Information Systems Architecture", IBM Systems Journal, 26, 276-292.

Zhang, S., Chen, X., Zhang, S., and Huo, X. (2010). "Cloud Computing Research and Development Trends", Second International Conference on Future Networks.

Index

Printed in the United States
By Bookmasters